Untie the Cords of Silence

Untie the Cords of Silence

Michael Huffman

Foreword by Anne Zaki

Afterword by Marisa Lapish

WIPF & STOCK · Eugene, Oregon

PAPERBACK ISBN: 978-1-6667-3001-2
HARDCOVER ISBN: 978-1-6667-2100-3
EBOOK ISBN: 978-1-6667-2101-0

12/21/21

For my daughters, Mikaela and Paulina. May you speak of Christ, and may your voices be heard.

*Your teaching signifies an entirely new world; for yonder
in the kingdom, men and women are equal.* [1]

—SAINT JACOB OF SARUG

(as translated by Joseph Amar)

*Nevertheless, in the LORD woman is not independent of man or
man independent of woman. For just as woman came from man,
so man comes through woman; but all things come from God.*

—1 COR 11:11–12 NRSV

1. Amar, *A Metrical Homily*, v. 43.

Contents

List of Illustrations and Tables

Figures

Tables

Foreword

by Anne Zaki

"Why not?"

THESE WERE THE INITIAL two words that led me down my odyssey of seeking ordination as a pastor. My nine-year-old tongue blurted the words during an intense discussion with my church elder, around the role of women in our church. The question was ignited by my witnessing for the first time a foreign woman pastor preaching and serving communion during a Sunday worship service in my local congregation in downtown Cairo. Growing up in the Presbyterian Church of Egypt, I had seen women serve in all sorts of ministries, but I had never seen Egyptian women teach or preach on a Sunday—as if Sunday was too sacred for women's participation—and I had certainly never seen them serve communion. A subtle dissonance was birthed in me, and I found myself wondering, "Why is it that we allow foreign women more freedom to serve than we do our own? Is this the honor of hospitality, the tyranny of tradition, or both?"

"Why not?" was the question that provided the common ground upon which Michael Huffman and I met, as he too discerned a similar dissonance in his local Plymouth Brethren Church in Northeast Ohio. We were from two distinctly different religious and cultural contexts, yet a corresponding experience of holy restlessness compelled us both to search Scripture in order to resolve the dissonance. Michael tells his journey in chapter 1, and he has graciously invited me to briefly share mine in the next few pages.

Loving God, Loving His Church

In *Blue Like Jazz*, Donald Miller says he disliked jazz until he watched a man on the street play the saxophone for fifteen minutes without once opening his eyes. "After that I liked jazz music," he says. "Sometimes you have to watch somebody love something before you can love it yourself. It is as if they are showing you the way."[1]

This is how it was for me growing up in the Christian home and church family of my upbringing. All throughout my childhood, and ever since, I have watched my parents and my brother love God and the church, and I have grown to share that love. I have also been inspired and affirmed by the spiritual leadership of so many faithful servants of God. Their faith and commitment showed me the way. Already encouraged to use my spiritual gifts for the edification of the church at a young age, I sought every opportunity to be more involved in ministry as I grew. But even then, I had tasted the joy of being a member of a serving community, of realizing that God's calling honors households and individuals, old and young, men *and* women.

You Shall Go and Speak: The Sparks of the Call

At age fifteen, during youth camp by the shores of the Mediterranean Sea, I first sensed my call to ministry when God spoke to me through his call to Jeremiah: "Do not say 'I am only a child [or, in my case, *only a female*]; for you shall go to all to whom I send you, and you shall speak whatever I command you'" (Jer 1:6–8). But the calling lay dormant for many years.

Later, while attending university in Michigan, I attended a church led by a woman pastor, where I sat under the outstanding preaching and leadership of this gifted woman of God. My sense of call to ministry was revived, and the dissonance that I had known early on grew. But my call was an impossible dream for my Egyptian Presbyterian context. Every summer, I would return to Egypt and serve alongside my brother at various youth camps. He, being the gifted speaker, would preach, while I would lead worship from the piano. Those summers brought me so much joy, and when added to the positive role model I had in my mother, who loved being a pastor's wife, I finally decided that the only way for me to resolve the dissonance, while still fulfilling my call to ministry, was to

---

1. Miller, *Blue Like Jazz*, ix.

marry a pastor whom I could serve through—and to become a professor, so that I could still teach adults.

This combination was certainly the most culturally appropriate choice. And to my good fortune, four months before graduating from university, God brought into my life Naji Umran, a Syrian-Canadian seminary student who was called to serve in the Middle East. Check! The first part of my calling was now fulfilled and I could proceed toward becoming a professor. Three years later, I completed a Master's in Social Psychology, and, shortly thereafter, I started pursuing a PhD in Christian Education. While taking some of the required courses, I grew in my desire to study theology and pastoral care in depth. Many of my professors and mentors urged me to consider becoming a pastor, but I refused, insisting that becoming a pastor was not my calling, since I really did love being a pastor's wife, and enjoyed devoting my personal and family life to ministry through my husband.

A Year of Discernment: Confirmation from Scripture and God's People

By the end of the first year of my doctoral studies, and after I had preached at our church, Naji encouraged and challenged me to prayerfully examine my call to ministry. He warned me that I could be objecting to a divine call simply because it was strange in my cultural context. "Are you sure," he asked, "that you are not letting your culture shape your call, instead of allowing your call to shape your culture?" I was not sure.

This challenging question sent me on a year-long quest in prayer and discernment, studying every Bible passage related to women's ministry and leadership, reading extensive books on the matter. I also intentionally surrounded myself with a group of mentors who held opposing views on the issue while I continued to share about my passion for ministry with family and friends. It was a long year of struggling with the issue, between confrontation and confirmation, but by year's end, through clear scriptural support, it became apparent to me that women's ordination is biblically acceptable. Here's a quote from a book that I found helpful in summarizing my research findings:

> I have come to see that Paul's prohibition against women believers teaching and exercising authority in the church is rooted not in a timeless principle of female subordination. Rather, it

is based on the timeless principle of not fostering unnecessary offense that would hinder the furtherance of the gospel by going against prevailing social conventions.[2]

It also became clear to me, through the overwhelming affirmation from many people, that God was calling me into full-time ministry. The dissonance disappeared the moment I surrendered, trusted, and obeyed. But the struggle would never disappear. It simply changed locations, from being trapped inside of me to surrounding me by its trap.

Back to School

Since being ordained in our Presbyterian tradition means committing to a thorough academic course of preparation, the first thing I did to respond to God's calling was to transfer from my doctoral studies to a Master of Divinity program. I wanted to pursue theological and pastoral training to equip myself for ordination. Four years later and after completing my MDiv, I was ready to be set apart by the church as one who gives pastoral leadership in church life. In 2008, I applied for ordination in the Presbyterian Church in Egypt's Synod of the Nile, and waited prayerfully for their decision. Meanwhile, my husband and I, along with our four sons, relocated to Western Canada, where I was privileged to share a ministry position, serving as a nonordained pastor alongside my husband.

Around the same time, the Fellowship of Middle East Evangelical Churches (FMEEC), a body made up of sixteen Middle East member denominations, including the Synod of the Nile, were concluding their twenty-year study of the topic. Finally, in January 2010, the FMEEC presented a detailed and clear report declaring the ordination of women as biblically founded and defensible, and therefore asking their member denominations, including mine, to reconsider established church orders, and to allow for the ordination of women pastors.[3] I continued to wait prayerfully for their decision, all the while hoping and trusting that our synod would not treat my request as a personal, isolated case to be decided upon. Rather, I prayed that they would see it as a church cause needing to be addressed. This became another piece of common ground upon which Michael and I would one day meet.

---

2. Boomsma, *Male and Female One in Christ*, 18.
3. See Van Marter, "Middle East Churches Assembly."

An Issue of the Church, a Matter of the Gospel

Michael had set out to prove that it is possible for a person who believes in the authority of Scripture to affirm the equality of men and women in ministry. But his employment of solid hermeneutics that were consistent with the whole testimony of Scripture, doctrine, reason, history, tradition, and experience also helped him to prove that this was a church issue driven by the gospel, and not simply a women's issue driven by a feminist and human rights agenda.

> If the church is the earthly witness to God's redemption of humanity in Christ, and if humanity is made in the image of God, the voices that speak for and to the church must represent the wholeness of that image. Our sisters' voices should be heard. This is not only for their own sake, but for the good of the church and, by extension, of humanity and all of creation. The issue is really that far-reaching.[4]

The half-truth of the idea that women's ministry is not a gospel issue—or a full church issue—is one of the many that this book brings into the light.

The Danger of Many Half-Truths

Half-knowledge is more dangerous than complete ignorance. Half-truth is more dangerous than a complete lie. It takes a keen eye, an alert mind, and a discerning spirit to expose half-truths. What Michael Huffman does so brilliantly and thoughtfully in this book is not only identify one half-truth after another, about women in ministry, but he also offers a corrective through a thorough and faithful study of the Bible.

- He exposes the half-truth about egalitarians not holding a high view of biblical authority, and the consequent assumption that they are driven by a feminist agenda. His brilliant and thoughtful study of Scripture throughout the book is a testament against that assumption. Through an in-depth Bible study, Michael proves that the obstacle to women's exercising the full range of ministries is not Scripture. In fact, Michael's argument echoes the results of a 1976 report by the Roman Catholic Congregation for the Doctrine of the Faith: The seventeen scholars of that assembly all agreed that, based on the witness of the New Testament alone, women could not be

4. Huffman, *Untie the Cords*, 214.

prevented from ordination as priests—this in contrast to a 15–12 vote against allowing for ordination when basing their decision on the witness of the whole of Scripture.[5] Despite the study's findings and these consistent majority votes, the final conclusion of the report was not determined by the biblical evidence; rather, the group's grounds for why the Roman Catholic Church will not authorize women's ordination as priests are traditional views of masculinity integral to the personhood of both Jesus and the twelve apostles.[6] However, some argued that if Jesus was a Jew and the twelve disciples Jesus chose were all Jews, shouldn't this mean that gentiles cannot be priests?

- Michael also exposes the half-truth about complementarians having a neutral view on hierarchy. Their insistence on inserting hierarchy in the creation account is simply unfounded. In God's original created design for the relationship between man and woman, as recounted in Genesis 1 and 2, no distinction is made either between the value of men and women or between the roles of men and women. Subjection of the woman to the man comes in Genesis 3, and is a result of the fall. But, if Christ has come to restore the relationships of a prefall paradise, then why is there an insistence on perpetuating the consequences of the fall? Egalitarianism believes that men and women have unique and distinct roles that complement each other, and so in that sense it poses a challenge to *hierarchicalism*, not complementarianism.

- He exposes the half-truth of equating complementarianism with conservativism. The fact is, complementarian theology is just as revisionist, just as influenced by modern thought, as egalitarian theology, and only dates to the later part of the twentieth century. Both of them have departed from some of the church's historic teachings, and thus neither group is actually conservative in the sense of preserving what the majority of past generations taught about women.

- He exposes the half-truth of assuming that all complementarians agree on the limits put on women. While they all claim to be biblical in their ministry practice, they hold diverse views on what women in ministry are permitted to do, leaving the distinctions between

---

5. NCR Editorial Staff, "Editorial."

6. See Šeper, "Declaration *Inter Insigniores*," especially sec. 5.

testimony, sharing, teaching, and preaching quite blurry. The only thing that actually unites them is their agreement that women should be limited somehow.

- He exposes the half-truth of associating ordination with hierarchy. Jesus redefined leadership as servanthood. When ordination means being set apart by the church to serve the church, and when service is the starting point and service is the telos of ordination, then we must stop and ask: What place does hierarchy have in a conversation about ordination?

Reading about all of these half-truths in one place, in the context of Michael's engagement of the most controversial passages, was both illuminating and encouraging.

The Waiting Place

In the years after 2008, I submitted numerous letters to the Synod of the Nile, repeatedly and respectfully requesting that they would recognize my credentials, and consider ordaining me as a pastor in our denomination. While I did receive encouragement from many pastors and church leaders in Egypt right away, I also suspected that this decision would take some time since it was the first request from a woman to be ordained as a pastor here.

I could have been ordained elsewhere, like the foreign women I'd observed as a child. But, I had refused ordination in the West because my husband and I knew that our call as a family was to return to Egypt eventually—and that call became a reality in 2011. Nine months after the January 25th Egyptian Revolution, my husband and I, along with our four young sons, returned to Egypt, obeying God's invitation to help raise the next generation of Egyptian church leaders, to replace the ones who had emigrated to the West in the midst of Egypt's political and economic unrest.

Even after returning to live in Egypt, my request for ordination continued to be discussed in Synod and Presbytery meetings, but no decision was reached. Two years later, in 2013, I applied and was offered a teaching position at the Presbyterian seminary in Cairo, as the first Egyptian woman to join the faculty in the 150-year history of the seminary. While thrilled to be hired, and to see God opening a door for me to fulfill the call for which we had returned to Egypt, sadly, the old dissonance returned. How could they trust me to teach pastors, but not trust me to become one? The inconsistency in the act of hiring me as a professor boggled me. If the Bible described me in my full womanhood as the temple of God, why could I not be consecrated as a temple servant of God?

Every year, from 2008 to 2016, at the Synod and Presbytery levels, my request and the issue of women's ordination as pastors was discussed, but no decision was made. And then, in 2016, the leadership of Synod decided to put a moratorium on all discussions of the issue for the next ten years! But the conviction that I am reading Scripture aright, and the ways this experience has both forged my God-given gifts, and taught me to lean into him, have somehow served to sustain my calling.

What Untied My Cords of Silence?

I was shocked. I was disappointed. Could not the church leaders see that by silencing half of humanity in the church, they were in fact denying the image of God in the whole? Could they not imagine how every part needs the other parts in the body of Christ? I felt that there was an unjust violation in my being silenced. But how could I keep silent, when the Triune God had called me to speak by the shores of the Mediterranean Sea?! So, I went back to that same calling place from where my journey had begun, and there . . .

The Creator God, who chose to create male and female in his image, untied my cords of silence.

The stories of Jesus' inclusion of women among his disciples untied my cords of silence.

The crucified Christ redeeming men and women from the curse untied my cords of silence.

The Holy Spirit, who gave gifts regardless of age, ethnicity, gender, or social status, untied my cords of silence.

The sign of the new covenant, baptism, that offered the same outward seal of the promise to both men and women, untied my cords of silence.

The doctrine of the priesthood of all believers, including men and women, untied my cords of silence.

The testimony of Scripture to women's ministry in the early church untied my cords of silence.

The example of godly men and women in history, and throughout my lifetime, who fully embraced and declared by word and deed three of the most powerful metaphors for total equality in Christ—*The image of God*, *the temple of God*, and *the body of Christ*—untied my cords of silence. All three images signify grace-based, not gender-, race-, economic-, or social status-based ministry.

Why Ordination in Egypt?

Instead of waiting until 2026 to bring the issue before synod again, some have advised me to get ordained in the West. To me, this is really a matter of calling. I believe that God places certain visions and passions on people's hearts, to serve him in a certain way or a specific place. My calling is to serve in Egypt, and my yearning is for the health of my native church. I am a daughter of the Egyptian Presbyterian Church, and I have immense respect for its leaders. It was they who nurtured me in my faith, who fostered my loyalty to the church, and who instilled in me my love for our Egyptian people. Thus, it is my prayer to follow in their footsteps, serving our church, society, and the kingdom of God, in whatever capacity God and this synod see fit. In the meantime, I also know that there are other women in our Egyptian church who feel the same way, and that they too are waiting for an opportunity to fulfill their calling. In some way, I know that my calling is also to help spark and sustain their callings.

Christ and Culture

Our Egyptian society is a traditional one, and I honor our cultural codes. Nonetheless, the church needs to remain *the* prophetic voice in our context, challenging cultural norms that counter the gospel. I understand that my request poses a challenge, not only to our majority Muslim context, but also to the various other patriarchal groups in Egypt, including conservative evangelicals, and Coptic Orthodox Christians. But it is my conviction that countercultural challenges are not necessarily bad. In the early 1900s, our denomination challenged cultural norms by establishing mission schools in the cities of Menia in the south and Tanta in the north to train women evangelists and preachers. We went further, challenging the patriarchal cultural traditions of the time by offering education to Christian and Muslim girls in Southern Egypt—a move that changed our entire society's perception of women (so much so that today we have women as governors, parliament members, and court justices). All of this is the result of Presbyterians in Egypt always having insisted that theology should guide practice, not the other way around.

Not Losing Hope

"Why not?" Those were the initial two words that led me down this odyssey, but *inconsistency* and *imagination* were the two words that have guided me on. I combat the former, while I cultivate the latter. Although it has been more than thirteen years since my initial request for ordination, I remain hopeful. History proves that whenever we take daring steps as a church, we will first need courage to address difficult situations thoughtfully and sensitively, through honest and open conversation. So, let us study the matter at hand—with its biblical and theological foundations and its cultural implications—and let us, together as a church, engage in honest, loving, and thoughtful conversations, offering light and leadership to our church, and to our world.

While Michael never intended for this book to be an exhaustive, scholarly work on the topic, it contributes significantly to the conversation because it contains a personal struggle to find God in the confusing maze of controversy, which I believe reflects and echoes the struggle of many others, including my own. In reading each other's stories, I believe there is pain that binds, truth that sets free, joy that revives, and hope that perseveres.

Preface

TRADITION HAS IT THAT, after Jesus' ascension, the apostles Thaddaeus (a.k.a. Jude) and Thomas went to Edessa, a city now called Urfa in southeastern Turkey, to preach the good news about the risen Jesus. The people of Edessa spoke Syriac, a dialect of Aramaic, the native tongue of the first apostles. It is said that Abgar V, Edessa's king, converted to Christ through the preaching and healing ministry of Thaddaeus, thus becoming the first Christian monarch. Abgar provided a haven for one of the most ancient Christian traditions to grow and flourish—the Syriac Orthodox Church.

As the Syriac church grew over the next few centuries, it came to revere a theologian and hymn-writer named Ephrem, who remains one of its most beloved saints. As I was in the midst of writing this book, my wife Isabel ran across a quote attributed to this celebrated saint on social media. The quote, in which Ephrem is addressing a group of Christian women, is recorded by a disciple of his, known as Jacob of Sarug. Here is what it says: *"Untie the cords of silence. Raise your voices. Speak out with the freedom that is yours by Baptism, the Body and the Blood of the Covenant."*[1] Isabel said to me, "This would be a good title for your book." I heartily agreed.

But I hesitated. "Surely," I thought, "a fourth-century theologian could not have been defending the full and free participation of women in the speaking ministries of the church!"

---

1. This quotation was borrowed from Amar, "Women Are Proclaiming the Word," para. 19. The quote summarizes and paraphrases several lines of Jacob of Sarug's homily in praise of St. Ephrem. Amar's complete, formal translation reads as follows: "Your silent mouth which your mother Eve closed, is now opened by Mary, your sister, to sing praise. The old woman (Eve) tied a cord of silence around your tongues; the Son of the virgin loosed your bonds that you may sing out. The married one put a muzzle of silence on your mouths; (but) the virgin opened the closed door of your tongues" (Amar, *Metrical Homily*, vv. 108–10).

I was right. Ephrem was not defending the complete freedom of women to use their voices in the church. But what he *was* defending made the quote all the more appropriate as a title for a book like this one. The question of how much, in what contexts, and by whom women's voices should be heard in the church divides it today more sharply than almost any other. But debates surrounding the voices of Christian women are not new. Rather, the specifics have merely shifted. Seventeen hundred years ago, Saint Ephrem found himself advocating for the singing voices of women before his opponents. The women to whom he said, "Untie the cords of silence," were church choristers. In retrospect, it seems Ephrem's position won out, at least in great measure, for nearly all churches today (with a few important exceptions) welcome the singing voices of women, especially in the context of a church choir. This reality gives me hope. The church *can* change!

The question I wish to pose at the beginning of this book is this: Did the good Saint Ephrem do all that needed to be done? Or, does his vision need expanding? Could it be that Ephrem only began a good work—a work that has yet to be finished? Somehow, Ephrem transcended the ostensibly biblical prohibition of women's (singing) voices in the assembly of God's people and persuaded his contemporaries to welcome them. I think the same Spirit that moved Ephrem still spurs us on to an even more complete freedom today. This book is my attempt to make that case. I write in hope and anticipation, knowing that I have a solid legacy to build upon. I am far from being alone.

Acknowledgments

SPACE, AND NO DOUBT memory, will fail me as I try to thank by name all those who, in various ways large and small, influenced the writing of this book. I wrote it over the course of such a long period of time—and much of that time without knowing that what I wrote would end up in a book—that I fear I may not remember all those who commented on the earliest versions of my evolving thoughts as they found their way into this document. Scores of informal conversations with friends contributed to this book. It would be impossible for me to name every friend who helped me refine my arguments on this topic, whether by agreeing with, disagreeing with, or questioning them. This book was written, truthfully, with them in mind.

I want to thank my wife Isabel Vera Zambrano especially, the woman who knows me better than any other. Isabel never ceases to believe in me, and to spur me on to be who I really am as a man in Christ. As will become clear in the following, it is unlikely this book would ever have come to be without her influence and backing. Isabel not only encouraged me to write; she also worked intentionally to make space in our busy family life for me to do so. She also read early drafts of this book and helped me refine it in numerous ways. She has been my devoted conversation partner as I've tried to refine my thoughts on this topic—and many others—over our decade of marriage.

My good friend Marisa Lapish also read multiple drafts of this manuscript and offered invaluable advice. She, perhaps more than anyone, has encouraged me faithfully not only to study this topic, but to share my discoveries with others. Laura and Zachary Balon, who pastored my home church in Istanbul, Yeni Ümüt Kilisesi, as I wrote the first draft of this work, provided priceless affirmation and support that goaded me to keep writing—affirmation made meaningful by their unwavering devotion to the health and thriving of Christ's church. I also want to thank my sister Susie Benz, friends David Erdel, Adam Hart, Samuel Lapish, Christina Muço, Wendy Yurkovich, Mary Longenecker, Samuel Killins, and Özlem Pelttari, all of whom commented on early drafts of my manuscript. Some of their suggestions resulted in substantial changes, others saved me from printing errors, and all made this a better book than it would have been. My diligent copyeditor, Brian Palmer, continued their work to the same effect. For the errors that remain, it is I alone who must ask for the pardon of my gracious readers.

I am profoundly thankful to Anne Zaki and Marisa Lapish, women who speak in the service of God's reign in two very different contexts, not only for their willingness to contribute their voices to this project, but for courageously speaking the truth about God's desire that women's voices be accessible to all God's people—including men.

I also wish to thank the friendly and helpful editors and staff at Wipf and Stock for their willingness to take on the work of a new author like me, and for working patiently with me to bring this book to print.

Abbreviations

BDAG   *A Greek-English Lexicon of the New Testament and Other Early Christian Literature*. Edited by William Bauer, et al. Chicago: University of Chicago Press, 2001.

BDB   *A Hebrew and English Lexicon of the Old Testament.* Edited by Francis Brown et al. Oxford: Oxford University Press, 1952.

DDD   *Dictionary of Deities and Demons in the Bible*. Edited by Karel van der Toorn et al. Grand Rapids: Eerdmans, 1999.

NPNF   *A Select Library of Nicene and Post-Nicene Fathers of the Christian Church.* Edited by Philip Schaff and Henry Wace. 28 vols. in 2 series. 1886–1889. Reprint, Peabody, MA: Hendrickson, 1956.

OED   *Online Etymology Dictionary*. https://www.etymonline.com/.

Introduction

WOMEN MAKE UP MORE than half of the church worldwide. Yet, the voices associated in public with the church are overwhelmingly those of men. Its authority figures, teachers, and preachers—the people who represent the church in the minds of outsiders when they think of Christianity—are nearly always men. Of course, the same could be said of other important institutions the world over. Governments, for example, are overwhelmingly male, even in the most self-consciously progressive countries. Even though roughly half of the world's population is female, males constitute the vast majority of leaders in nearly every sphere.

Many Christians are not disquieted by the world's historic acceptance—or, at least, tacit tolerance—of disproportionately male leadership. For them, it reflects God's design. In the human economy, man was made to lead, woman to follow. It is no surprise, therefore, that men tend to take leadership roles more than women do both in the church and in wider society, and that women tend to follow their lead.

Such Christians find ample biblical support for this hierarchical arrangement. God created Adam first, then Eve. Furthermore, Adam named Eve, not vice versa.[1] With only a few exceptions, men tend overwhelmingly to be the political leaders, religious representatives, and ordained spokespersons among God's people in the Hebrew Bible. In the New Testament, Paul tells women on several occasions to submit to their husbands (see Eph 5:22, 24, and Col 3:18), and Peter teaches the same (1 Pet 3:1). Paul appears not only to tell women to avoid teaching and leading men (1 Tim 2:12), but also to be silent in the church (1 Cor 14:34). Throughout the Bible, it is argued, God's design for men to be leaders and women to be their helpers is consistently maintained.

---

1. But, see the last chapter.

Despite all of this, some Christians today have started to teach and practice male-female equality both in their marriages and in the church. Some major denominations within the past century have even begun to ordain women to pastoral roles, as well as to other positions of ministry that involve speaking to whole congregations. The question is: Why is this happening?

The Bible is often used to confront such Christians. As we noted, there seems to be a lot of biblical precedent for the idea of male authority. If the Bible teaches that men are the leaders of their wives, their families, and the church, to say otherwise is to set oneself over against biblical teaching. Many Christians who think this is what the Bible clearly teaches genuinely want to know why other professing Christians seem to be ignoring what the Bible says. Why do some Christians believe men are *not* women's authorities? Why do some Christians believe that women can preach and teach in church? Why do some Christians believe that women can be pastors? This book is an attempt to answer those questions in a simple, straightforward way.

I should mention something about the terms I choose to use in this book. Because I think that the so-called complementarian position really is a case of wanting to have one's cake and eat it too, I have sometimes chosen not to use the word "complementarian" to describe it. This is not to be spiteful, but to be clear. Like the heart's relationship to the lungs, two different things can complement each other without being arranged in a hierarchical relationship. Women and men are different, and offer different, equally human gifts to the family, church, and society. Therefore, every Christian would acknowledge that God intends for women and men to complement each other. The word "complementarian," thus, does not really capture the crux of the matter. That is, it doesn't really distinguish this view from any other Christian position. For that reason, I will sometimes choose to use the word "hierarchicalist" to describe the position that sees male-female hierarchy as basic to humanity's design. It would simply be confusing for me to argue *against* the complementarity of male and female when, in fact, this is precisely what I want to affirm! I want to challenge hierarchicalism, not complementarianism as such. Generally, when I refer to specific people who call themselves complementarian, I go ahead and use their preferred term. However, when I argue against the overall *idea* to which those complementarians hold, I generally prefer the word hierarchicalist instead.

There is a growing number of excellent books on this topic. Indeed, I admit that there will likely be some readers who won't find this book very helpful because they will have already heard most, if not all, of the interpretations and arguments I will present. In the past fifty years or so, a wealth of books has been published by Bible scholars, theologians, and other authors on the topic of women in ministry, and I have benefitted tremendously from this surge of interest in this topic. Though there are a few I have not personally encountered elsewhere, I doubt there are any truly new ideas or arguments in this book. For that reason, it would be appropriate for me to give a brief explanation about what I hope this book will add to the conversation.

I should first say what this book is *not* trying to do. I admit that I have *not* engaged with everything that has been written on this topic. This is not intended to be a scholarly contribution. Rather, the primary purpose is to give my readers the kind of resource that would have been helpful to me at the beginning of my own journey to a change of mind about male-female equality. This book is a simple, step-by-step and question-by-question, approach to coming to terms with who we are as men and women in Christ.

I was raised in a Christian home and church that most would describe as conservative (a term I've come to dislike), in which the Bible carried tremendous authority. While my understanding of the nature of that authority has not remained static, I continue to hold to a high view of Scripture. Through my many conversations with other Christians about women in ministry, I have found that I am not alone in this regard. What I and most of my Christian friends really want to know is: Can I, without trying to uphold a contradiction, stay true to the teaching of the New Testament while also affirming male-female equality, not only as an idea, but also in practice? Many people hesitate to affirm male-female equality because they are waiting to see evidence in favor of it in their open Bibles. In the following I do my best to give good arguments for just that kind of person.

But I also try to go a bit further. I try to show that the biblical witness not only frees us to affirm male-female equality, it also urges us along in that direction. In a nutshell, here is my thesis: *The biblical testimony to Christ's work both frees Christian women to speak and also men to hear their voices.* I hope that women who read this book will be liberated from the burden of constantly wondering whether or not they are crossing gender-role boundaries by using their speaking and leadership gifts in the service of Christ and the church. I hope that men who read this book will be freed from the burden of allowing their own sense of masculinity to be threatened by the voices and leadership of women. The church has everything to gain from rejecting the fears that both sexes harbor toward the other in favor of embracing the oneness and wholeness of humanity as redeemed by God, filled with the Spirit, and sent out into the world to proclaim the victory of Jesus.

A second purpose I hope this book will serve is to help bring clarity to the questions at stake about the silencing of women. I hope that pastors and others who teach the Bible will find in this book something to aid them in their teaching, particularly when it comes to explaining certain so-called "problem" texts to their congregations, Sunday schools, Bible study groups, youth groups, etc. If I succeed in my purpose, a pastor, teacher, or even youth leader who reads this book will come away not only having appreciated the gospel's overall message to men and women more, but also having gained the necessary confidence to open their Bibles and explain what those difficult passages mean to those they are called to shepherd. My goal is to show that, when these passages are read within the context of Christ's work for and message to the world, they become a part of the gospel's liberating light.

Many times, even within churches that affirm the mutual equality of men and women, one gets the sense that the passages we will examine in what follows are more of an embarrassment or, at least, a source of confusion, than part and parcel to the liberating message of God's reign in the world. As a result, those texts are often avoided or passed over. I presuppose in my writing—and assume that most of my readers agree— that *every* word of Scripture is there for a reason, even when we don't see the reason right away. Moreover, that reason comes from God, and is therefore good, life-giving, and holy. It appears to me that some biblical texts have been, on the one hand, read over and over by some Christian groups to the disastrous effect of variously silencing or muffling the voices of Christian women. Meanwhile, the same texts appear to function like a thorn in the side of other Christian groups—a source of annoyance to their commitment to welcoming women's voices in the church. As a result, some Christians are using these texts in a misguided way (to put it generously), while other Christians sideline or ignore them. Neither of these two approaches respects these texts for what they are, for they are part of holy Scripture. These passages should lead the church, *alongside the rest of Scripture*, to the worship of God as the earthly representative of a redeemed humanity.

Most of this book focuses on those New Testament texts that are often used to silence women in the church or to subject them to male authority. Before we get into those more detailed arguments, I want to make some general observations about Jesus' place in this discussion.

A Word about Jesus

The only substantive record we have of Jesus' behavior toward anyone—whether men or women—is in the New Testament. Jesus never silenced a woman. Not even once. That is important. There is also plenty of evidence in the New Testament that Jesus had female friends and disciples. It is important that we make this point before we delve into the biblical texts that often take center stage in the debate about women in the church's speaking ministries. I'll say it again just to drive home the point: Jesus *never* silences a woman in the New Testament. That is just not something Jesus did.

But we can make a stronger point than this. Not only did Jesus refrain from silencing women, we have evidence in the Gospels that he would, with some frequency, purposely draw the attention of men to women in such a way that those men who had ears to hear would learn from them.[2] That is, Jesus intentionally looked for ways to show men that they should learn from women. So, here's a question: If we have no record of Jesus ever silencing a woman, and if we have multiple examples at our disposal of Jesus intentionally drawing people's attention—including that of the men around him—to the voices of women, why don't most churches in the world today behave similarly toward women? The church is the body of Christ. We are here to represent the living Spirit of Jesus in God's world. If that's true, it follows that whatever we can say truthfully about the character of Jesus we should also be able to say about the church, because we are his body. But when it comes to how we have treated women historically, I don't think we can. The church will, of course, always fall short of fully embodying the ministry of Jesus. After all, we are not God incarnate; he is. No Christian would argue from that fact, however, that we shouldn't at least try to be like Jesus. But when it comes to what we

---

2. See Matt 9:18–26; 15:21–28; 26:6–13; Mark 5:21–43; 7:24–30; 14:3–9; Luke 7:36–50; 8:40–56; 10:38–42; John 4:1–45; 16:21.

teach and practice as the body of Christ with regard to women, are we even trying to be Christlike?

Suppose a local church made the following resolution—"We want to treat all women in exactly the same way that Jesus treated them when he was on earth"—what would be the result? How much silencing would occur? How much would such a church emphasize male authority? Jesus *never* taught anything close to the idea that men are women's authorities. Suppose Jesus' relationship with the famed (yet unnamed) woman at the well in John 4 was carried on and developed in the ongoing ministry of the church for generation after generation. Jesus sat with this woman, educated her theologically, and then, in effect, sent her off as a preacher of the gospel into her home town. Suppose a church were to say, "How can we mimic Jesus here? How can we prepare women theologically and make good preachers out of them?" What would happen? So much of the church is actively discouraging women from preaching and teaching today that it may be difficult to imagine what would happen.

Here is another broad observation about Jesus' relationship to women. Everyone knows Jesus had enemies, and everyone knows that Jesus had friends who failed him in his hour of deepest need. But, how many of Jesus' enemies were women? As far as we know from the Gospels, not a single woman who encountered Jesus during his lifetime ended up opposing him. As we will note in the last chapter of this book, the crucifixion of Jesus could have been avoided if one arrogant man, Pontius Pilate, had been willing to listen to his wife's advice—and she never even met Jesus! I'm not trying to say that all women get it just because they're women. But, it's hard to deny, based on what we know about Jesus from the stories of his interactions with women in the Gospels, that women who encountered Jesus, almost as a matter of course, became his disciples. And, we can legitimately make an even more radical claim about women based on what we see in the Gospels: they were arguably better disciples than the men, at least in a general sense. It was the women who followed him *all the way* to the cross,[3] and it was the women who, in God's providence, first proclaimed the message of the empty tomb.[4] I wonder, if it hadn't been for women, would we even know that the tomb was empty, and the stone rolled away? They are the witnesses we have. Sure, Jesus appeared

---

3. See Matt 27:55–56; Mark 15:40–41.

4. See Matt 28:1–10; Luke 24:1–12; John 20:11–18.

to his disciples later. But the strongest *historical* basis for the resurrection of Christ is the empty tomb.

When it's all said and done, it really doesn't matter whether a man or a woman first encountered the risen Jesus; what is important is that Jesus is risen! I am merely drawing certain facts to the fore that are often missed in conversations about the Bible, Jesus, and the "role" of women. For me as a man, the observations I made above about Jesus and women from the Gospels have a sobering effect. Jesus was a man, and on the surface that reality might make it seem like I, as a man myself, am in a better position than my sisters to understand him. But based on what we see in Scripture, the opposite seems more likely. Women, overall, seemed to understand Jesus more readily than men did. This may sound like an extreme assertion to make. But I actually think it's fairly obvious. The Gospels don't come out and say it like I just did, but if we draw a few interpretive conclusions from the stories recorded in the Gospels, I don't think I could be accused of making a far-fetched claim. Generally speaking, women who knew Jesus understood who he was and responded appropriately despite the fact that, quite often, crowds of men around them remained variously puzzled, clueless, or hostile.

Of course, it is also a fact that most of the women Jesus personally encountered were members of marginalized groups, far from the halls of power. It is likely that a woman like Herodias, the dastardly wife of Herod Antipas who manipulated her daughter into requesting John the Baptist's severed head on a platter, might have colluded, if given the chance, in the murder of Jesus if she had thought it would serve her interests.[5] I'm not trying to set the stage for a men-versus-women schemata here, or trying to argue that the female psyche is somehow more naturally pristine or predisposed to recognizing God incarnate than its male counterpart. My observations above may, in the end, point more clearly to a truth about the kinds of people—whether men or women—who tended to recognize Jesus rather than an observation about one gender's ability, as such, to do so. As Jesus himself implied, his gospel was one most easily understood and received by the poor,[6] not the wealthy and powerful. Nevertheless, the point still stands: the women Jesus encountered personally—women who, in their society were the marginalized sex *within* the marginalized

---

5. See Matt 14:1–12 and Mark 6:14–29.

6. See Matt 4:18; 19:23–24; Mark 10:25; Luke 4:18; 6:20; 7:22; 18:25.

classes—tended to be more discerning witnesses to his identity than their male contemporaries.

From a Christian's perspective, Jesus is at the center of Scripture. The purpose of the Bible is, ultimately, to point us to him. I've shared these broad observations about Jesus right up front because I want them to color everything I say in the following arguments. We are going to dig deeply into interpretations of individual biblical texts in this book. But Christian readers of the Bible should be wearing Christ-colored lenses as they do their interpreting. If the end goal of Bible interpretation is to lead us to Christ and, indeed, to transform our character and thinking to be more Christlike, our interpretations should leave us looking more like Jesus when we are finished. If that doesn't happen, something has gone quite wrong.

This is only the introduction. I'm not saying these broad generalizations should be the end of the matter. But, the fact that we find such disparity between what we know about Jesus' behavior toward women and the behavior of many churches toward women over the past two millennia should give all of us pause before we start declaring the Bible's prohibition on women preachers, or the clarity of the Bible's teaching about male authority. We need to keep Jesus right in the middle, because that is where he belongs. When we find Jesus is becoming more like a loose cog in the wheel of the church than the axis around which the whole wheel turns, we need to stop and have a serious conversation about realigning ourselves. Such a realignment could be called a reformation, to borrow a familiar term.

All this is to point out that reading the Bible is not an end in and of itself. The Bible has a purpose. This book, because it is essentially a book about interpreting certain parts of the Bible, should have that same purpose. I pray it does.

My Own Silence

In our first chapter, I would like to tell my own story about what led me to begin changing my mind about God's intention for women in the church and Christian home. My story may not be of interest to some of my more eager readers, who should feel free to skip to the next chapter where I begin my formal arguments.

A Time to Speak

I spent my first eighteen years deeply involved in the vibrant life of a small Plymouth Brethren church in Northeast Ohio, in the United States. My uncles, aunts, grandparents, and some of their like-minded friends started that church. Growing up, my seven siblings and I learned to call it, "the assembly." We never said, "I'm going to church" because we insisted "the church" was not the building but the people. Still, the building was important to us. I remember many a "work day" when the majority of the church would show up to spend half a Saturday or more cleaning it and caring for the parking lot and lawn. We did it all ourselves. In fact, we built that building with our own hands. We had a construction contractor who was a regular attendee. He contracted the work, and we spent numerous weekends building while we rented another place for our weekly worship services. Our "assembly" was extremely important to us. Of course, as a child I never appreciated this as much as I do now that I have been involved in other churches.

Like other Plymouth Brethren assemblies, ours was actively engaged in Bible reading and study. We hosted weekend Bible seminars frequently. We invited itinerant Bible teachers to come and we'd have potluck meals together and listen to hours of Bible teaching. What's more, people brought their Bibles to church—*their* Bibles. And they took notes in the margins of their Bibles and had them open on their laps during services. We called most of what we heard from the pulpit "preaching," but it was actually pretty meticulous theological lectures that we heard most of the time. I have never seen a church since then that has achieved the emphasis on personal Bible study that we had in our assembly. The Bible-centered culture was so strong that as a teenager I would awake regularly at 5 a.m. to pore over my *Scofield Reference Bible*, with my *Strong's Exhaustive Concordance of the Bible* ready at hand.

Our church didn't have a youth group. In fact, due to a particular philosophy of child-rearing to which my parents held, I was not even sent to the Sunday school our assembly offered (except for special programs). Instead, I stayed in the adult meetings—all three of them, each an hour long (or more), every Sunday morning.

I loved going to church because when I went, my presence mattered. The Brethren have a custom of celebrating the Lord's Supper—or communion—every Sunday. Unlike churches I have attended since that time, the communion services at that church lasted an hour and were entirely unplanned except for the ending, which is when we ate the bread and drank the grape juice. For this weekly "remembrance meeting," as we called it, the saints would gather at 9 a.m. and sit in silence until someone—anyone[1]—was moved by the Spirit to stand and suggest a hymn to be sung, read a passage of Scripture, or share a devotional thought about God's work in Christ on the cross. We were not afraid to be quiet and solemn. It was completely normal in these meetings for ten minutes to pass without anyone's saying a word—except, of course, a baby or small child. We were not a charismatic church, at least as the term has come to be defined in the past century. Actually, we believed that certain miraculous gifts of the Spirit, like prophecy and speaking in tongues, were only for the earliest generation of believers. Still, in *that* meeting, we believed the Spirit was moving, and often commented afterward on how the meeting had taken on a Spirit-inspired theme, even though no one had planned any such theme beforehand. There was no prescribed method.

---

1. Not quite, but we'll get to that.

In eighteen years I never heard instructions on how it was to be done. It was more like a culture. Everyone knew what to do, and when new people came they learned quickly simply by observing and participating.

That hour was never boring to me, even from a very young age. Far from it. I looked forward to it weekly. Of course there were regular participants, but there was always a sense of anticipation in the room. One never knew beforehand what would be said or who would speak. I always hoped that someone would share who had never shared before—perhaps a young person or someone who was new to the assembly—and I think almost everyone felt similarly. There was something exciting and ever-fresh about that hour. I've not been a part of a Plymouth Brethren church since my childhood. I have never experienced anything quite like this in other churches I've attended. I won't deny that I miss it, sometimes profoundly.

I learned to participate vocally in that meeting by the time I turned thirteen. Through that meeting, I learned that my voice was welcome in our church. Very often an older person would approach me afterward to encourage me. "Michael, I was blessed by your words in the Lord's Supper this morning" or, "Michael, it is wonderful to hear a young person who has a heart for the Lord share with us." At other times, a person might provide correction as well. "Michael, thank you for speaking today. I wanted to caution you about something you said . . ." But even in correction the tone always communicated approval. I never felt that anyone preferred not to hear my voice.

The elders of the church noticed my interest in what we called, "the things of the Lord" when I was in my early teens and allowed me to enter the rotation to lead the Wednesday night Bible study. By age fourteen, I was preparing to say something at church almost every week. Later, I was invited to lead congregational singing and to preach in the Family Bible Hour (the third Sunday morning meeting) several times as well. While not all the young men in the church shared my passion for vocal ministry, I did not see these opportunities as abnormal. Our assembly emphasized what I later learned was a key doctrine that had driven the great Protestant Reformation in fifteenth-century Europe—the priesthood of all believers. Because *all* believers were priests—not only a clergy class—it made sense to me that my age should not hold me back from using my voice at church. I knew that God could speak through me just like God could speak through someone older than I. I did not fully appreciate how unique my situation was until later when I began attending churches of other traditions.

From the Brethren's point of view, the rest of Protestantism had actually failed, in practice, to carry out the doctrine of the priesthood of all believers to its practical implications. "If *all* believers in the new covenant are priests to God, why should they not *all* be represented in the life of the church?" we wondered. We decried the folly of churches where the pastor did all the work, and we were roundly critical of any hint of a clergy-laity distinction between members of the body of Christ. Why would we accept the vocation of a pastor or other clergy person, when before God we are *all clergy*?! We had elders, but the elders were there for purposes of government and order and for nipping false teaching in the bud. They were not ordained by anyone, but were simply recognized as elders because of the function they served. It was emphasized over and over that, as a Brethren assembly, we did *not* have a separate clergy class.

I'm about to say something critical about this church and also report some serious errors that it made. However, I want to preface this by saying first that what happened in my church would not necessarily happen in other Plymouth Brethren congregations. Further, it is hard to deny that the church of my childhood memory got a lot right. The culture of personal Bible study and devotion that it fostered in me wasn't a gimmick—a slick program that made Bible-reading more attractive to young people. Not at all. It was simply the culture of the church. Everyone had his own Bible, and everyone read it and studied it and talked about what he[2] had learned. Cultures have the values they have for a reason. I cannot think of a better explanation for the culture that our church was able to cultivate than our stubborn belief that all Christians are priests to God and are, therefore, equal before God, both with regard to rights as God's children and with regard to responsibility as God's servants. *It was ultimately because of that belief that I knew my voice was worth hearing,* but all of that changed for me one day when I was told to stop speaking in church.

A Time for Silence

In 2002, serious conflicts arose within our assembly. Due to some scandals that came to light in that year, two of the church's leaders—an elder and a deacon—were placed under church discipline. First Corinthians 5:11 was applied directly to them and the entire congregation was instructed

---

2. And she, to a more limited extent, but I'll say more about that shortly.

to avoid these two men completely, with the exception of necessary business interactions. As I got caught up in the ensuing conflict—which in my case was unavoidable—I began to develop disagreements with the elders about how they were handling the situation. I expressed my disagreement with the elder whose personal charisma and conviction was obviously stronger than the others, but I was shut down. He told me flatly that the matter was not up for discussion. I also expressed my opinion about their handling of the conflict with several friends.

Then I made a decision to go directly against what the elders had told the congregation to do. On a summer Sunday morning, I approached one of the regular attendees of the church and asked him to contact one of the men who was being shunned. These two men were friends, I reasoned, and friends need to support one another during hard times. After I had made my request, the man said to me, "Michael, do you realize what you are asking me to do?" I did. I was asking him to disobey the elders' instruction out of concern for his friend. Doing that would come at a certain cost.

When they learned I had talked with another church member about the matter, the elders called me aside after the worship service into one of the Sunday school classrooms. I remember it like it was yesterday. They confronted me about my disobedience to their instructions and asked me to repent. When I persisted in challenging them, they told me that, because of my rebellion, I was not allowed to speak openly in the church until a future time when I would, hopefully, repent of my disobedience to them.

I still remember that meeting quite clearly—the meeting in which I was told I would not be permitted to use my voice in church. It was just me and the three elders. Two of them tried to tell me gently. In fact, they seemed to think it would not be a very difficult thing for me to hear. But it is difficult—maybe impossible—to silence a person without hurting him. Indeed, the feelings that followed—a garbled mixture of shame, anger, disillusionment, and frustration—were not easy to leave behind once they entered my soul. It was the most emotionally challenging experience of my life and I don't think I've quite gotten over it yet. As a homeschooled young person in my late teens, that church was my primary community beyond my family. It was the place where I shared my deepest thoughts about God, and a place where people listened to what I had to say. How many people can say they have a place like that? I took it for granted then, but now I know that very few teenagers—or adults for that matter—have the privilege that I had then to use my voice so freely in the church (or anywhere, for that matter). But in that moment, as the elders told me that my voice was not welcome, at least until I had met their requirements for what they called restoration, I felt the full value of that gift. I'm sure we've all heard the popular proverb that says, "You don't know what you have until you've lost it." I think that's true.

Racked with guilt, within a few days I called one of the elders to confess that I had, in fact, registered my disagreement with the elders with several people, not only that one person whom I had asked to contact the shunned man. Upon my confession, I heard the elder's half-frustrated, half-dismayed sigh on the other end of the line. His first words to me were, "Michael, may God have mercy on your soul." My defiance proved weak in the end and I complied with that elder's request that I write about a dozen apology letters to all the people to whom I had spoken about my disagreements with the elders.

After sending out the letters, it seemed I had met the elders' requirements for repentance; for a few weeks thereafter I was told I could participate audibly in church services again. I had been restored.

But I did not want to exercise a spiritual gift that could be taken away from me so easily. I decided that, for the time being, I would simply be quiet. In the end, I never participated aloud in another meeting in that church again. A little over two years passed. While I was away at college, that little assembly closed its doors permanently. Like me, so many people had been silenced that there were not enough voices left to justify a gathering. That church no longer exists to this day.

Those who have been kind enough to listen to my story since then often respond with compassion and sympathy. They sense something inherently unjust in my silencing and can understand why I felt violated, even though many have not experienced something like that themselves. It is not a happy story—not the kind of childhood tale one enjoys sharing with friends over dinner. For that reason, some of my gentle readers might find solace in the belief that my story is fairly unique—that few people have gone through what I underwent, and that most churches do not silence people the way I was silenced.

But actually, the opposite is true. People are silenced on a regular basis in many churches across the world. Unlike in my case, in which I was silenced for an offense I had committed—and for which I could achieve restoration by completing a few specific tasks—in these cases people are being silenced *because of who they are.* They are women—lots of women—and they have voices that, in many churches, are not welcomed, or at least not to the extent that men's voices are. In reality, my status in my assembly on that summer's Sunday was reduced no further than to that of every female attendee. I left out this part of my description of my childhood church above because I wanted to bring it in here for dramatic effect. In our church we believed that the doctrine of the priesthood of all believers led to the inclusion of all *male* voices in the church. Strangely, we also believed that women were priests to God, just like men. The Bible, after all, is clear on that point. Yet, even though the doctrine of the priesthood of all believers led to our welcoming every man to participate, we somehow saw no logical flaw in our prohibition of the same for women. At my church, women's voices were almost *never* heard during meetings. The only exceptions to this rule were that they could ask for prayer during the Wednesday evening prayer meetings (though they couldn't pray aloud), could teach Sunday school to the younger children, and could sing solos on a Sunday morning or on a special occasion. Other than that, they could not speak publicly during our meetings. I remember a few occasions in which women who were newcomers to the congregation participated audibly during the remembrance meeting. I knew that when that happened an elder would approach the woman after the meeting and explain what we perceived to be the biblical teaching about how women ought to be silent in the church. This took care of it. Some women were puzzled by the idea, but I never heard a woman complain about its being inconsistent with the teaching about the priesthood of *all* believers. I never heard of any woman objecting to the church's policy—questioning, yes, but not actually objecting.

Somehow (to my embarrassment now), I never saw a contradiction between the doctrine of the priesthood of all believers and our practice of silencing women either. This, after all, was what everyone around me said the Bible taught, and that was good enough for me. Churches that had a clergy-laity separation were certainly doing something wrong by limiting the voices heard to those of the clergy. They were quenching the Spirit, we said, by limiting the free use of God's gifting in the church. Still, it never occurred to me that our church was missing out on anything by silencing women. I embraced this perspective without any doubts until I went to college, where I discovered that, actually, even among conservative evangelical churches in America, my church's practice was considered a bit extreme.

A Time for Questions

In 2004, I enrolled in the Biblical Studies program at The Master's College (TMC)—now The Master's University—in Southern California. John MacArthur, the college's president at the time, is a leading proponent of what has come to be known in the past several decades as complementarianism, and this is the official position of the school as well. But on campus, I quickly learned that a church like the one in which I had been raised was considered extreme in its literal application of the New Testament's instructions about women's silence. I had been wounded by my church and, therefore, was happy to poke fun with my college friends at its strict practice of silencing women in the assembly. Nevertheless, in the back of my mind I wondered if something was wrong. "If the Bible is God's word," I thought, "and if it says that women should be silent in church, why should a church that applies the text directly to its practice be considered extreme? If women are not *actually* supposed to be quiet in the church, then what *is* the proper application of Paul's teaching in 1 Corinthians 14:34?"

I began to discover that the answers available in my new social sphere were far from clear. Even though all the churches that students at TMC attended claimed to practice biblical guidelines for gender roles (they were all hierarchicalist), no one seemed to be able to nail down what this was supposed to mean in practice. In some of these churches, women taught in Sunday school classes for children until they were teenagers, but not afterward. This made sense to me, because it is "men" not "males" over whom they should not have authority according to 1 Timothy 2:12. But I noticed that in other churches women led small group Bible studies in which men also participated. In others, even if they were not leading the study, women sometimes participated vocally, which seemed not only to violate 1 Timothy 2:12 but also 1 Corinthians 14:34. This puzzled me. For my friends in college, this seemed entirely normal and reasonable. They somehow saw no inconsistency between this practice and the teaching about women's silence in Paul's letters. But for me it was not so easy because I had been taught to take the Bible at face value. The Bible says women should be silent, and not only that, but they should not lead either. Why, then, should it be considered normal for them to speak, especially when men were present? (Keep in mind, I was for the first time mixing with Christians who called their church leaders pastors instead of elders, and who required people who preach and teach regularly to have some kind of formal training in a Bible school or seminary.)

Other churches drew a distinction between sharing or giving a testimony on the one hand, and preaching or teaching on the other. A woman might be invited to share something, even to the entire congregation of both men and women, but because she was not teaching according to a certain definition of the word (though, it seemed to me that people were indeed learning through the process), this was deemed permissible. I had trouble making sense of such reasoning. On the face of it, the Bible says women should not speak, and it does so without specifying distinctions between testimony, sharing, preaching, and teaching. Further, it seemed to me the sermons the apostles preached, as recorded in the book of Acts, were largely based on testimony—they were stories that connected God's work with what the apostles had themselves seen and experienced with Jesus. "Isn't testifying before a group about what God has done at least *a kind* of preaching?," I wondered. Some talked about a difference between authoritative teaching or preaching and other types of vocal public address that women were allowed to do. But when it came to actually demonstrating such a distinction between these various ways of talking about God in front of a group from the Bible, no answer was forthcoming. I'd been taught my whole life to pay close attention to the words of Scripture. But I didn't see any such fine distinctions—whether between authoritative versus nonauthoritative teaching, or between preaching and testimony—anywhere on the pages of my open Bible.

This variety in practice and application of the doctrine of women's silence in the church was new to me and, frankly, I had considerable trouble grasping the slippery explanations that were offered. All the churches talked about being biblical in their ministry practices, yet they varied wildly from each other when it came to how they limited women in the church's speaking and leading ministries. The only thing that actually united them was their agreement that women's voices should be limited *somehow*. The rest was left up to the individual churches to decide. The lines between what was biblically supported and what wasn't were blurry at best.

The other point of tension I began to experience resulted from the fact that I was learning from women professors. I had been homeschooled up to the day I entered college. My mother, therefore, was the only woman under whose teaching I had sat in an academic context on a consistent basis until then. For some reason—whether because she was my mother or because I was not yet a full-grown man—this was acceptable. In college, however, I found myself learning from women instructors in traditional classrooms, and the enrichment I enjoyed by submitting myself to their instruction was undeniable. In fact, the professor who mentored me the most closely of all my instructors during my college years was Dr. Lisa LaGeorge, a woman professor from whom I took several classes in crosscultural ministry and who mentored me in earning my certificate to teach English as a foreign language. I was definitely learning from women while in college, and much of what I learned was inseparable from my Christian formation, including the formation of my theology. Further, because TMC was a Christian college, *all* of the professors were expected to integrate themes of Christian faith into their teaching. It was virtually impossible to take any class at TMC without sitting under teaching that in some way touched upon the gospel and the Bible.

For students accustomed to a school environment, the involvement of women professors seemed to present no contradiction in the face of a belief that women ought not teach men in church. But for me, the school environment *itself* was new, and it proved impossible for my mind to separate the idea of learning in a school under a woman professor from the idea of learning under a woman's teaching in a church context (or anywhere else, for that matter). The Plymouth Brethren had taught me carefully that the building in which we met on Sundays was *just a building*. It was not a sanctified space; it was no holier than our home living room, a backyard, or a storefront. Indeed, when my father, brothers, cousins, friends, and I would go camping on a weekend, we would celebrate Holy Communion together in the forest around a campfire on Sunday morning. Thus, I had a harder time than many of my classmates did in distinguishing between classroom space and Sunday morning church space. It was all the same to me—and if a woman could not teach about God, the Bible, and Christian life in a church building on a Sunday morning, I found it difficult to understand why she could do so in a classroom on a Monday afternoon just because the setting was different.

To compound it all, I had been homeschooled in the first generation of a burgeoning homeschooling movement in the United States. The pioneers of that movement homeschooled with purpose. For them, homeschooling was not just a good, alternative way to educate; it was *the right way* to educate. Theirs was a resistance movement. They were bucking the system. One part of the conventional education system they were resisting was its tendency to bracket out learning from the rest of life. "Children don't have to sit in a classroom to learn," they argued. For my parents, and others who followed the same philosophy, *the whole world was a school*. Our family vacations *always* had an educational flavor. We visited historical sites and museums; we avoided amusement parks and anything akin to them like a plague.

While I'm on the topic, I should say something more about how my experience of growing up in the early homeschool movement probably prepared me for a change of mind about women's voices in the church later. Homeschooling parents are in constant education mode. As I mentioned before, the entire world becomes a schoolhouse for them. Because mothers, who were often full-time homemakers in the homeschooling families of my generation, usually filled the educator role more than fathers did, I interacted constantly with women who tirelessly tried to facilitate innovative educational opportunities for their children. The result was a culture in which nearly every grown woman I knew was constantly reading, thinking, discussing, and searching. It wasn't until later that I realized how creative, intelligent, and driven these women were. I later had no trouble recognizing how effective women can be at teaching. I had experienced it my whole life.

Perhaps for some, an upbringing void of an institutionalized school experience might sully one's view of the traditional classroom. For me, however, it had the opposite effect. Once it became available to me in college, I devoured traditional classroom learning. I loved every minute of it. For me, the classroom was and still is an extension of the real world. As I write this, I am a high school teacher, and it still, as far as I'm concerned, all goes together. For me, the classroom is a wonderful, sanctified place set apart for teaching and learning. I know of no other place like it. A preacher has about fifteen to forty minutes once a week to deliver a sermon to the gathered congregation. A teacher, on the other hand, can have up to four or five hours a week with a comparatively smaller group of people. The influence of a teacher or professor is nothing to be dismissed! For that reason, again, I was confused as a student at a Christian college about why it was alright for women to teach in a classroom from behind a lectern, but not in a church from behind a pulpit. I couldn't see the difference.

Apart from chatting about it with friends on campus, this dissonance between doctrine and practice did not reach the forefront of my attention for most of my time in college. No one around me seemed to be struggling with these questions. Also, as a man, I must admit, I sadly did not see a need to confront the status quo. The problem didn't have a direct bearing on me, I seemed to think, so I didn't delve very deeply into questioning it.

Still, the issue was there, even though it was not primary, and I had occasion to be reminded of it from time to time. One incident in particular stands out. I took several pedagogy courses on how to teach English as a foreign language. The instructor was a woman who had spent nearly a decade overseas as an EFL teacher. She was also an alumna of the college and a devout Christian, and she took her role as a teacher very seriously. It was common at TMC for professors and instructors to open class in prayer, and sometimes with a short devotional thought (especially if it was a three-hour evening class, as these classes were). This instructor informed the class on the first evening that this was her intention as well. But, she felt that giving a devotional meditation at the beginning of class in front of the male students would risk violating her biblical role as a woman. While the college had no policy forbidding her from giving devotions in her classes, her commitment to following Scripture compelled her to ask the male students to sign up for a rotation to present short thoughts from Scripture at the start of each class. I am almost certain that no one in that class would have been offended or uncomfortable had she chosen to open her Bible before us, or had she put the whole class—not just the male students—on a rotation to share. But her conscience directed her otherwise. She felt it was not her place to teach the Bible to men, and she knew that giving a devotion at the start of class from an open Bible would be doing just that. Actually, she was right—giving a devotion would have certainly put her at risk of teaching us men something from the Bible!

As I recall, this did not strike me as unreasonable at the time. In fact, it made sense to me given the interpretation of the biblical texts about women's being silent that I had been taught up to that point. Nevertheless, I remember wondering about the consistency between that instructor's practice and her belief. What was it about an open Bible on the lectern in front of her that changed everything? She felt comfortable—even called by God—to train both men and women in her classroom to the best of her ability. She was clearly taking a position of authority over us male students. That is what teachers do. It could not have been a matter of roles. Further, it was not the act of teaching men itself in which she felt she should not engage. Her femaleness neither prevented her from teaching nor from having authority over us men. It was much more specific than that. She believed that she should not teach specifically *the Bible* to men.

She could teach virtually anything else, so long as she had the requisite qualifications to do so. But as soon as a Bible was open in front of her, she felt she needed to be silent.

I cannot remember exactly when, but at some point this incident became the departure point for the discovery of more inconsistencies in what I had been taught. I began to realize that I had been a student of women throughout my life. It had not begun in a college classroom.

I already mentioned that I had been homeschooled, and that my mother was my teacher in that "school." So, that's enough for starting. I remember in a moment of tension during my early teenage years my telling my mother that, actually, she should be listening to *me* teach *her* because I was a man and she was a woman. If that sounds absurd, it's because it is. But in my youthful folly, this was my hermeneutical approach. In reality, I was struggling with the fact that I had been my mother's student my whole life, and I was trying to square this—albeit in an inappropriate manner—with what I had been taught the Bible says.

But my mother was only one of several women from whom I learned a great deal. In my late teen years, I was blessed to have been surrounded with more than a few adults who took an interest in my spiritual development. From among these, however, one person stands out in my memory as the most influential in terms of my training for future ministry. Though I did not realize it at the time, my Aunt Debbie was my primary ministry mentor as a teenager. She was the one who taught me how to teach the gospel to children. For four years, I learned from her as I assisted in her after-school Bible clubs for children during the school year, and in her front-yard Bible clubs during summer months. Because of her influence and teaching, I teamed up with my younger sister Susie to start two after-school Bible clubs in other elementary schools in the city of Ashtabula, which we eventually ran on our own for two years. To me and my sister, this felt like a normal way to spend one's summer free time and after-school hours. Why did giving our time to sharing Bible stories, songs about God's love, and the gospel message with children seem so normal to us? It was largely because of Aunt Debbie's mentorship. As I looked back at that experience while in college I began to think, "If it was wrong for women to teach men, how could it be right for men to learn from them? How could it be right for me to have learned so much from Aunt Debbie?"

Perhaps Aunt Debbie's mentoring me could be dismissed as unproblematic because she ceased to play that role in my life by the time

I became an adult. Someone could note that I was still a child then, and therefore Aunt Debbie never really engaged in mentoring a man. However, the contradiction only became more palpable the more I emerged into adulthood. More and more, women became key players in the story of my spiritual formation. And, far from avoiding it, I embraced the influence of mature women of faith in my life.

To highlight a key example, shortly after college I worked for a year as a discussion facilitator (part-time) in a one-year Bible and ministry program called INSIGHT. The director of the branch where I worked was my friend, Marisa Lapish. Marisa has ten children and she homeschooled all of them. She was one of those homeschool mothers I mentioned previously whose creativity, energy, and grassroots pedagogical thinking prepared me to see that women's speaking ministry in the church should be welcomed. When Marisa asked me to help her in the INSIGHT program, I eagerly accepted. This meant, however, that whereas previously I had learned only informally from her, now she was officially my mentor. She was mentoring me while we both were mentoring the students in the program. Neither of us is involved in INSIGHT anymore, but our mentor/mentee relationship has continued. Even after I moved away from Northeast Ohio, Marisa's advice and counsel continued to be important for me as a youth director and seminary student in New Jersey, and I still seek her out frequently for spiritual direction and guidance now in my work as a teacher in Turkey.

Few self-proclaimed Christians would say that I had done something wrong by allowing myself to be influenced by the teaching of women in the contexts I mentioned above. However, some would want to offer a word of caution. They would say that it is perfectly fine and even good to learn from godly women. But, a man needs to be cautious if a woman begins to acquire a role of spiritual authority—a pastoral role—in his life. This presents a problem for me because, as I look back over my life, it is undeniably clear this is precisely what has happened. Before college, though I had never attended a church that had women pastors or elders, both men *and* women had, in effect, been spiritual authorities to me in various ways. No pastor position existed in the Plymouth Brethren church in which I was raised. My spiritual mentors and teachers had *always* been laypeople. And, they had been *both* men *and* women. According to what has come to be called the complementarian position, a young man should gradually begin backing away from such mentor/mentee relationships as he approaches adulthood. But for me this never happened. I continued to be mentored spiritually by women and, by the time I went to seminary, was fully ready to receive direct instruction from women theologians, Bible scholars, historians, and pastors. I even sat under the direct mentorship of three experienced women pastors in practical ministry contexts during my seminary field education—Jennie, who was my supervisor in the program; Eleanor, a Presbyterian pastor in Cape Town, South Africa; and Karen, a Foursquare Church pastor in New Jersey. As far as I can recall, I never spoke about the issue of women in ministry at any length with these three pastors because we were too busy talking about issues related to ministry itself. Of course, I have sat under the teaching and mentorship of many godly men as well. But the point I'm making here is that, in light of the amount of influence faithful women have had on me, I don't know who I would be if I had never submitted myself to their leadership.

In my Plymouth Brethren church, we did not talk about women's roles very much. Instead, the focus was on functions. Basically, women could not do anything that required their speaking to groups in which men were present. Of course, by extension, this excluded them from being elders since elders had to be able to teach. But when I went to college, I began to hear a lot of talk about a woman's "role" in the church and Christian marriage. Far less emphasis was placed on a woman's *functions* (that is, specifics about what she actually does) in the church than on her role. The primary thing to avoid, from this new point of view, was women's being in *positions* of authority over men, not really women's speaking—or even teaching—*per se*. This seemed to be how these complementarians were justifying the fact that women were doing a lot of teaching in their circles, and often when men were present. As long as the teaching was not authoritative in nature, it was permissible. But this, again, struck me as odd because I had always been taught to take the Bible at face value. "If it says women shouldn't speak, that's what it means," I reasoned. Nevertheless, in the absence of anyone pushing me to ask questions, I was content overall to move along without voicing too many concerns.

But then something changed. I began to consider marriage. Isabel Vera Zambrano and I began dating in our senior year of college. What attracted me to Isabel was not only her electric personality, her mischievous laugh, her nearly permanent, bright smile, or her lightning-fast sense of humor. Isabel was a sincere, committed follower of Jesus who lived to serve others, especially the poor and vulnerable. Her working philosophy was something she called, "incarnational ministry." It was a practical way of applying the biblical doctrine of the incarnation of God in Christ to Christian ministry. Isabel didn't want to just serve the poor and marginalized from a distance; she wanted to live with and among them, to be their friend and companion in life's journey. She wanted to learn *from* them as well as to teach them what she knew about God. I noticed that whenever I spent time with her I came away a better person than I had been before. It wasn't guilt. I don't remember comparing myself to her. Rather, there was something about her spirit and singular focus that made me feel accepted and inspired at the same time. During her studies, Isabel joined a program offered through the college called Los Angeles Bible Extension, which involved her living and serving in a poor (and dangerous) area of downtown Los Angeles through a ministry of the First Evangelical Free Church in the city. I was also interested in crosscultural ministry, and I wanted to learn Spanish, so I volunteered once a week as a tutor of Central American immigrant children through the same ministry.

Isabel and I became friends by serving together in that ministry, but eventually I began to wonder if there might be a way to extend Isabel's influence on me. One evening I asked her to go for a walk with me along Placerita Canyon Road, which runs through the middle of the The Master's University campus, and I asked her about the prospect of our considering a future together as a married couple. She agreed to consider it, and we began spending time together. (Some might call this dating, but to be truthful we didn't go on many dates. We mostly just did homework together, but I'm sure it was romantic in its own way.) At that time I assumed that Isabel held to the same hierarchicalist views to which, as far as I knew, everyone at TMC held and that, as I believed at the time, were taught in the Bible. "Of course, if Isabel were married, she would accept the Bible's teaching about her husband's authority," I thought. "If we get married, she will see me as her leader, and I will see her as my follower. I'll be captain of our marriage ship; she'll be first mate."

Well, I was in for a surprise. I don't remember how the subject came up, but one day she told me very clearly that, actually, she didn't buy in to the hierarchicalist view of things that was taught at our college. She believed that women could teach men—in church or anywhere else. Furthermore, should she ever marry, Isabel told me that she did not plan to see her husband as her authority. While she expected to submit to her husband, she did not expect the submission to be one-sided—she hoped her husband *would also submit to her!* Isabel was, thankfully, quite forthright with me about this. She cheerily and openly expressed her views, all the while smiling and laughing as she usually did (and still does). Strangely (to me), our disagreement about this issue did not seem to bother her very much.

But for me, this was a point of immediate and enduring anxiety. I knew that, unless we agreed about who was going to be the leader in our marriage, it would not be advisable for us to marry. The problem was, I really liked Isabel. My desire that she and I would someday marry brought the questions that had formerly only bothered me occasionally right up to the front of my consciousness. Suddenly, this issue became personal and extremely important. *One of us was going to have to suffer a change of mind if we were going to have a future together.* In the beginning, I fully expected it would be her. I knew the Bible's teaching on this, and if only I showed her the relevant passages and explained them to her, she would see that I was right, or so I thought. As it turned out, it was my mind that would change.

Conclusion

I have this crisis to thank for finally sending me on the journey that has resulted in my change of mind about the question of women's place in the church and Christian home—and ultimately to writing this book. This story is long enough already, so I'll just say that Isabel and I have been married for ten years now, and she hasn't changed her view about this! But I have, and here's why.

2

Silent in the Churches

THE POSITION THAT WOMEN should not speak in certain settings in the church due to their gender is sometimes referred to as the traditional view. But some proponents of that position do not like the term traditional because it makes it sound as if it is based on tradition alone, as opposed to biblical teaching. The result, which has come about within the past half a century, has been quite literally the adoption of a new word—*complementarianism*. It comes from the word "complementary" (*not* complimentary) and has to do with the idea that men and women are two parts of a complete whole.

New Words, Old Ideas

There is another important reason for creating a term other than "traditional" for this position. Complementarians believe that women and men are equal before God. This is why they emphasize the word "roles" so much. They want to be sure that people understand that women are not inferior to men in any way that relates to their nature as human persons. They insist that women are every bit as intelligent and capable as men are. In terms of their value as Spirit-filled members of the body of Christ, women are equal to men entirely. Furthermore, and most importantly, complementarians affirm unequivocally that *both* men *and* women are made equally in the image of God. Women and men differ only in terms of the roles they fill in the church and home.

Unfortunately, however, the belief and teaching that women and men are equal in these ways was not emphasized nearly so much in the Christian church in the past, to put it generously. To the contrary, many theologians in past generations taught that women were the weaker sex both spiritually and intellectually. They are, furthermore, more susceptible to temptation than men. As a result, they are in need of constant male guidance and protection from false teaching.

In fact, some prominent theologians even taught that women were either not made in God's image or that they bear the image God in a secondary way, inferior to the way men do. Among the many who taught this are influential theologians like Augustine, Thomas Aquinas, Ulrich Zwingli, and John Calvin. According to Calvin, for example, "women *are* in God's image. But on account of their eminence, men are much more so—so much more, in fact, that Calvin saw God as more glorified in the birth of a boy than in the birth of a girl."[1] This kind of reasoning is ubiquitous in the Christian theology of the past. It is so offensive to our postfeminist-movement way of thinking about women that one can easily understand why even a self-proclaimed conservative group of today's church leaders would want to distance itself from it. The fact is, even though complementarians often accuse biblical feminists—the term often used by complementarians for Christians who oppose their doctrine—of ignoring the church's historic teachings in deference to feminist ideology, complementarianism is also a new idea, and it contrasts starkly with what many prominent theologians in past centuries taught about women. *Neither* group is actually conservative in the sense of preserving what the majority of theologians in past generations taught about women. As New Testament scholar Alan Padgett points out, "Complementarian theology is just as revisionist, just as influenced by modern thought, as the egalitarian point of view," and only dates to the later part of the twentieth century.[2] This is why a new word—complementarianism—needed to be coopted to describe a position that preserved some of the past generations' *practices* of requiring the silence of women while rejecting their *beliefs* about the inferiority of women to men.

The problem with this let's-make-a-new-word approach, however, is that past generations' practices of silencing women in the church were directly connected to the belief that women were inferior to men. But

---

1. Thompson, *Reading the Bible*, 130 (emphasis original). See Calvin, *Sermons of Master Iohn Calvin*, 54–55.

2. Padgett, *As Christ Submits*, 9.

once the foundational belief of women's inferiority has been taken away, is it possible for practices that were formerly based on that belief to continue unchanged? It is sufficient for now to point out that this is, at best, an unusual way of doing things. Normally, beliefs should guide practice, and as beliefs change, practices should follow suit.

The opposing position in this debate has come to be known as *egalitarianism*, from the word "equal," because of its emphasis on avoiding gender-based restrictions on ministry functions. "We are equal before God," the egalitarian argues, "so, we should be equal in ministry as well." Egalitarians contend that the *belief* that women and men are equal leads naturally to practices that affirm this belief.

A challenge with using "egalitarian" or "equality," however, is that some seem to confuse it with "equivalence." Men and women are not equivalent to each other, as if one could just be swapped out for the other. No egalitarian would suggest that a woman could be a husband, or that a man could be a daughter. Being a son, mother, wife, or grandfather involves intrinsically being one sex or the other, and there is no confusion about this among biblical egalitarians.

However, introducing the concept of roles into a discussion about what men and women should (and should not) feel free to do in the church and home has caused a tremendous amount of confusion. Complementarians have been eager to use the word role to explain how women can be equal to men in essence yet unequal to men in practice. The reasoning seems to go roughly like this: "A woman can't be a father, even though a man can. How is this different from excluding women from the role of a pastor?" The problem is that identities like father, mother, sister, brother, aunt, uncle, etc. *are not roles at all,* while vocations like pastor, elder, or deacon are. Being a man or woman is a matter of biological[3] reality, and therefore the identities that human beings acquire by virtue of their sex— like grandmother, aunt, uncle, or brother—are not the same as identities that we acquire by performing certain functions within a society.

Let's take the identity of uncle as an illustration. Every man, in principle, has the potential to become an uncle (though there is no guarantee, of course). And, if my sister or brother has a child, I *will* be an uncle. I cannot avoid it. But, what I *do* as an uncle is quite flexible. In some cultures, an uncle is considered responsible for finding a spouse for his niece. In other cultures, an uncle should take his nephew fishing every

---

3. Even if sex also has a spiritual dimension, such that a disembodied "soul" could be male or female, the argument here still holds true.

once in a while. In other cultures, an uncle is expected to buy choco-lates for his nieces and nephews. But, match-making, fishing guide, and chocolate-supplier are identities that an uncle can only acquire by per-forming certain functions; it *could be* that a given man whose sibling has a child won't play any of these roles. In addition, we can observe right away that an aunt *could* conceivably perform them. There is a difference between roles that we play by choice or because of the expectations of our cultures and the identities that we acquire simply by being male or female in certain circumstances. I'll mention here my sister-in-law, Jessica. Jess is an expert welder and mechanic. She can build a pickup truck or mo-torcycle from the ground up in her garage. Stereotypically, at least in the rural American culture of my upbringing, auto mechanics is something that a brother-in-law might be interested in, not a sister-in-law. But, Jess can't become a brother-in-law to me by being an auto mechanic any more than she can become a sister-in-law by being a good cook (another of her many skills). Jess *is* a sister-in-law, but she *plays the role* of an auto mechanic (at least on the weekends). The role a person plays in a given society is not the same as her intrinsic identity.

Consider the etymology of the word "role," as described by the Online Etymology Dictionary. It has a theatrical background. An actor's lines were written on a roll of paper. Gradually, the word became a stand-in for the things the actor himself did in the play—that is, the actor's role. Later, social psychologists who were trying to find ways to describe how the various actors in a society function adopted the word.[4] A character in one of Shakespeare's plays famously says,

> *All the world's a stage,*
> *And all the men and women merely players;*
> *They have their exits and their entrances,*
> *And one man in his time plays many parts*[5]

That seems to be the idea behind using the word "role" to describe people in real life as opposed to people who are merely acting. So, take a movie like *Sherlock Holmes,* in which actor Robert Downey Jr. plays Holmes and Jude Law plays his assistant, Dr. John Watson.[6] Let's as-sume that, in real life, these two actors are equals, but for the sake of the movie, they choose freely to take on two different roles in which one is

4. *OED,* s.v. "role."

5. Shakespeare, "As You Like It," Act II, Scene VII, Lines 142–45.

6. Ritchie, *Sherlock Holmes.*

subordinate to the other (if we can think of Watson and Holmes's complicated relationship in this simplified way). The complementarian reasoning seems to go as follows: "While women and men are *really* equal, they should choose to play roles in life in which one is subordinate to the other." But such a premise is a nonstarter for the simple reason that, in real life, *we are not actors!* In fact, Jude Law could have played Holmes's role in the film if he had been asked to do so. Roles, by definition, are not tied to reality as such. Instead, we take them upon ourselves, whether on the set of a movie or play, or on the stage of life.

A few months ago, as I was putting my daughters to bed, my older daughter Mikaela, who is seven years old, said to me, "Daddy, I don't know what I should be when I grow up. I don't know if I should be an astronaut, a dentist, or a hunter." Of course, as I knew every good father should do in such situations, I suggested to Mika that she could be anything God would call her to be, and also added that she had plenty of time to decide. Mika was trying to discern what role she should play in life. In her society, the roles of astronaut, dentist, and hunter (apparently) were available for her to fill, and she was pondering how she might fit in, given her interests, abilities, and gifts. But if Mika had asked me, "Daddy, I don't know if I should be a man or a woman," what would follow would be a very different kind of conversation. Why? Because man and woman are not roles people fill. One simply *is* a man or a woman. Certainly, society *expects* certain behaviors of men and women—behaviors a given man or woman may or may not perform—but whether I fulfill society's expectations or not, as an adult male, I remain a man. Perhaps my male readers have heard the admonitions, "Be a man" and, "Man up." But the truth is, a man cannot be more or less a man than he already is. The same could be said of animals. Dogs are just dogs—they can't be otherwise. A dog can play the role of a pet, or a sheepherder, or a seeing-eye dog, but she can't play the role of a dog *per se*, because that's simply what she *is*. Mika is a girl, so whether she becomes an astronaut, a dentist, or a hunter, she will be a female version of it. Her sex is part of who she is, while her future occupation is a role she will fill.

This is why talking about women and men in terms of roles causes more confusion than clarity. If a society decides that women should *always* play a subordinate role, in that case women are not taking on the role of a woman *per se*, but rather that of a servant, slave, follower, or some other subordinate—because in that given society this is what is expected of her. One might argue that God created women to be men's subordinates, and that therefore they should always take on roles that are subordinate to men. But if that is the case, in what sense are women *really* men's spiritual equals? In what truly meaningful way can we assert that men and women are essentially equal?

Saying that men and women are different—a truth that no one in this debate denies—does not lead automatically to the conclusion that men should be leaders and women followers, or that men should speak and women should be silent. Men and women could be different in a host of ways and still participate in the church's various speaking ministries. The issue is not whether or not men and women are different. Rather, it's about whether or not women's gifting, calling, and preparation should be enough to determine what ministry roles they fill in the church. There is nothing biological that prevents a woman from standing behind a pulpit and delivering a sermon, for example. Maybe she can't lift the pulpit and carry it away. But, so what? The barriers that prevent women's voices from being heard in the most prominent speaking-and-listening contexts in the church have nothing to do with anything inherent to femaleness.

In places heavily influenced historically by European cultures—ones we might call Western (though I prefer to use "Westernized" because the geography is a bit scrambled at this point)—it is common for women to take on speaking and authority roles in a wide variety of public contexts. Women are managers of companies, university professors, school administrators, journalists, lawyers, judges, police officers, government officials, even prime ministers and presidents of entire nations. In such contexts, there is clearly nothing intrinsically offensive to the wider culture about women's being in leadership positions over men. The wider culture does not object, at least overtly, to women speaking to and even educating large groups of people that include men. Churches in such societies, therefore, can no longer claim that asking women to be silent in the church is supported by the culture around them. In other words, they cannot say that a woman's role needs to be a silent one in those societies. It would have to be shown, rather, that women's speaking to or leading men specifically *in church* is uniquely problematic. Many churches that practice the silencing of women nevertheless encourage their young women to pursue authority roles outside it. In fact, it is difficult to find a Christian college or university that does not advertise itself as a leader-shaping institution. Egalitarians point out that this is inconsistent. If women are not supposed to be leaders in the church, it is inconsistent to encourage them to be leaders elsewhere.

Having said all that, I applaud complementarians' affirmation of men and women's spiritual and intellectual equality. This is undeniably a move in the right direction. Now, we should *all* take the next step and also affirm male-female equality in practice.

Navigating the Debate

When one first begins reading the numerous books and articles that have been written on this subject over the past few decades one can easily become befuddled. It can seem like there are as many interpretations of the relevant Bible texts as there are interpreters! Indeed, this is surely one of the reasons why so many books have been written on this topic. Are all the scholars simply representing themselves individually? Or, are there really two, distinct sides to this debate?

There *are* two sides. While daunting at first, the answer to this question is actually quite straightforward. Here it is: the complementarian believes women's ministry in the church should be limited based on their gender, and the egalitarian believes it should not. It's really that simple.[7] The distinction between the two sides in this debate—perhaps paradoxically—does *not* revolve around a certain interpretation of a selection of biblical passages. Instead, the distinction revolves around the *practice* of the church. Recognizing this is important because, actually, both egalitarian and complementarian scholars disagree among themselves, at least in the details, about how the relevant Scripture passages should be understood. What really keeps them on the same team is a matter of praxis, not Bible interpretation *per se*.

A quick perusal of only a few books that have been published on this topic bears this out. Craig Keener, Alan Padgett, and Cynthia Long Westfall are three scholars known for defending the position that women should be free to use their gifts in the church without gender-based limitations. But, they do not agree about how the relevant Bible passages should be interpreted. Take 1 Corinthians 11:1–16 as an example. Keener thinks it was the women at Corinth who wanted to remove their veils, and that Paul instructs them against doing so. Padgett also thinks that it was the women who wanted to remove their veils in the Corinthian

---

7. Of course, some people think women should be quiet because they're innately inferior to men. I assume that someone who holds to such a view would not be interested in reading a book like this, so I'm intentionally ignoring it.

church, but thinks that Paul is actually arguing in their defense. That is, according to Padgett, Paul wants them to be able to remove their veils if they think it best. Westfall, by contrast, argues that it was the *men* at Corinth—not the women—who wanted the women to remove their veils and that Paul is defending the women's desire to keep on wearing them! These are very different interpretations of a pivotal passage in this debate.

But, notice carefully that all three of these scholars agree on this: women should not be limited in ministry due to their gender. They arrive at the same practical conclusion, even though the interpretational paths they trod to arrive there are different.

The same could be said of complementarian interpreters. They also vary with respect to this or that text's interpretation. However, complementarians face an important problem that egalitarians do not. As I mentioned before, complementarians are *by no means* united with regard to the practical implications of their position. They all agree that women should be limited in ministry *somehow,* but precisely where the boundaries of women's ministry should be set varies drastically from one complementarian interpreter to the next.

For example, notice how difficult it is to apply in practice Douglas Moo's version of complementarianism. This careful and well-respected complementarian scholar's conclusion after interpreting 1 Timothy 2:8–15 is this: Christian women "like men, have been given spiritual gifts (1 Corinthians 12:7–11). Women, like men, are to use these gifts to minister to the body of Christ (1 Peter 4:10); their ministries are indispensable to the life and growth of the church (1 Corinthians 12:12–26)."[8] But, Moo explains, Scripture limits Christian women in ministry according to 1 Timothy 2:8–15 in two key ways. First, he claims, Christian women are "not to teach Christian doctrine to men" and, second, they are "not to exercise authority directly over men in the church."[9] This may sound clear enough on the surface. But, what are the implications of this for the practical life of worship in a local congregation?

The Music Problem

Anyone who has attended church on a regular basis will agree that the Christian doctrine enshrined in hymns and songs is some of the most

8. Moo, "What Does It Mean?," 233.

9. Moo, "What Does It Mean?," 235.

remembered and cherished. Scripture recognizes music as a form of teaching (see Col 3:16). Many of the most beloved hymns were written by women. Fanny Crosby is probably the most famous American hymn-writer of all time. Hymns like, "Blessed Assurance" and, "Pass Me Not, O Gentle Savior" were theological products of her feminine mind. "Take My Life and Let It Be" was written by Frances Ridley Havergal. Jennie Hussey wrote, "Lead Me to Calvary," and Charitie L. Bancroft wrote the recently repopularized hymn, "Before the Throne of God Above." Here are a few more examples of hymns I grew up singing:

- "All the Way My Savior Leads Me," "Jesus, Keep Me Near the Cross," "Take the World, But Give Me Jesus," "To God Be the Glory," and "Redeemed," by Fanny Crosby

- "Who Is on the Lord's Side?," by Frances Ridley Havergal

- "He Will Hold Me Fast" and "Will the Circle Be Unbroken?," by Ada Habershon

- "Help Somebody Today," by Carrie Breck

- "His Eye Is on The Sparrow" and "God Will Take Care of You," by Civilla D. Martin

- "I Am Not Skilled to Understand," by Dora Greenwell

- "I Need Thee Every Hour," by Annie S. Hawks

- "Jesus, I Am Resting, Resting," by Jean S. Pigott

- "More Love to Thee," by Elizabeth Prentiss

- "Break Thou the Bread of Life," by Mary A. Lathbury

- "All Things Bright and Beautiful," by Cecil F. Alexander

- "Have Thine Own Way, Lord," by Adelaide A. Pollard

This is, of course, a short sample of a much longer list of hymns and praise songs written by women that have been used by the church over the past several centuries. I became familiar with all of these hymns as a child, and can sing a few of them from memory. Such hymns have served to shape Christians' thoughts about God for generations. This means that not only are the words of Christian women proclaimed from the pulpit, *the entire congregation has also memorized a great deal of doctrine that has been taught to them by women—and these women continue to teach the church through their hymns, even posthumously!* There is probably not a church in the world (with the exception of those churches that do not include music in their services) whose members have not been taught by women through hymns and praise songs.

Likewise, most churches welcome the ministry of women through live music. Even in the Plymouth Brethren church which I attended as a young person, women could sing solos in front of the congregation. If the measure of whether or not teaching has occurred is the learning of those who sit under that teaching, it seems obvious that singing—and certainly the writing of songs for others to sing—*is* a form of teaching. Yet, no complementarian wants to purge church hymnbooks of hymns written by women or ban women from music ministries. How is it possible for a church to simultaneously hold that it is unbiblical for women to teach Christian doctrine to men on the one hand, while on the other hand repeatedly leading its congregation in the singing of hymns that were written by women?!

Let's do a thought experiment. Suppose someone were to claim that, based on 1 Corinthians 14:34–35 and 1 Timothy 2:12, women should not sing in church choirs. How could a complementarian (virtually all of whom would disagree with this) respond? Let's put this fictional scenario in dialogue form. The person opposing women in choirs will be called "A" (for "Against") and the complementarian person defending women in church choirs we will call "P" (for "Pro").

> A: Women shouldn't sing in church choirs because Paul says women should be silent in church.
>
> P: Singing isn't really speaking.
>
> A: Yes it is.
>
> P: But it's not speaking in a formal sense.
>
> A: Yes it is. It's the most formal way of speaking one can imagine. It's entirely scripted!
>
> P: But, Paul is not worried about speaking in and of itself. He is worried about women teaching in the church.
>
> A: Paul implies in Colossians 3:16 that the singing of songs and hymns is a way of teaching, and common experience would say the same. People remember songs a lot better than they do lectures and speeches. Singing words is definitely a way of teaching them.

P: But there are instances of women singing, and even leading worship, in the Bible. For example, think of Miriam after the Red Sea crossing, and of Mary's "Magnificat."

A: God can make exceptions to a general rule. But for the church, we need to follow what the Bible says in 1 Corinthians 14:34–35 and 1 Timothy 2:12.

At this juncture in our imaginary conversation, "P" has a choice. He can either acknowledge that "A" has a point and that, in fact, the singing of hymns *is* an authoritative, formal way of teaching. Or, he has to continue searching for a good reason why women *should* be included in the church choir, despite what the Bible says. Suppose he chooses to pursue his defense of the practice further. What will his argument be?

This fictional scenario may appear farcical at first, and someone might wonder why we would engage in a thought experiment that would never happen in real life. But this scenario is not as ludicrous as it might appear. It actually represents a real issue, albeit an issue that probably falls outside the experience of many of my gracious readers. With reference to common practice in the early centuries of Christianity, historian Susan Ashbrook Harvey writes, "In Greek and Latin churches . . . women were often frankly discouraged even from congregational singing."[10] Because women's singing voices are accepted by probably every Christian reading this book, it is worth emphasizing how controversial women's choirs were in the church's past. In a fascinating chapter on the subject, my former professor, historian Kathleen McVey, provides several telling quotations from church fathers on the matter. She is worth quoting at length. I have put key portions in italics.

> [Other church fathers] were critical of women's participation in congregational song as well as in separate women's choirs. They invoked the Pauline . . . injunction against women's speaking in church *to oppose women's voices being heard at all* in the church. Cyril of Jerusalem (c. 315–86) specified for catechumens awaiting exorcism that men and women be segregated: then the men might read to one another, "The assembly of virgins, however, should be gathered together, *quietly reciting psalms or reading, so that their lips move, but the ears of others do not hear—'For I do not permit that a woman speak in the Church'* (1 Cor. 14:34). And the married woman should do likewise: she should pray and move her lips, *while not allowing her voice to be heard.*"

10. Harvey, "Singing Women's Stories," 174.

According to Isidore of Pelusium (d. 435), women were permitted to sing psalms in church only to prevent them from gossiping, but since this privilege has been abused, women should be prohibited from singing in church ("and also from loitering in the city") since "the majority of the people . . . misuse the sweetness of melody to arouse passion, thinking that it is no better than the songs of the stage."[11]

In his work against Pelagius, a false teacher, the church father Jerome likewise argued that women should not sing in mixed company in the church (as Pelagius had allegedly permitted) because this would legitimize such women as "teachers." Here is the quotation:

> "For you [Pelagius] add and set down the thesis: 'Women should also sing psalms to God.' But who does not know that women should sing psalms in their own cells, and apart from the company of men, and the gathering of crowds? Namely, you allow them to sing out what should be performed by them secretly and without any witnesses, *as though they were lawfully constituted teachers.*"[12]

The question of whether or not women's singing voices should be heard in church is still under debate in some parts of the church today, even if Protestants do not participate in the discussion. Some Christians still hesitate to allow women to sing in church choirs, and to thereby participate in leading the church's worship. Theologian Donna Risk Azdourian explains the situation thus,

> In the Syriac Church . . . women chanters date back to the fourth century, where they were first employed in divine liturgy by St. [Ephrem] the Syrian. The Armenian Orthodox Church also has a long history of women chanters, and several instances of female choir directors. Today, Greek, Russian, Ethiopic, Antiochan and [Russian Orthodox Churches outside Russia] use women chanters, even if there is not a unanimous set of standards for them, and some local parishes of these jurisdictions are averse for such positions. The Coptic Orthodox Church does not have any women choirs (with the exception to one official group in the Western Hemisphere), and typically does not endorse them.[13]

11. McVey, "Ephrem the Kitharode," 238.

12. McVey, "Ephrem the Kitharode," 238–39.

13. Asdourian, "Women for the Church," para. 4.

The luxury of being able to bracket out women's singing voices from discussions about whether or not women should function as pastors or teachers in the church is largely, therefore, a modern and culturally bound one. In turns out that, while the little dialogue I invented previously between "P" and "A" was fictional, a very similar one could easily materialize in real life. What could a Christian, wanting to stay true to Scripture, say in defense of women choirs—whether today or fifteen centuries ago? What, as it were, can "P" say in response to "A?"

As divine providence would have it, an example of just such a defense from the fifth century has survived for us to learn from. Saint Ephrem, whom we met previously in the preface of this book—and who provided its title—is probably the most beloved theologian of the Syriac Orthodox Church. In a poem he wrote in praise of Saint Ephrem, a later theologian of the same tradition called Jacob of Sarug makes a remarkable statement. Lauding Ephrem, he writes,

> Our sisters also were strengthened by you to give praise; for women were not allowed to speak in church. Your instruction opened the closed mouths of the daughters of Eve; and behold, the gatherings of the glorious (church) resound with their melodies. A new sight of women uttering the proclamation; and behold, they are called teachers among the congregations. Your teaching signifies an entirely new world; for yonder in the kingdom, men and women are equal. You labored to devise two harps for two groups; and you treated men and women as one to give praise.[14]

The good Saint Jacob has more to say about this. McVey summarizes thus,

> [B]y far the most important message of the memra[15] is Jacob's spirited defense of the custom of having women's choirs sing St. Ephrem's hymns. His argument is implicitly based on the following points: First, this liturgical role has been traditional for women since St. Ephrem himself. Second, the saint's innovation was itself based on Scripture . . . Third, women's choirs are useful in combating both heresy and idolatry. Finally, women are indeed redeemed equally with men and therefore ought not only to give praise aloud but also to cease from veiling their faces.[16]

14. Amar, *Metrical Homily*, vv. 40–44.

15. "Memra" was a term that refers, roughly, to a poetic sermon on a biblical passage.

16. McVey, "Jacob of Saruge," para. 8.

Notice that Jacob's defense of women in the church's music ministry is based not just on tradition, but ultimately on the oneness that male and female share in Christ. Historian Joseph Amar stresses the point further,

> [F]or all his encouragement to women to claim their rightful voice, [Ephrem] never advocated for their ordination . . . He did something considerably more. He based their role on one Baptism, one Body, and one Blood, not on ordination. It was a vision that did not depend on the clerical institution that was already becoming top-heavy in Ephrem's day, but on the gifts freely poured out on all believers, regardless of gender.[17]

Here, then, is the argument that Saint Jacob of Sarug and Saint Ephrem can lend to "P" in our fictional dialogue above: "Women should be encouraged to lead the worship of God in church because they, just like men, have been redeemed and baptized into one church. *That* is why 1 Corinthians 14:34–35 and 1 Timothy 2:12 should not be used to silence their singing voices."

My readers will doubtless have already guessed where I'm going with this: *The only argument available for defending women singers would lead logically to a defense of women preachers and teachers as well.* Most Protestant hierarchicalists will never encounter a Christian who thinks women should not participate in church choirs. But in the off chance that they did, the best defense they would be able to marshal in favor of the practice is also the best defense in favor of women preachers and teachers. Equality in Christ entails equality in *all* the worship and ministry of the church. Those who want to be theologically consistent can't pick and choose. Either women should be encouraged to teach—through song or otherwise—or they should not.

The Learning Problem

Some hierarchicalist Christian women have written books intended for mixed audiences as well. Surely these authors hope to teach their readers something through their writing, and those who read them hope to learn. In order to justify this, these women authors would need to show that teaching men through books is somehow different from doing so in person. As seminaries and universities have gradually sought to give women a place at the scholarly table over the past half century or so, it

17. Amar, "Women Are Proclaiming the Word," para. 18.

has gotten to the point now that learning from women Bible scholars, historians, and theologians is virtually unavoidable for any person who wants to earn a degree in any area of biblical or theological studies, particularly at the graduate level. In practice, it is hard to deny that women teach Christian doctrine to men quite often in the church and elsewhere, and it is probably happening more now than ever before.

When confronted with puzzles like this, advocates of complementarianism tend to respond that it is actually acceptable for women to teach men as long as they do not do so in a direct or authoritative way (see Douglas Moo's second principle above). For example, in response to a man's question about whether or not he should read books written by the reputable Christian author and Bible teacher Beth Moore, famed complementarian pastor and theologian John Piper responded that there was no problem with a man's benefitting from the teaching of a woman, so long as he guarded against that woman's beginning to take on the role of a pastor in his life.[18] It is not difficult to see why this man felt the need to ask Dr. Piper such a question. He probably realized that he was sitting under the teaching of a woman by reading Moore's books. It is hard to see why doing this would not be off limits for a complementarian man.

On the face of it at least, it seems that there is a considerable amount of confusion in churches that try to prevent women from engaging in the somewhat vaguely defined activities of exercising direct authority or providing authoritative teaching. One church might only allow women to teach Sunday school to males until they reach adolescence. Another church might designate the cutoff age sometime in early adulthood. Another church will ask women to teach Sunday schools or lead small groups no matter what the age of the group's members, having decided that a Sunday school teacher's role is not really authoritative like a preacher's. Another church might ask women to preach from the pulpit from time to time (like on Mother's Day), having decided that the role of a pastor is authoritative, but not the act of preaching itself. Another church might reserve the pulpit for men only, but will ask women to lead congregational singing, having decided that a worship leader's role is not authoritative like a preacher's is. Another church might hire a woman to provide marriage counseling to couples, reasoning that a counselor's role is not an authoritative one.

18. QABible, "Is It Wrong?"

This variety in complementarian practice extends beyond the walls of the church. Many Christian educational institutions employ women as teachers and professors. Christian colleges and seminaries that officially hold to complementarianism often hire women professors of theology, biblical studies, evangelism, missions, and other areas of study in which Christian doctrine is explicitly taught. I recently spoke with a woman professor who teaches biblical counseling at such a Christian university. She shared with me that she has to be careful when teaching male students to avoid being as direct as she is when she is teaching women. Indeed, it is not difficult to understand her predicament. The New Testament says that many of the first people to hear Jesus' teaching were amazed because he taught as "one who had authority, and not like the scribes."[19] But Christian women professors at complementarian institutions need to develop the skill of teaching *without* authority!

Perhaps the most immediately obvious problem with complementarian practice is in the area of evangelism outside the church or Christian institution. Any woman who shares the gospel with a man is teaching him Christian doctrine. This is impossible to avoid. No matter how humbly she proclaims the lordship of Christ, her words will be authoritative—at least from her point of view—simply by virtue of the content of her message. In practice, complementarianism is far from consistent. There seem to be no clear guidelines for how its principles are to be applied in daily life.

Conclusion

The problem of inconsistent practice in and of itself does not disprove complementarianism's claim to be the correct, biblical position. Indeed, many questions of right and wrong are more clear in theory than in practice. Still, given the clarity with which many complementarians claim the New Testament speaks to this issue, it is surprising how little agreement they can find with each other regarding how the biblical teaching should be put into practice. This problem was what initially caused me, as well as many who have changed their minds about women in ministry, to first wonder if the complementarian position was actually tenable. This pushed me to reread the relevant biblical texts. It's time now to open our Bibles and look at what is there. My good readers may want to have a Bible near as they read the next several chapters.

19. See Matt 7:29 and Mark 1:22.

3

Who We Are to Each Other

(Genesis 1 & 2)

THE GOSPEL OF MATTHEW recounts a time when a Pharisee asked Jesus about the Mosaic law's allowance of divorce. In his response, Jesus acknowledges that God indeed allowed men to divorce their wives. Then he adds, "[B]ut it was not this way from the beginning" (Matt 19:8). Although we are not talking about divorce here, our question nevertheless relates to the nature of the male-female relationship at creation: Whom *did* God create us as men and women to be to each other? Jesus seems to base his argument for faithfulness in marriage on the ideal presented in Genesis. It makes sense for us to start in the same place in our discussion about whether or not men are women's authorities. Do Genesis 1 and 2 present a hierarchical relationship between the sexes, or not?

Because all parties involved in this debate are Christians, they share many fundamental beliefs about human nature. Most importantly, complementarian and egalitarian Christians all believe that humans bear the image of their Creator, that we have fallen away from a right relationship with our Creator, and that we need the reconciling work of Christ to have that relationship restored. In other words, all Christians agree basically about how human beings were made to relate to God.

However, complementarians and egalitarians differ in their beliefs about how men and women were created to relate to each other. Virtually without exception, modern complementarians agree that the Bible teaches that men were created to be in authority over women and that women were created to be their subordinates. This relationship of authority and subordinate is part of the created order. From a complementarian's point of view, along with the undeniable reality that male and female comprise humanity comes the equally undeniable fact that men are made for authority and leadership while women are made for submission and compliance with authority. The hierarchy between the sexes is built into the nature of humanity. Thus, no matter how much complementarians differ among themselves with regard to the details of how this or that text should be interpreted, they all arrive at this basic theological conclusion.

Biblical egalitarians, on the other hand, think that there is nothing about the created nature of male and female that necessitates an authority and subject relationship. Egalitarians are not opposed to authority in and of itself. Some of the most hierarchically structured of the Protestant traditions (the ones with bishops and archbishops—like Methodists and Anglicans) are egalitarian in their understanding of God's design for male and female. The point is not to avoid *all* authority structures, but to avoid authority that is based on gender. Almost all churches recognize the need for authority structures. In an egalitarian church, those placed in authority positions should (1) be called by God, (2) evidence pastoral gifts, (3) have the moral character and integrity that is needed for leadership, and (4) be equipped to serve through training, study, and mentoring. There are many important qualifications necessary for leadership, but being male is not one of them. It could be that gender might be taken into consideration in an egalitarian church. For example, a church might want to have both women and men serve on their elder board for the sake of balance. Such churches might therefore look specifically for people of one or the other gender for that reason. But, an egalitarian church is open to submit to the leadership of anyone who meets the qualifications mentioned above, regardless of that person's sex. Egalitarians acknowledge that submission is a central part of Christian discipleship. But unlike complementarians, they require it equally of *all* the faithful, not specially of women believers.

Here is the crux of the matter: if authority is God's created intent for men and submission for women as such, then hierarchicalists are right to try and find ways to ensure this principle is expressed in the structure and practice of the church. But if there is nothing about authority that is intrinsically male and nothing about submission that is intrinsically female, according to God's created order, then egalitarians are right not to see maleness as a qualifier for authority positions in the church. All Christians agree that the church is a community that should express

God's original, created intent for humanity. But, what *is* that intent specifically with regard to male-female relationships? Does the Bible teach
that men are women's authorities by virtue of their gender, or not?

The most natural place to begin exploring for an answer to that question is the creation stories in Genesis chapters 1 and 2. This was one of the
first passages I reread when I decided to critique my own view of what
roles were appropriate for women to fill in the church and home. What
I discovered astonished me. I found that I had been reading against the
grain of the text. I won't be able to say this with as much confidence about
the other Scripture texts we will consider in chapters to come, but in the
case of Genesis 1 and 2 there is virtually no contesting the matter; those
who see a created hierarchy between the sexes in these passages are clearly
bringing something to the text that is not there. Let's look at them.

The Image of God

Genesis 1:1 is a well-known verse. It says, "In the beginning God created
the heavens and the earth." God then proceeds to describe that creation
as "good." Anything that God makes would have to be so, for God is all-
good. When God created human beings, the creation was not corrupted.
There was no sin; only goodness. The creation was not perfect (or complete), as if God wanted human beings to simply leave things the way
they were. God expected human beings to work within creation. God
expected them to share in God's ongoing creativity. It might be helpful
to think of God's original creation like we often think of newborn babies.
They are innocent, clean, pure, and good. But, as every parent discov-
ers, they represent a tremendous amount of work! It seems to me that
creation was like this. God placed human beings in a fledgling world and
entrusted it to their care. They had an immense amount of work before
them as soon as they came into existence.

What the Bible says clearly about God's intent for human beings
can be observed in human nature. If left to themselves, human beings
tend to work. When people find ways of taking care of the basic needs
of food, water, and shelter, they soon get about the business of discovery
and creating. If we encounter someone who does nothing but sit around,
eat, and sleep, we think, "There is something wrong with this person. He
needs help. He should *do something with his life.*" Why do we assume
there is something wrong with his doing nothing at all? There are surely

various ways of answering that question. But from a biblical point of view it's clear that God intended people to be creative. Not many would be upset at a pet cat or dog who does nothing but the minimum necessary to survive because we don't expect anything more from animals. But from humans we expect creative engagement with the world, and when people are content merely with surviving, we think something is wrong with them. Either our instinct about this is right or the Bible is wrong, at least at this point. That is, we really were made for something. We really do have a purpose in the world. This purpose is not imposed on us from the outside like a master imposes a slave's labor on her. Rather, God simply created people whose nature is like God's own. As Genesis 2 puts it, God made human beings as God's own representatives—God's image—in the world. Therefore, we create. It's an inextricable part of who we are.

All parents eventually realize that children are creative. My children (three, five, and seven years old when I wrote this) are constantly making new worlds. It's a challenge, in fact, to get them to stop doing so in the evening when it's bedtime, or when we sit down for a meal. They stack things, draw things, make up stories with their dolls (or even a handful of soup spoons—it doesn't matter), build houses with blocks, Duplo and Lego bricks, dance, sing, make new noises. Actually, children are very busy people! But they never think of it as work. It just comes out naturally. That, I think, is how God made people—adults included—to be.

All of this has relevance to the topic at hand for the following reason: the Bible doesn't merely say that God created the world and that we, in turn, as image-bearers of God, are creative by nature; the Bible also tells us *how* God did it. Genesis 1:2 says, "And God said . . ." This phrase is repeated ten times in chapter 1. Christians affirm the doctrine of creation *ex nihilo*—creation "out of nothing." We believe neither that God is the universe, nor that the universe was created out of any part of God. We should think for a moment about the implications of this doctrine for our interpretation of the Genesis creation story, particularly as it relates to women's speaking in the church. If God created the universe out of nothing, why does the author of Genesis go to the trouble of repeatedly describing creation as the result of God's speech? This obviously cannot be a literal description of how the universe was actually formed by God. God is spirit, which means God does not have a mouth and tongue or vocal cords or lungs. God has no material existence at all, in fact. The significance of the Bible's describing God's creative activity as a series of speech acts, therefore, must be metaphorical or symbolic.

But of what? The Genesis creation story could have used any number of analogies to talk about *how* God created the world. It could have said that God molded the world out of clay, or that God gave birth to it, or that the world emerged from God's body in some other way (like other ancient creation stories say). It could even have said that God imagined the world into existence. But instead, creation is depicted as an act of God's speaking. Creation is the product of God's word—God's great act of communication.

This is instructive for our discussion about women's voices in the church. If God made human beings to be creative, and if this is a key way that human beings reflect God's nature, and if God's creative actions are purposely depicted in Scripture as a product of God's speaking, it seems to me that human speech, broadly defined, must also be a special sign of our bearing the image of God. If this is true, what is the significance of limiting women's voices in the church due to their gender?

Further, Jesus, the one who demonstrates what true humanity is, is described in the New Testament as the "Word" of God. God in the flesh—the true humanity made new—is described as the communication of God. It cannot be an accident that God is depicted in Genesis 1 as creating through a series of speech acts, followed closely by the formation of the one creature who is said to be made in the divine image. There must be something special about humanity's communicative ability that relates closely to its being God's image-bearer in the world. It's probably obvious where I'm going with this point: If bearing God's image is connected to speaking, limiting someone's opportunity to speak because of her gender would entail suppressing the full manifestation of God's image in humanity. I realize that this is a serious accusation, and I don't make it lightly. But as far as I can tell, this is an inescapable conclusion grounded in basic Christian theology.

On the one hand, bearing God's image in humanity is a fact—an inescapable reality. "Human beings do not simply *have* the image of God," observes Jamar Tisby, "we *are* the image of God, thoroughly and holistically . . . no part of ourselves is separate from our image-bearing."[1] Nothing that a human being does, and nothing that is done to a human being, can change this reality. Our created purpose is to represent God in creation, just like any image represents whatever its maker made it to represent.

---

1. Tisby, *How to Fight Racism*, 29 (emphasis original).

But on the other hand, it *is* possible for us human beings to obscure or mar God's image through our behavior. The image of God is not a mere abstraction that is never touched by human choices. Rather, we can observe that image to greater or lesser degrees, depending on our activity in the world. A person who knows my father might meet me for the first time and say, "Wow, you look just like your dad." All such a person is doing is making a superficial observation about the marvel of how genetics works. But a person who knows both me and my father well would be able to say, "You are so much like your father." What the person means in this case is illustrated by popular proverbs such as, "Like father, like son" and, "The apple doesn't fall far from the tree." A person who says this about me means that I resemble my father's character and personality, not just his appearance. There was nothing I did to bear a physical resemblance to my father. But, in all the other ways that I resemble him my whole person is involved, including my willful decisions.

By analogy, just as I cannot avoid resembling my father in one sense, human beings cannot avoid bearing the image of God in one sense as well. We do not bear God's image in any physical way—no one will approach me and say, "Wow, you look a lot like God!" Nevertheless, we all *represent* God in the world, and that's a reality that can't be avoided. Just by being human, we are the image of God in the world. But, in another sense, just as my will is involved in my becoming the kind of person that I am under the influence of my father's example and instruction, so human beings can to a greater or lesser extent reflect God's character. We can be more or less faithful to that image depending on the way we live our lives. It is possible, therefore, to live more—or less—truly to who we really are.

The concept of the gods' having images was, of course, ubiquitous throughout the world in which the Bible was written. The second of the Ten Commandments was, "You shall not make for yourself a carved image." There are at least two problems with idolatry. The first problem—the one all Christians learn about in Sunday school—is that idols are not worthy of human worship. They lead to polytheism and, therefore, divert worship away from its proper object.

The second problem with idolatry is just as important as the first, but is not discussed as often and thus requires a little more explaining. Idols are intended to represent a deity. Technically, those who worship idols are not actually worshipping the image itself, but the deity that the idol represents. The idol is their way of connecting with that deity. It is a physical representation of a nonphysical or otherworldly entity. If a person defaces or otherwise disrespects the idol, this is considered the same as defacing the god that the idol represents. My sister Susie had an encounter with a coworker that illustrates this point. She writes,

> I had an interesting experience once during which I teasingly "stole" my Indian (and devout Hindu) coworker's phone and another friend and I replaced her background with our picture rather than the picture that was originally there, which was an image of Ganesha (a beloved Hindu god). She explained that she was offended by that because, as she stated, "That is my god . . . I have to have that picture on my phone." I learned a lot from her.[2]

Susie's experience with her friend shows how interconnected reverence for a deity is with that deity's image. Something similar happens with images of people. If someone were to tear apart a piece of blank paper in front of me, I wouldn't think twice about it. But if that piece of paper had an image on it of one of my family members or another person that I love or respect, I would be rightly offended, disturbed, and probably angered. In other words, idols do not acquire their sacred status in and of themselves; they become sacred by virtue of the god or goddess they represent. This fact exposes the second big problem with idolatry: idol-based modes of worship distance religious devotion to God from inter-human relationships. By locating God's image in a stone or metal sculpture, idolatry sets the stage for religious devotion, or worship, that is separate from moral requirements toward one's neighbor. An idolatrous worldview allows a person's relationship with God to exist independently from her relationship to other human beings, and to creation as a whole. By contrast, the creational monotheism of the Bible—of both the Hebrew Scriptures and the New Testament—fuse these two things together. Love of God and love of neighbor cannot be separated in biblical religion, even a little bit.[3]

This fusion of devotion to God and love of neighbor in biblical religion relates directly to the Bible's teaching about God's image in human beings. While the Bible forbids idol manufacturing, it does *not* erase the idea that the immaterial being of God may be represented through a material image. The Bible *affirms* God's being represented in images—just not sculpted, manmade ones. The only image for the divine that God accepts is humanity itself. This truth is crucial, even though it is often

2. From a comment on an early draft of this book, made on March 22, 2020.

3. See Lev 19:18; Matt 22:34–40; Mark 12:28–34.

skipped over when we teach the Ten Commandments in Sunday school. Even as the defacing or marring of an idol would be a blasphemous violation of the sacred to an idolater, so any action that I take in relation to my fellow human being that mars or diminishes his or her humanity is an action against the God whose image that person is. If we are the image of God, we are sacred objects. The whole world has become a temple to house God's images—all the people. I have a choice. Every action I take to promote human flourishing is an act of religious devotion to, or worship of, God. Conversely, every action that I take to suppress the humanity of others is sacrilegious and blasphemous. It is not merely a legal or even a moral offense; it is an afront to the Creator of the universe. With reference to humanity's being made in God's image, Archbishop Desmond Tutu writes, "[E]ach of us is a God-carrier, God's viceroy, God's representative. It is because of this fact that to treat one such person as if he or she were less than this is veritably blasphemous. It is like spitting in the face of God."[4] In the same vein, Rashi, the great eleventh-century Jewish rabbi, wrote, "Because man is made in the image of his Creator, to humiliate his body is to demean the Heavenly King."[5]

When one thinks about it, there is really no time when human beings come closer to creating something *ex nihilo*—"out of nothing," like God does—than when they speak. Whenever I speak, no matter what I say, something new comes from nothing. The world is forever changed. Those words never existed before, but now they do. So long as someone hears, sees (as in sign language), reads, or otherwise comprehends them, my words have created something *out of nothing*! As human beings, we are no more like God than when we speak.

Maybe that thought alone doesn't tell us who should be in the pulpit next Sunday morning. But, like every stage needs a backdrop, this idea needs to be there even if it can't bring us to a conclusion by itself. Now let's look more closely at the creation story.

Humanity (Genesis 1:26–31)[6]

In 1972, NASA launched a satellite into space called the Pioneer 10. A few months before launching, Carl Sagan suggested to NASA that they

4. Tutu, *No Future*, 93.

5. As quoted by Weintraub, "Torture and Torah," 130.

6. For a summary of this explanation of Gen 1:26–31, see Table 3.1 in the appendix.

include a message from humanity on the outside of the satellite in view of the slight chance that it might come into contact with intelligent extraterrestrial beings.[7] The result was the making of a plaque to be fastened to the outside of the satellite.

The trouble with communicating with extraterrestrials, of course, is that we don't have any idea what their language(s) might be like, and even if we did know we wouldn't know what script(s) they use. Thus, the message on the plaque had to be as clearly understandable as possible, but apart from the use of words. Several symbols were chosen, but the most striking on the plaque were the figures of a naked man and woman. If we want the aliens to know us, the minimum that they must know is that we as a species come in two parts—male and female. Apparently, the aliens had to know about both sexes or they would not understand who we are.

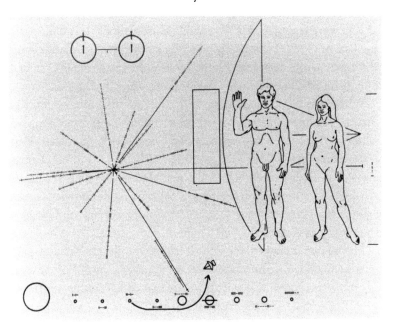

Plaque fastened to the frame of the Pioneer 10 space probe in 1972

The Genesis creation story likewise emphasizes that humanity is a two-part composition, each of which cannot exist without the other. The first thing we notice upon reading Genesis 1:26–31 is that male and female are made *together* in the image of God. At first, this might sound like the same thing as saying that both men and women bear God's image

7. Rosenthal, "Pioneer Plaque."

equally as individual persons. That is true, but this is not the emphasis of this particular passage. Rather, Genesis 1 teaches that male and female bear the image of God *together* as the two parts of one, single humanity. The text is not talking about two images—one male and one female; it is talking about one image—humanity. After all, there is only *one* God! The Hebrew word translated "man" in verse 27 is *adam*. This word is used in English only as a proper name. But in Hebrew it simply means "man." In verse 27, it is clear that the author does not mean "man" as a male human being (there is another Hebrew word for that, the word, *'iyš*), but refers to man as humanity in general. It is right to translate *adam* here with the word "man," but only insofar as the English word "man" means "humanity" or "mankind." This is made clear by the rest of verse 27, where the author has added, "male and female [God] created them." The author was talking about God's creation of humankind as a whole.

This is by no means a controversial claim. Both egalitarian and complementarian Christian scholars agree that the *adam* in Genesis 1:27 is *not* a person named Adam. Instead, the word refers to "man" as humanity or humankind comprised of its male and female parts. Biblical scholar Bruce Waltke confirms, "*adam* means 'humankind.'"[8] Biblical scholar Aida Besençon Spencer rightly notes, "[I]n order to understand God's nature, males and females together are needed to reflect God's image. The image of God is a double image."[9] The notion, held by some Christian theologians in the history of the church, that men bear the image of God in a more complete manner than women do is not supported by this passage.

The importance of this point for a right understanding of human nature should not be overlooked. It is obvious to us all that the two sexes are necessary for the survival of our species. Even at a biological level, we understand that humanity must exist as two parts of a whole. But Genesis takes this biological reality and invites us to see it in a symbolic, relationally and spiritually profound way. While every individual human being is made in God's image, Genesis 1 emphasizes humanity's corporate nature. We, as male and female, represent God *together* as *adam*. God is not represented merely by autonomous individuals, but by the whole of the human community—and in its most basic and condensed form, humanity is represented by its two interdependent sides, male and female. Just as we can only truthfully say, "Look, *here* is humankind!" if we have *both*

8. Waltke, *Old Testament Theology*, 254.

9. Spencer, *Beyond the Curse*, 21.

a man *and* a woman standing in front of us, so we could only truthfully say, "Look, *here* is the image of God!" if we are referring to humanity as a whole, as represented by its two most basic representative parts. If Carl Sagan's would-be extraterrestrial friends developed an interest in theology and asked us, "What is the image of God?," we could show them the picture on the plaque fastened to the side of Pioneer 10.

In verse 28, God lists the tasks that the man and woman will do in God's creation. There are four of them: (1) be fruitful and multiply, (2) fill the earth, (3) subdue the earth, and (4) rule over the animals. In each case, God is addressing both the male and the female. The tasks were meant to be shared completely. There is no division of labor, and there is certainly no authority structure between the man and the woman, at least at this point in the narrative. Likewise in verse 29, God gives the same gifts to both male and female.

And that's all! It is a short passage, but very important. It teaches us that, in the beginning, all the responsibilities and gifts that God gave to humanity were given to both men and women. There is no evidence of a hierarchical distinction, no evidence of an authority structure between the sexes.

Christians have traditionally called sin's entrance into the world, "the fall." In order to determine whether or not God's design for human beings involves male authority and female subordination, we need to observe what we can about how the male-female relationship is described in a prefall world. This being the case, it is telling that there is no hint of male authority or female subjection in the creation story. Male authority only appears *after* the effects of human disobedience emerge in Genesis 3.

Nevertheless, some hierarchicalist interpreters think they find hints or whispers of male authority even in this text. One scholar, for example, thinks that the text's use of the word *adam* to refer to humanity suggests male authority because it is a gramatically masculine word. He writes, "God's naming of the race 'man' whispers male headship,"[10] and continues,

> God did *not* name the human race "woman." If "woman" had been the more appropriate and illuminating designation, no doubt God would have used it. He does not even devise a neutral term like "persons." He called us "man," which anticipates the male headship brought out clearly in chapter two, just as "male and female" in verse 27 foreshadows marriage in chapter

10. Ortlund, "Male-Female Equality," 123.

two. Male headship may be personally repugnant to feminists, but it does have the virtue of explaining the sacred text.[11]

A response to this remarkable claim will take a bit of explaining, so bear with me.

In English, words that carry gender are nouns that have to do with the gender of persons or animals. For example, we know that mothers, wives, and daughters are female, and that fathers, husbands, and sons are male. The nouns woman, man, boy, girl, lad, and lass are other words that imply gender in English. The only other words in English that carry gender are the pronouns—*he* and *she*, *him* and *her*, *his* and *hers*. Words like chair, table, house, apple, tree, and antidisestablishmentarianism are neither feminine nor masculine in English. They are all neuter—or "it"—in the minds of English speakers. That seems so clear that some of my patient readers might be wondering why I would even say it out loud. Here is why:

In some languages, including the so-called Semitic languages like Hebrew, Aramaic, and Arabic, nearly all words—nouns, adjectives, verbs, adverbs, etc.—have a gender, not just those that refer to male and female animals or pronouns. In the Romance languages, like Spanish, Italian, and Portuguese, nearly all nouns, pronouns, and adjectives carry gender. For example, in Spanish *casa* (house) is feminine while *arbol* (tree) is masculine; *bote* (boat) is masculine while *silla* (chair) is feminine; *naranja* (orange) is feminine while *zapato* (shoe) is masculine, and so on. This obviously has nothing to do with the biological sex of these things; it is simply a grammatical feature of the language. We call this grammatical gender, because it is just a function of grammar.

I grew up speaking only English, so this concept was difficult for me to grasp when I started learning ancient Greek grammar in college and later learned to speak Spanish. I've since learned to speak Spanish fairly well. My wife Isabel is from Ecuador, so we speak Spanish in our home. But even though I've been speaking Spanish every day for years now, I still mix up the genders of words frequently! My English-thinking brain just hasn't fully embraced the idea of a grammatically gendered language. In an English speaker's mind, it does not make any sense to think of a ball, a table, a meeting, a door, or dinner as being feminine, but in Spanish these are all feminine nouns. Likewise, the sky, the weather, hair, and breakfast are all masculine in Spanish. Why? Who knows?! One thing is

---

11. Ortlund, "Male-Female Equality," 123 (emphasis original).

certain, however: the genders of these nouns have nothing to do with the sex of the things to which they refer.

Hebrew likewise is a grammatically gendered language, even more so than Spanish or Greek. Not just the nouns and adjectives but also the verbs in Hebrew carry gender. There are virtually no neuter words in Hebrew—almost *every* word is either masculine or feminine.

When we hear the word "man" in English we naturally think of a male person. We know that man can be a collective noun referring to humanity or humankind as well, but it is still hard for us to separate the idea of maleness from the word man, no matter how we use it. However, if we were speaking Hebrew, we would know that *all* nouns carry gender. Therefore, the word *adam* would not necessarily conjure up the idea of maleness if we knew that the word was being used, in a given context, to signify humanity or humankind. Even if the author of Genesis had wanted to use a nongendered or neuter word—like our English word "human"—*it would have been impossible because virtually all Hebrew nouns are either masculine or feminine!* Claiming that *adam* in Genesis 1:26–27 "whispers" male authority is like claiming that the Hebrew word *nefeš* ("life" or "soul") whispers something about the essential femaleness of the human soul—because *nefeš* is a feminine word in Hebrew! The fact is, the reason that *adam* was used in Genesis 1:26–27 to describe humankind is simply because *adam is* the proper Hebrew word for the concept of humankind, humanity, or mankind. There is no whispering message hidden just beyond earshot. The scholar quoted above suggests that the author of Genesis could have come up with a neutral term like "person" if he had wanted to avoid emphasizing male authority. But the problem is, there simply is no such thing as a neutral Hebrew noun. In fact, if one looks up "person" in a modern English-to-Hebrew dictionary, the Hebrew word provided is *adam,* the same word used in Genesis 1:27–28. When it comes to grammatically gendered languages like Hebrew, there are no neutral terms available.

Since we're on the subject, I'll mention that the Spanish word for humanity—*humanidad*—is feminine. A person speaking Hebrew is no more whispering male authority by referring to humanity as *adam* than a Spanish-speaker is whispering *female* authority every time she says *humanidad!* Likewise, in Spanish the word for person—*persona*—is feminine. But this does not mean that everytime a Spanish speaker refers to a person she is whispering something about female leadership. Here is the bottom line: arguing that the word *adam* in Genesis 1:26–27 somehow hints at male authority just because it is a masculine word commits the logical fallacy of special pleading. The fact is, the word simply means humanity in this context, with no emphasis on the priority of the male over the female.

But suppose, for the sake of the argument, that Hebrew *did* have a neutral, nongendered word for *person*. Even then, the author of Genesis makes clear that *all* the responsibilities and *all* the gifts of the original creation were given to "them"—that is, to *both* the man *and* the woman. In other words, in terms of function in creation, there is still no difference between male and female in Genesis 1. Actually, Spencer gets the application of this text to male and female right when she writes that, for male and female, "not to jointly rule would be to disobey God's command."[12] If the story emphasizes anything about the male-female relationship at creation, it is their mutuality and togetherness. The text neither shouts nor whispers anything about male authority over women.

Genesis 1 sets the stage for the rest of the Bible. If there is a place where we should turn to begin an investigation into God's created intent for human relationships, this is where we should start. It does not say much about male and female, but what it does say decidedly emphasizes equality. There is not even a hint about male priority in any way.

Man and Woman (Genesis 2:7, 18–25)[13]

In Genesis 2 we encounter again the word *adam*. This time, however, the word is being used to refer to an individual male person. At first, this may seem to challenge our observation of how this word was used in 1:27–28. However, this only shows the versatility of this word. The English word *man* has similar qualities. For example, one of the verses of Eric Wyse's hymn, "Wonderful, Merciful Savior," ends with the phrase, "O, you rescue the souls of men!" Of course, Wyse wanted God to be praised for rescuing the souls of *all* people—both men and women. But he was free to use the word "men" in his hymn because one of that word's meanings is "people."[14]

12. Spencer, *Beyond the Curse*, 23.

13. For a summary of this explanation of Gen 2:7, 18–25, see Table 3.2 in the appendix.

14. This is not to say that using "man," in English, to refer to humanity, has not been problematic. For a discussion on this, see Barr, *Making of Biblical Womanhood*, ch. 5.

God's first declaration in relation to male and female in this passage is that it is "not good for man to be alone" (v. 18). He needs a "helper." Perhaps "not good" is meant to contrast with the repeated declaration of "good" over the creation in chapter 1 (vv. 4, 10, 18, 21, 25, and 31). God says that to remedy this condition, God will make a "helper suitable" for Adam (v. 18).

When we hear the word "helper" in English, we might think of an assistant, a butler, a servant, a maid, or a sidekick—someone whose role is to help another person accomplish something that the person is already doing. We think of a helper as someone in a secondary or subordinate role. Genesis 2, however, has something quite different in mind. The Hebrew phrase translated "helper suitable" is from the root words *ezer,* which means "help, succor," and *neged,* which means "in front of, corresponding to." A standard Hebrew-English lexicon notes that this phrase in Genesis 2:18 is literally translated, "I will make him . . . a help *corresponding to* him i.e. equal and adequate to himself."[15] These terms carry no undertones of subordination. To the contrary, they explicitly portray equality and mutuality and agree beautifully with the account in chapter 1. Spencer notes that the "early church father Irenaeus (second century) also says that God made 'a helper equal and the peer and the like of Adam.'"[16] There is little dispute here regarding the meaning of these words. The picture here is *not* one of God making a sidekick for the man to help him accomplish a mission—like Robin is for Batman. Rather, the man and the woman are to share the mission as partners. The work belongs to both of them.

When I was growing up, I remember very clearly thinking of a wife as being essentially a man's personal assistant in marriage. I was taught that the man was the leader—the head of the house—and that the wife was there to help him accomplish this mission. I thought the word "helpmeet" (I used the King James Version when I was younger) was basically a specialized term for a wife. The husband was the captain of the ship, the wife was his first mate—no pun intended. I was literally taught using this very analogy. When I began investigating what Bible scholars had written about this term, however, I discovered that my understanding of the word had been based on a common (though mistaken) use of helpmeet, and not on the meaning of the Hebrew term in its biblical context. What the Bible actually says is that the woman completes the man. They are two

15. BDB, s.v. "דגנ."

16. Spencer, *Beyond the Curse,* 25.

equally crucial parts of a whole. Nothing about either being subordinate to the other is implied in this text. If anything is implied, it is the opposite.

While we often talk about Adam and Eve as the prototype for marriage, they actually represent the relationship between male and female humanity generally. Thankfully (for the rest of us), Adam and Eve decided to have children together. In retrospect, we could say they got married, even though that would be an anachronistic way of talking about it. But in the larger scheme of things, God's commands and charges to the first man and woman carry over to all men and women today, whether they are married or not. All men and women, together as the two essential parts of the human family, are responsible to care for and promote the flourishing of God's creation. Of course, ideally, the reproduction part should be left up to married couples. But that is only one part of what God told the first humans—and what God tells us today—to be about. In Genesis, God tells the man and the woman to do *everything together,* not simply conceive offspring together.

If God's declaration was that the woman is a *helper suitable* or *helper corresponding* to man, what was the man's response? Did he recognize her as his subordinate, or as his equal?

Verse 23 is the only prefall statement made by a man about a woman present in the Bible. Consistent with all we've observed in the Genesis creation story up until now, "Bone of my bones and flesh of my flesh" seems to emphasize the equality of the sexes. What Adam calls the corresponding creature—*woman*—emphasizes his being her source; he states, "for she was taken out of man." Paul alludes to this statement in 1 Corinthians 11:8 where he notes that, just as woman finds her origin in man, so man is born of woman. Paul teaches there that, "In the Lord . . . woman is not independent of man, nor is man independent of woman . . . but everything comes from God" (see also 1 Cor 11:11–12)—another clear statement emphasizing the mutuality and equality of man and woman according to God's created design.

The Hebrew word used for "man" in the phrase "for she was taken out of man" in the second part of verse 23 is not *adam*. Rather, it is the word *'iš*. The word for "woman" here is *'ishā*. While they are not the same as the words used for "male" and "female" in 1:27, it seems the man referred to here—that is, the *man*, Adam (see also 2:15)—is not to be taken generally as humanity. It is not that *the human* is naming the human's helper as if she were a supplement to himself. Adam is not giving the woman a name at this point. Rather, he is comparing her to himself.

He is describing his relationship to her. *She is, he says, made of the same stuff*—of the same bones and flesh—as he, for she came from him. She is the perfect companion for him. She corresponds to him, fits him, is good for him. Adam is recognizing the benefit of her presence in poetic language. This is not, as hierarchicalists often claim, an assertion of his authority over her. The man is not happy to have a supplemental helper, but a corresponding companion. Furthermore, he cannot do the task of being human by himself. Her "help" is not an extra thing; it is an absolutely essential thing. Again, our minds immediately go to the reproductive essentiality of the two sexes. Yes, that is part of it. But I hasten to reiterate, it is *only a part*. The human vocation involves far more than that—and according to Genesis 1 and 2, the human vocation is for both men and women.

Verse 24 is portrayed in our English translations as a commentary by the author. The man will leave his father and mother in order to "cleave" (KJV) to his wife "and they become one flesh." This command (or prediction?) runs contrary to the practice in the majority of cultures throughout history in which the woman is expected to leave her family and move to her husband's locale instead of vice versa. Paul references this short comment in Ephesians 5 where he instructs Christian husbands about how they should treat their wives (v. 31). The purpose in context is clear. Paul wants to connect following Christ, who brings the new creation, with God's intention for humanity in the first creation. In both, the man was made to give selflessly to his wife, subordinating his own priorities to hers. We'll look at Ephesians 5 later in more detail.

But does our perception of the prefall relationship between the sexes need to affect our understanding of the postfall relationship? To the Christian, restoration of the original goodness of creation is basic to the doctrine of redemption in Christ.[17] If there was a hierarchy between male and female before the fall, redemption necessarily involves restoring or maintaining that original hierarchy in the church, for the church is called to be the embodiment of God's redeemed creation in the world. Conversely, if there was functional equality between the sexes before the fall, redemption necessarily involves embodying, as far as is possible, that new reality in the church in order to more fully represent the image of God to the watching world. This is where the tension arises between the two sides in this debate. Our presuppositions, taken from how we view

17. See for example Rom 8:19–23; Gal 6:15; Col 1:15, 23.

the state of male and female in God's created design, tint the lenses we use to interpret all postfall passages of Scripture on this topic.

As we noted, even though popular understanding of the English word "helper" (or "helpmeet") implies subordinate status, the Hebrew term carries no such connotation. For that reason, the most careful hierarchicalists do not use the word "helper" to argue for women's subordination. Instead, they appeal to the pattern of creation. They present primarily two arguments. To illustrate the first, we'll use a quote from a highly respected complementarian biblical scholar, Bruce Waltke. He writes,

> As Paul notes in a passage dealing with the role of men and women, one that demands its own study, "man did not come from woman, but woman from man; neither was man created for woman, but woman for man" (1 Cor. 11:8–9). In other words, Paul gives governmental priority to the man by the sequence of the creation of man and woman and by the purpose for which the woman was created. Is it not plausible to assume that if God intended equality in government, he would have formed Eve and Adam at the same time and made them helpers suitable to each other? If he had wanted a matriarchy, would God not have formed Eve first and created the husband to be a suitable helper to his wife?[18]

Complementarians tend, thus, to appeal to the "sequence" of creation to justify their position. God made the man first, then the woman. That the man was created first implies, on this reasoning, his authority over the woman.

It is actually fairly easy to spot the flaw in this argument. As New Testament scholar R. T. France rightly notes, "If the logic is simply that the first to be created must necessarily be the superior, one might wonder why human beings are not subject to the rest of the animal creation."[19] In chapter 1, the animals are created before human beings! Further, in chapter 2, the animals are created before the woman. If being created first implies higher authority, the woman ends up at the bottom of the hierarchical order—under the giraffe, the chameleon, and the hedgehog! The argument for male authority based on the sequence of creation is founded, I think, on a misreading of Paul's comments in 1 Timothy 2, and I'll try to demonstrate this later. It is sufficient for now to note that the logic does not match what we see in Genesis 1 and 2. God's creation of the

18. Waltke, *Old Testament Theology,* 242.

19. France, *Women in the Church's Ministry,* 67.

woman in chapter 2 *after* and yet *from* the man far more likely emphasizes the man's need for an equal, yet different, partner. He didn't need a
sidekick. As my friend Dave notes, "The story in Genesis 2 has man being
made first to stress that when only males are in charge, without equal
women partners, things are 'not good.'"[20]

A second argument hierarchicalists marshal that relates to the early
chapters of Genesis is based on anthropological findings. Waltke notes
that cultural anthropology has consistently shown patriarchy (that is,
male-centered societal structure) to be the norm in virtually all cultures
of the world throughout history. He writes, "This truism of anthropology
suggests that nature tends to validate Scripture that men, not women,
were created to lead."[21] New Testament scholar Robert Culver presents a
similar argument when he claims,

> Old Testament history supports the eminence of men over
> women in every kind of leadership. Genealogical lines are ordi-
> narily traced only through the male line. Women are introduced
> as the complements and helpers of their men. This is so over-
> whelming that no special documentation is required. The same
> was true of all ancient peoples.[22]

Thus, the reasoning goes that God's intent for male-female relationships is manifested in cultures that prioritize males in the home
and that, in turn, develop male-dominated governments. For hierarchicalists, this reality is evidence of God's design. That is, male-centered
governance is prominent in the world because this is the natural—or
created—order of things.

The problem egalitarians have with this argument is that it is based
on a false premise. The argument seems to say that the way things are
is the way God wanted them to be. It fails to respect the distinction between what *is* and what *ought* to be. Christians believe that all human
relationships are broken, having been corrupted by that mysterious thing
(or *anti*-thing) we call sin. From a Christian perspective, it would not be
the least bit surprising if humanity had consistently done things wrong
since the beginning of recorded human history! The male-female difference is the most basic difference that exists between human beings. Given
human beings' historic ability to find ways to exert power and violence

---

20. David Erdel, conversation about this book, April 13, 2020.

21. Waltke, *Old Testament Theology*, 242.

22. Culver, "Let Your Women Keep Silent," 37–38.

along lines of tribal, national, ethnic, and a host of other lines of difference, it actually makes sense that the male-female difference would provide occasion for the wrongful use of power throughout the cultures of the world.

For an example of the importance of distinguishing between what *is* and what *ought* to be, take monogamous, lifelong marriage. Christians today, for the most part, think that marriage should be both monogamous and lifelong, insofar as this is possible. I don't think I would be exaggerating to claim that a large majority of people in the Westernized world, whether they are Christian or not, still take these strictures for granted, even in a world where sexual libertinism is often celebrated. We have learned to assume that when people marry there should be only two partners involved, and those two people should do their best to keep their sexual activity within that relationship alone—that they should do all that they can to be exclusively faithful to the marriage "until death do [them] part." So deep and wide has this assumption run that we Westernized folk often have the audacity to call this the traditional view of marriage. But, before Christianity became a major global influence, *this was by no means the traditional view of marriage* in many, if not most, cultures. Particularly, polygamy has been habitually practiced in many cultures all over the world, as well as a variety of other marital arrangements. Thus, the monogamous, permanent view of marriage did *not* used to be a description of the way things are. Indeed, it still isn't in many places. Yet, most Christians would agree that God designed human sexuality to remain within that very strictly defined bond.

If we want to be consistent, therefore, the way things are cannot be our guide to understanding God's intention for human relationships, including (and perhaps most importantly) relationships between men and women. In the end, the hierarchicalist argument based on the way things are is, thus, moot from the beginning. It could be, in fact, that the disproportionate dominance of men over women in cultures all over the world is evidence of sin's pervasive *corruption* of creation rather than being evidence of God's design.

Actually, it turns out that Genesis all but says just that. In chapter 3 God foretells what will happen to creation as a result of humanity's rebellion. One of the consequences God mentions there is that the man will "rule over" (3:16) the woman. There is no way to construe this as a positive development. It is couched in the famous text in which God pronounces a list of curses on the ground and on the snake. The weight of the textual support clearly favors the egalitarian reading in this case: male dominance is *not* God's design; rather, it is a consequence of humanity's corruption. Again, the hierarchicalist interpretation seems to be reading against the grain of the text, while the egalitarian reading enjoys much more consistency and cohesiveness.

A well-known complementarian scholar writes the following: "Radical feminists should give up and quit. Normal, universal, female human nature is against them. Most women prefer things the way they are, at least wherever biblical norms have prevailed."[23] This statement is astonishingly inaccurate on several levels. For one, wherever biblical norms have prevailed—that is, wherever the gospel has spread and had time to influence a culture—the status of women has historically been improved, and women's rights have been brought closer to equality with those of men.[24] In my home country, the roots of the early feminist movement can be traced directly back to the movement to abolish slavery. "If no person should be enslaved because we are all equal under God," some women thought, "why should men be entitled to rights not also granted to women?" Granted, the opposition to those movements also claimed biblical backing. But, the basis for equality was consistently the same—*all* people are made in God's image and, therefore, should be treated equally. Further, this scholar's comment betrays misguided assumptions about women. While I cannot prove it, I suspect he is equally wrong in assuming that "most women prefer the way things are." My suspicion is that many women the world over would prefer to have equal rights to men, and would prefer to be seen as men's equals. As education and career opportunities formerly closed to women open up to them from place to place around the world, women tend to participate in filling them (even when they don't do so in equal number to men).

I'm not suggesting that we should expect a fifty-fifty male-female ratio in every field. Some fields may always be dominated by one or the other gender. For example, according to a study published on the website of the National Center for Education Statistics, only about 24 percent of teachers in public schools in the United States are men, even though the

23. Culver, "Let Your Women Keep Silent," 41.

24. I am speaking here about how the status of women changes in a society when the gospel *first reaches* a culture. I am aware of the woefully numerous instances in which thoroughly Christianized cultures reverse that transformation, using the Bible as a tool to put women down rather than lift them up. Indeed, this is largely why I am writing this book!

teaching profession is wide open to men, and that percentage is lower than it was two decades ago.[25] At this point in history, it looks like public education will continue to be dominated more and more by women. But, we should note that 24 percent of those who become public school teachers are *still* men. And, they are no less men for it! Suppose we all agreed today that women can be pastors of churches, and yet twenty or 100 years later only 24 percent of pastors were women. This would in no way prove that women should not be pastors! It would merely show that only 24 percent of people who find their way into pastoral positions are women. I'm painting an unlikely hypothetical picture here. The reality is that the percentage of women who would go into full-time pastoral ministry if given the opportunity (*and the encouragement*) to do so would almost certainly be higher! My point is merely that, even if the practice of prohibiting women from being pastors robs the church only of a small number of gifted women leaders, such a practice is nevertheless worthy of resistance.

But suppose, for the sake of argument, that I'm wrong and the scholar I quoted above has a point. Suppose "[m]ost women prefer things the way they are." Would it prove anything about how we should interpret the Genesis creation stories? No, not really. Fallen mankind is very often all too content with its fallen state. Note again that the argument is *not* based on the wording of the text itself but on an assumption about what women happen to prefer in a world corrupted by sin.

Looking at the world around us can tell us how things are, but that alone cannot tell us how things *ought* to be. While it is true that most cultures are male-centered, it is also true that at least some people within every culture have to struggle and sweat to grow food (see Gen 3:17–19). Yet, hierarchicalists would neither argue that God intended life to be this way, nor would they object to the development of better technology aimed at making farming easier. The more consistent position is to see the subordination of women as a result of the fall, not God's intent. God's original intent seems to be clear in Genesis 2:18—equality, correspondence, and mutuality.

To be fair, modern complementarians only endorse the subordination of women insofar as it is done lovingly and in the mutual best interest of the man and the woman. Further, they only support it when women submit voluntarily to male authority, not when they are forced to

25. "Characteristics of Public School Teachers," para. 2.

submit. Complementarians often argue that the problem with male-over-female hierarchy is not the arrangement itself but our lack of ability to imagine a mutually beneficial authority structure in a sin-tainted world. For example, Susan Foh contends,

> Our objections, whether philosophical or emotional, to this hierarchical system arise because we do not know what a sin-less hierarchy is like. We know only the tyranny, willfulness and condescension that even the best boss-underling relationship has. In Eden, none of these perversions existed.[26]

Fair enough. But, notice what Foh does when she explains how such a sinless hierarchy would appear in practice:

> The man and woman knew each other as equals, each in God's image and each with a personal relationship with God. Neither doubted the value of the other or of himself or herself. Each was to do the same work, with husband as head and wife as helper. They functioned as one flesh, one body without discord. Does the rib rebel against the head or the head mistreat the rib?[27]

In order to describe a sinless hierarchy, Foh must employ the word "equal," and speak of "one body without discord." She omits the word "authority" altogether, and sticks to the biblical metaphor of "head." What is interesting about this is that Foh is describing the male-female relationship in virtually *the same terms that an egalitarian would do so*. If someone were to ask an egalitarian scholar how she thinks God created men and women to see themselves in relation to each other, she would agree with everything Foh states in the above quotation (with the pos-sible exception of a few translation differences). It seems almost like what Foh means by sinless hierarchy is the same as what egalitarians mean by male-female equality.

The problem with Foh's description of her position is that it is not consistent with complementarian practice. Literally all complementar-ians limit women's speaking ministry in the church in some way. Of course, one could point out that all churches limit the speaking ministry of everyone. After all, even the preacher (usually) has a time limit on Sunday morning! But complementarians limit women *because of their gender*. This is what makes the difference.

---

26. Foh, "Head of the Woman," 73.
27. Foh, "Head of the Woman," 73.

Waltke, who also holds that men were made to be women's authority, suggests that we should *invent new terms* altogether to describe male authority. He writes,

> Christian hierarchy, it must be insisted, is unlike worldly hierarchies. It is a government of mutual, active, voluntary submission. Leaders among God's people, on the one hand, love and serve others and become their slaves; they do not lord it over the governed. They abhor the worldly concepts of "having the last word" and of defining hierarchy as a "pecking order" (Matt. 20:25–28). Those who are led, on the other hand, actively, independently, and freely submit to this leadership. *Hierarchy, obedience,* and *submission,* are red-flag words because we invest them with worldly meanings, not with biblical ones. We need to sanctify them or *invent new vocabulary.*[28]

Similarly to Foh, Waltke also seems to be wary of using words that emphasize male authority. But the only alternatives he presents are words that emphasize male-female equality and mutuality! Waltke's description of the Christian community in which leaders lead with love and people serve one another and submit to leadership is *precisely the same as what egalitarian Christians believe the church should be like.* In fact, now that we're talking about inventing new words, we should throw the word "complementarian" itself back into the mix. This word actually fits the egalitarian position perfectly too—because egalitarians believe the differences between men and women complement each other and, therefore, we should seek to have both men and women present in every sphere and at every level of the church's ministry.

The other problem with Waltke's desire to avoid words like *hierarchy, obedience,* and *submission,* and the idea of having the last word, is that complementarians actually *do,* at times, teach that wives should submit to the last word of their husbands when there is a difference of opinion. In fact, the last word—or tiebreaker, as I call it—example is so commonly given in hierarchicalist circles that many do not know where it came from. "If the husband is not the authority," so the reasoning goes, "no one will have the last word in arguments, and *somebody* has to have the last word!"

As far as I can tell, the tiebreaker argument came from C. S. Lewis's classic work, *Mere Christianity.* Lewis is such an influential Christian thinker that anyone who wishes to argue that he was mistaken about something

---

28. Waltke, *Old Testament Theology,* 243 (emphasis original).

should think twice before doing so. Still, at the risk of sounding impetuous, I'm going to do just that. In *Mere Christianity* Lewis argues that, so long as there is no disagreement between a husband and wife, there is no need to worry about who is in charge. But, suppose the husband and wife talk an issue over, and suppose they have to make a choice, but in the end they still disagree. What then? Lewis has the answer. He writes,

> Surely only one of two things can happen: either they must separate and go their own ways or else one or the other of them must have a casting vote. If marriage is permanent, one or the other party must, in the last resort, have the power of deciding the family policy.[29]

Characteristically, Lewis provides a logically sound argument for the point he is making. Indeed, if voting were the way decisions were made in marriage, Lewis's argument would be irrefutable. But this is why I think Lewis is wrong: voting is *not* the right way to make decisions in marriage. Marriage is not a democracy; it is the merging of two lives into one flesh. In a marriage, everything is more complicated than things would be if two individual, autonomous persons were simply trying to live together. Marriage is not two parallel lives; it brings two lives together such that, over time, the identity of the two individuals therein become so intertwined that their confluence becomes a new entity of its own. This is what makes marriage so unique among human relationships and, to be honest, one of the things that makes it so challenging. This is how Genesis portrays marriage and, as I will argue later, how the Bible as a whole portrays it.

My friends Marisa and Jim have ten children and have worked in Christian ministry for several decades.[30] They have made their fair share of challenging family decisions. About eleven years ago, before I was married, I asked Marisa pointedly about the tiebreaker problem. "What do you do," I said, "when you and Jim can't agree about something? How do you make a decision when that happens?" Her reply came without hesitation. "We don't," she said. "We pray and wait until we come to an agreement." To be truthful, I found her response dubious and even a bit frustrating at the time. It seemed like a copout. But, after ten years of being married myself, I would say precisely the same thing. For either a husband or a wife to make an important family decision over the top

---

29. Lewis, *Mere Christianity*, 113.

30. Marisa wrote the afterword for this book.

of the other is, at best, unwise. At worst, it can be catastrophic for the harmony of the marriage.

Actually, I think that many complementarians would agree that Lewis's democratic, tiebreaker view of decision-making in marriage was not quite right. Theologian John Stackhouse, who argues in favor of an egalitarian view of men and women in Christ, notes, "[W]hen I have asked complementarian couples how often in years or even decades of marriage they have ever had to resort to this [tiebreaker] device, the answer almost invariably comes back, never."[31] In writing about how he believes husbands and wives ought to seek agreement in decision-making with each other, the prominent complementarian theologian Wayne Grudem recounts an anecdote from his own life. He and Mrs. Grudem were considering relocating to another part of the United States. The two of them were each, he says, "concerned for the other person's welfare." He adds, "I think that's how marriage is supposed to function." Agreed! He continues,

> What should the final decision be? We prayed and talked and went for walks and talked some more. Finally Margaret said, "I have made up my mind what to do about this decision." I said, "What?" She said, "I have decided that you should make the decision!" I smiled, but I also felt the burden of responsibility. It seems to me that that is how marriage is supposed to function—prayer and love and conversation, and each caring for the other, but then, finally, the husband as head of the household has responsibility to make the decision. My decision was that we should move, for the sake of Margaret's health.[32]

Actually, this is precisely how people in healthy egalitarian marriages often make decisions—one person chooses to leave a decision to the other. The only difference is that, in an egalitarian marriage, sometimes the wife will lead the decision-making. In an egalitarian marriage the yielding of responsibility to the other, so wisely exemplified by Mrs. Grudem in the above anecdote, can be done by the husband as well as by the wife.

31. Stackhouse, *Partners in Christ*, 76.
32. Grudem, "Foreword," 12.

Conclusion

C. S. Lewis poses other arguments for husbands' authority over their wives that haven't enjoyed the same popularity as his tiebreaker proposal. He writes, for example, that a man needs to be in charge in order to "protect other people from the intense family patriotism of the wife."[33] I've never heard that argument repeated in my conversations with my many complementarian friends. Lewis's tiebreaker argument is the one that has gotten the most traction. Still, Lewis did *not* try to prove his point from the Genesis creation narrative. His arguments are based largely on his own experience and observations. Insightful as Lewis was—and indebted as I am to his rich literary legacy—I think he really missed the mark here, and I wish many of his readers had read him a little more critically here. The fact is, no created hierarchical relationship is portrayed in Genesis 1–3. With all due respect—and much is due—Lewis would have done well to employ his erudite analytical skills to a careful reading of Genesis 1 and 2 before venturing to give his democratically driven marital guidelines.

But the texts to which Lewis *does* refer in *Mere Christianity* are in the New Testament. As we will see, a lot of mistakes can be avoided when we read the Hebrew Bible first, on its own terms, before reading New Testament references to it. Having built our foundation in the beginning of the Bible, we are ready to turn to the New Testament. Most of the texts that comprise the foundation for hierarchicalist arguments against women's speaking in the church are found there. To these we now turn.

33. Lewis, *Mere Christianity,* 114.

4

The Word of God

(1 Corinthians 14:34–38)

IN CHAPTERS 4 AND 5 we will examine the two texts of the New Testament that are used most often to argue for the silencing or limitation of women's voices in the church: 1 Corinthians 14:34–38 and 1 Timothy 2:12–14. Honest complementarian and egalitarian interpreters alike acknowledge that these two passages contain elements that are challenging to understand, even to the most erudite interpreters. Because of this, the rest of us might be tempted to say, "Better safe than sorry—I'll let the scholars interpret these for me." I should address this sentiment before we go any further.

There are two problems with invoking the "better safe than sorry" logic in this context. The first is that it assumes one knows which side would be the more "safe" vis-à-vis the other. "Better safe than sorry" is only a valid argument when we can *foresee* that taking one course of action is safer than another. For example, I may choose to wear a seatbelt because I can foresee that, in the event of a road accident, I will be safer if I do so. Similar reasoning might lead me to pay extra for a refundable airline ticket, or to buy life insurance. In other words, the only situations in which a "better safe than sorry" argument is valid are those in which one knows beforehand what the safest arrangement would be in the case of some undesirable, but nevertheless possible, turn of events. Rock climbers often tether themselves with ropes for this reason, and sky divers jump with a spare parachute.

By contrast, in cases in which one genuinely does not know which of two or more choices would be safest, the "better-safe-than-sorry" logic becomes invalid. One time my wife and I were hiking in the forest at the Delaware Water Gap National Recreation Area in New Jersey. It was a lovely, sunny day, and perhaps for that reason we weren't paying close enough attention to the choices we were making as we walked along the trail. Eventually, we found ourselves walking along a part of the trail that we had already traversed, and we realized we had been walking in a circle. By and by, we came upon a fork in the trail.

Now, suppose that at that moment Isabel had turned to me and said, "Which way do you think we should go?," and that I had responded, "We should go to the left." Of course, Isabel would want to know why I thought we should go left instead of right. Suppose, then, that I had replied, "Well, you know, better safe than sorry." In order for such a reply to make sense, there would need to be some reason why going left would be the safer of the two options. Isabel would want me to provide her with some explanation about *why* taking the path on the left was the less risky option. If I truly had no idea which path had been more likely to lead us to the place where we had parked our car, my invocation of the "better safe than sorry" argument would be worthless.[1]

Similarly, churches and individuals who think the Bible is authoritative in life have to choose one way or the other. There is no safe way! Even the act of letting other people deal with the issue is a choice that could represent greater or lesser risk.

Someone might reason, "But, look at how many godly, highly educated scholars defend this view! Surely, they are unlikely to be wrong about this." The problem is, there are upright, devout, highly educated scholars who defend *both* sides of this issue.

Others might point out that women have taken subordinate roles throughout most of recorded church history. Isn't it safer to trust the traditional practice of the church? Again, not necessarily. First of all, there have been many exceptions to the general practice of discouraging women's speaking in church over the past two millennia. But even more significantly, one of the most important traditions that the church should uphold is the practice of revisiting the Bible in every generation to test what has been passed down. This should be particularly important to Christians in Protestant churches, all of which confess the preeminence of Scripture *over* church tradition. "Better safe than sorry" is not a valid

1. To reassure my kind readers who might be worried about our safety in the predicament described above, I should mention that eventually we found our way out of the forest.

option in this debate. Like Isabel and I out hiking in the woods, we are well on our way into this journey, and we have reached the fork in the trail already. We have to choose one way or the other—either we choose to limit the voices of women in the church (to whatever degree) based on their gender or we encourage them to speak.

I don't want to give the wrong impression with my hiking analogy here. I *do* think there are certain interpretations of 1 Corinthians 14:34–35 and 1 Timothy 2:11–14 that are demonstrably better than others, and I hope to show this shortly. But, if my readers are like me they will wish these texts were *just a little bit clearer* to us modern readers than they are. No doubt, these texts were quite clear to their original readers. But for us, reading them in a different language, from a different cultural perspective, in (for most of us) a different geographic location, and on the other side of nearly 2,000 years' worth of convulsive historical change, their meaning is not as readily accessible as we might like it to be. With that in mind, in the following I am going to make a case for what seems to me the most consistent, reasonable explanations of these texts. I have to acknowledge that even among the most knowledgeable biblical scholars, these texts are notoriously difficult to interpret. But I have no choice. If I'm going to be an active part of the church, I simply must develop an opinion about this to the best of my ability, and so must my gracious readers.

What It Doesn't Mean

Even if we cannot determine exactly what a passage of Scripture means, we can often determine what it definitely does not mean. One such passage is 1 Timothy 2:15 (upon which we will comment later). The passage says that a woman "will be saved through childbearing." While it may not be clear to us what the passage means (at least upon first reading), we can right away eliminate an interpretation that would connect salvation from sin and death with the act of giving birth to babies. Why? Because such a teaching would contradict too much of the theology taught in the rest of the New Testament. All Christian scholars would agree about this.

Such is the case with 1 Corinthians 14:34–35. It is possible, even before settling on a particular interpretation, to know that this text is not eliminating women's voices entirely from the church's worship services because just a few chapters before, in 1 Corinthians 11:5, Paul allows for women's voices to be heard. In addition, there is evidence in the New

Testament that both Paul and others in the early church received the vocal ministry of women.[2] As we observed before, virtually no complementarian interpreter would disagree with this. Women in almost all churches have some sort of voice in the life of the church. The question cannot be, therefore, "Should we allow women to speak in church?" Rather, it has to be something like, "What *kind* of speaking is forbidden in 1 Corinthians 14:34–35?" As we will see later, this may not be the correct question either. The point for right now is that it is possible to eliminate at the outset the idea that Paul demands the *complete* silence of women.

In the following I provide two possible ways of reading this text. Some of my readers may find it strange that I've chosen to offer a second interpretation. Their puzzlement might increase once I admit that I find *both* of these interpretations plausible, even though they are basically mutually exclusive. Some of my careful readers might ask, "Shouldn't one's application of Scripture come *after* one settles on the right interpretation?" It's a valid question, and I feel I ought to explain myself.

In my own journey to changing my mind about women in speaking ministries, I sometimes struggled because I couldn't land exclusively on one single egalitarian interpretation of some of the relevant Bible passages. I struggled because I was looking for the *only* plausible interpretation. Instead, I found (and, truthfully, I still do find) myself drawn to various readings. As I mentioned before, egalitarian scholars interpret these passages differently from each other and, because of that, I wavered on my way to embracing the egalitarian position. But eventually I realized that the reason it was sometimes difficult to choose between various egalitarian interpretations was because they seemed so equally reasonable to each other. By comparison, the hierarchicalist interpretations I read consistently made less sense of the text. I realized that, in order to affirm women in speaking ministries in the church, I did not need to commit once and for all to any one particular egalitarian reading; I merely needed to be convinced that the two or three egalitarian ways of understanding the passages that seemed persuasive to me were clearly *more* plausible than the hierarchicalist alternatives.

Both interpretations of 1 Corinthians 14:34–38 that I will offer result, practically speaking, in freedom for women to fully participate in the speaking ministries of the church, provided they are called, gifted, and qualified—the same requirements for men in the same ministries. As

2. See, for example, Rom 16 and Acts 18:26; 21:19.

I mentioned previously, it is possible to distinguish between interpretations that do a good job of taking into account all the factors at work in a given Scripture text from interpretations that don't do as good a job. By saying, "This text could mean this, but it could also mean this," I am not saying that anything goes—that a person can haphazardly choose an interpretation at random. Rather, I am arguing that, even though some interpretations are clearly better than others, we still have to recognize the limits of our knowledge. I will argue that so-called complementarian interpretations are demonstrably inferior to *at least some of* the egalitarian interpretations available. When we choose from among the most carefully formulated interpretations available, the result in practice will be freedom for women to use their gifts and abilities in all ministries of the church.

Explanation A: It Was a Matter of Disruptive Noise[3]

The movie *A Quiet Place* is a fascinating (but scary—not to be watched with small children) story about a family trying to survive after the world has been invaded by monstrous, man-eating creatures.[4] The film begins after the monsters' arrival. The viewer has to guess what happened before, and how the creatures arrived in the world. The family's daughter is deaf, and this seems to have been the impetus for the family's learning sign language before the monster invasion and takeover of the area. This works to the family's advantage because the monsters do not have eyes. They only have extremely sensitive hearing, and they pounce with lightning speed upon any living thing that makes a noise. One aspect of the film that makes it unique is the long segments that have almost no sound. Lots of communication happens between the family during those segments, but it happens in silence.

There are different ways of being silent. When the elders silenced me as a teenager in our assembly, they were not concerned about my making too much noise in the church meetings. From a noise-making point of view, they really didn't silence me at all. They never accused me of disrupting a church service. And truthfully, if I *had* been making disruptive noises in the church services—say, by drumming the back of the

---

3. For a summary of "Explanation A" of 1 Cor 14:34–38, see Table 4.1 in the appendix.

4. Krasinski, *Quiet Place.*

chair in front of me with my fingernails or humming Handel's *Messiah* during the meetings—they would have been right to ask me to be quiet. They didn't stop me from making noise; they stopped me from communicating. There is a difference between telling someone to be quiet out of concern for them—like in *A Quiet Place*, in which the loving father has to remind his children to be quiet so they don't get eaten by the savage monsters—and telling someone to be quiet because one thinks her voice itself is unsafe for people to hear.

I do not know how to communicate via sign language. But, in a way, reading and writing are a form of sign language. As a teacher, I frequently have occasion to tell my students things like, "Please, be quiet and work on your writing assignment." Note that I am *not* telling these students to refrain from communicating. Instead, I am asking them to refrain from making audible noise because their doing so disrupts the development of their own communication skills. Actually, I am trying to maximize my students' communication potential by facilitating a quiet learning environment. To that end I, at times, literally silence my students.

Similarly, suppose I were a teacher in a deaf school, where I taught my lessons using sign language. In that case, I would no doubt at times need to tell my students to stop signing to each other so that they could focus on what I, as the teacher in the room, was signing. Even though the issue would not be noise in a deaf classroom *per se*, I would need to arbitrate my students' communication in order to maximize learning. In a deaf classroom I wouldn't silence my students with respect to noise, but I would have to silence them at times with respect to communication.

When we talk about the act of silencing someone, it is important to know what kind of silence is in view. Did Paul tell the women in Corinth to be quiet because he was trying to get rid of excess, disruptive noise *for the women's own benefit*—so that they and others, for example, could learn? Or, was he telling them to be quiet because their voices were unsafe for the church to hear?

Let's imagine for a minute that the women in the church at Corinth knew how to communicate using sign language. In this case, their communicating would not disrupt the service because there would be no noise. Would this have changed anything about Paul's instruction to them?

In a hierarchicalist interpretation, it would not have. For most hierarchicalist interpreters, Paul is not worried here about women being disruptive; he is worried about their communicating ideas to the congregation—particularly the men. Their communicating in and of itself is the hazard from which Paul wants to safeguard the Corinthian church. The problem, from a hierarchicalist reading, is not that these women were making noise, but that they were *female people* trying to communicate something to the congregation.

But suppose the problem being addressed in this passage is not a breach of gender role protocol, but disruptive noise. Let's work through the text and see if we can back up this proposal with sound textual arguments. First of all, we need to look at the word translated "silent" in verse 34. The word is *sigáō*, and it means simply "to be silent," in the sense of not making any noises, including speaking. This text's instruction to women has to do with actual sounds, not communication. As we will see later, Paul uses a different Greek word when he wants to speak of "silence" in the sense of being tranquil or calm. Here the text is not telling women to be more serene; it's telling them to be quiet. If that sounds rude, I apologize. I'm not necessarily defending the text's abrupt style. I'm just clarifying what it says.

This fact brings a key point to the forefront of our discussion. In 1 Corinthians 11:5, Paul mentions women who were, apparently, "praying and prophesying" in church services, and he seems to approve of the practice. There, the topic at hand is head coverings. The fact that Paul does not forbid women from speaking in chapter 11 leads hierarchicalist and egalitarian interpreters alike to agree that Paul cannot be forbidding women from speaking *entirely* in church in 14:34. He is not giving a blanket, absolute commandment. Rather, Paul *must* be telling women to refrain from certain kinds of speaking in church. Again, hierarchicalists and (most)[5] egalitarians agree about this. The real question is not about what the text says, but about the context. In what context, and for what reason, is Paul telling these women to be silent?

For the hierarchicalist, Paul is telling women to be silent with regard to authoritative speaking ministries—ministries like preaching and teaching. That is, most hierarchicalists imagine that the context around Paul's instruction here is ultimately about a female person's place in the hierarchical order of the church. Women should be sure that they are not usurping their proper male authorities, and this involves being silent under certain circumstances in which their voices would sound too imposing. In this view, the danger from which Paul is trying to protect the church at Corinth is the authoritative voices of women.

---

5. See "Explanation B" of this passage below.

Egalitarians who interpret this passage in the way I've just described imagine a different context. They imagine that Paul's concern is not hierarchy but orderly church worship. In this view, the danger from which Paul is trying to protect the Corinthian church is not authoritative female voices but disorderliness. Paul is trying to teach this young church how to worship together and develop as a Christ-centered community. Which imagined context makes the most sense of the text?

There are at least three reasons why the hierarchicalist interpretation is less plausible. First, the hierarchicalist reading requires us to import the category of authoritative speaking, like preaching and teaching, to the text even though there is no indication *in the text itself* that this is what Paul had in mind. Paul doesn't mention teaching or preaching at all, much less authoritative speaking; he only uses the word "speak," a word that would include preaching and teaching, but also any other kind of speaking. If we just look at the words on the page, it appears that the verses are forbidding speaking of all kinds. Why say "speak" if the issue is only preaching and teaching, or some other authoritative kind of speaking? It just doesn't fit.

Second, the very idea that Paul considered some kinds of speaking gifts as more authoritative than others is questionable at best. The fact is, there is no biblical evidence that the early church categorized spiritual gifts such that some gifts were ranked higher than others in terms of authority. Of course, there were certain *positions* of authority in the churches—elders, bishops, apostles, deacons, etc.—but the spiritual gifts are not placed one over another, nor are those who exercised them. The only possible exception to this claim might be 1 Corinthians 12:28, where Paul does in fact put some gifts in sequential order. But ironically, Paul puts prophets *before* teachers! So, even if I'm wrong and Paul actually *does* think some spiritual gifts are more authoritative than others, it turns out that prophecy would be closer to the top than teaching or preaching, and, as we saw, Paul seems to accept women's use of the gift of prophecy in 1 Corinthians 11:5. Thus, the view that Paul is trying to prohibit women from only authoritative kinds of speaking in 14:34 cuts against the natural flow of the letter. As we will see later, it also cuts against the grain of Paul's practice.

Third, and perhaps most importantly, there is simply no evidence in the rest of the Bible, and especially in Genesis 1 and 2, that men and women were created to live in a hierarchical relationship. Thus, a concern for that relationship could not function as a sound foundation for silencing women.

As a young person growing up among the Plymouth Brethren churches, I always assumed this text was telling women be silent only when men were present. As I related before, in my church women were not allowed to lead Bible studies or preach to the general congregation. But, women were encouraged to teach groups of other women. I was taught that this was what Paul was getting at in 1 Corinthians 14:34—"Women can teach other women, but they should not teach men." But later I realized that I had been reading something into this passage that is not there. First Corinthians 14 doesn't say anything about women not teaching men as opposed to other women. It simply says women should be silent, regardless of the gender of the listeners. If I had been a Christian in ancient Corinth reading this letter, I would have had no basis for assuming that Paul meant women should be silent only when men were present.

Some might suggest that this text should be read in light of 1 Timothy 2:11–14, where Paul *does* mention teaching in relation to telling women to be quiet (though, as we will see, this is a different kind of quietness), and where a woman teaching a man is specifically mentioned. However, as Keener notes, "[T]he Corinthians could not simply flip in their Bibles to 1 Timothy [2:12] (which had not been written yet) to figure out what Paul meant, and unlike prophecy and tongues, teaching is not even mentioned directly in the present context!"[6] If we want to understand Paul's Letter to the Corinthians as the Corinthians understood it, we will look for the interpretation that makes the most sense of all the elements of the passage within this letter *first* before looking elsewhere for clues to its meaning. This is especially true in this case since 1 Timothy was written almost a decade after 1 Corinthians. There is no way the Corinthians could have read 1 Timothy.

So, if there is no evidence that teaching and preaching are the specific kinds of speaking from which Paul is asking women to refrain in this verse, what is the better alternative? Assuming that this is not an absolute prohibition of women *ever* speaking in the church, what imagined context flows more naturally and coherently with the text's grain instead of pushing against it?

We don't have to look far for the answer—it's in the very next verse! Verse 35 says, "If there is anything [the women] desire to learn, *let them*

6. Keener, "Learning in the Assemblies," 163.

ask their husbands at home. For it is shameful for a woman to speak in church." There it is! *The context includes question-asking.* Why import something from outside the text when a certain type of speaking is right there on the open page? Paul wants women to save their questions for later. Instead of warning against women teachers, Paul is actually *advocating for* women students. The only act of speaking that is explicitly mentioned in the text is question-asking, which is most naturally the activity of a learner, not an instructor. Far from telling all Christian women everywhere that they must forever abstain from becoming teachers in the church, one can coherently read this passage as Paul trying to facilitate women's learning. Keener makes the same observation. He writes, "Paul here actually opposes something more basic than women teaching in public: he opposes them learning in public. Or, put more accurately, he opposes them *learning* too loudly in public."[7]

As a teacher myself, this makes sense. We may think the language of the verse is a bit terse, but that doesn't change Paul's goal, or the meaning of the text. His goal is that these women conduct themselves as good students because he wants them to learn. We'll see later that this is consistent with Paul's instruction elsewhere in the New Testament.

These observations pose an obvious interpretive problem for those who read this passage as restricting women from filling teaching and preaching roles in the church. These readers claim that 1 Corinthians 14:34–35 is about gender roles. But as we have observed, the only actual role this text suggests these women were filling—or even trying to fill—was that of a learner or student, *not* an instructor or teacher. I feel I should say it again: *this text does not mention teaching or preaching.* Further, a reading that sees these women in a student's role makes sense of the normal meaning of the word *sigáō* ("to be silent"). It is the right word to use when a teacher is addressing his students. It is the right word to use when a teacher is trying to maximize learning by, for the time being, telling her students to refrain from communicating with each other. "There will be a time for questions later," Paul is saying. "But at church, please be quiet during the service."

These observations also make sense of the accompanying command to "be submissive." Every teacher and every good student knows that in order to learn one has to submit oneself to the learning process as well as to the teacher's instruction. The same can be said of worship.

---

7. Keener, *Paul, Women & Wives*, 80 (emphasis original).

If a worship service is going to be orderly, its participants *must* submit themselves to whomever is leading the service, and also to the order of the service as a whole.

This interpretation also agrees with what Paul is trying to teach overall in 1 Corinthians 14. It turns out that the word *sigáō* only appears four times in all of Paul's writings, and three out of those four are in this chapter. Paul actually tells three groups of people to be quiet. He addresses the first group in verses 27 and 28: "If anyone speaks in a tongue, two—or at most three—should speak, one at a time, and someone should interpret. If there is no interpreter, the speaker should keep quiet in the church and speak to himself and to God." Notice that in these verses Paul is correcting disorderly behavior. He is trying to teach the Corinthians how to order their worship services so that every member can benefit from them, so that the members can build one another up. Paul knows that context matters. He is trying to cultivate an orderly worship environment. The second group that should "be silent" appears in verses 29 and 30 where Paul says, "Two or three prophets should speak, and the others should weigh carefully what is said. And if a revelation comes to someone who is sitting down, the first speaker should [be silent]." Again, orderliness in worship is Paul's primary concern when he silences a group in the church. Verse 33 says, "For God is not a God of disorder but of peace."

Now think about this: If verse 34 is actually about silencing women because they are women, Paul is abruptly changing his line of thought. Instead of continuing with his concern for orderliness in worship through verse 34, Paul, in this view, is very suddenly changing the subject to gender roles. Of course, it is possible for Paul to change the subject abruptly, and if there were no plausible alternative interpretation available one might have to conclude that this is what Paul did here. But, as we have seen, there *is* a plausible alternative interpretation! One could consistently interpret that Paul silenced these women for the same reason he silenced the other two groups of people shortly beforehand in the same chapter—to foster orderliness in the worship service.

First Corinthians 14:34 ends with "as the law says." This little phrase creates a conundrum for the modern reader. For one thing, as we know from Paul's writing elsewhere, simply referencing the Torah (the Law) would not have been the end of the matter for Paul. Paul saw Jesus as fulfilling the law, and this implied that the people of the New Covenant had a new relationship to the Torah, which in at least some cases meant freedom to depart from the letter of the law in order to follow its spirit (see 2 Cor 3:6). But the biggest barrier to knowing exactly why Paul refers to the Torah here is that he doesn't provide any clues about which passage of the Torah he has in mind. One might expect to be able to find a passage in the Torah that tells women to be quiet after reading 1 Corinthians 14:34. But the Torah simply says no such thing. There is no command in the Old Testament enjoining or even encouraging female silence, much less passage that connects teaching with a lack of submission. The fact is, there are several pivotal moments in the Torah when women of faith *speak profound theological truths* that have instructed readers of the Torah for millennia. Think of Miriam, who was called a prophetess and who led the people of Israel in worship after God delivered them from Pharaoh's vengeance at the Red Sea. Think of Hagar, who is the first person in the Bible to encounter that mysterious person called, "The Angel of the LORD," and to whom God gave a promise about her descendants that was strikingly similar to the one God gave Abraham. Think of Moses' mother and the midwives of the Hebrews who, by the wisdom of their words, protected the baby Moses from Pharaoh's murderous hand. Think of Zipporah, whose wisdom in a crucial moment saved Moses from God's anger.[8] And there are more such women whose voices found their way into Scripture in the rest of the Hebrew Bible. It's impossible that Paul could have been referring to a text in the Torah that forbids women from speaking. No such text exists!

Unfortunately, I do not have a thoroughly satisfying explanation for the presence of the phrase, "as the law says," in this passage. But I would prefer to continue searching instead of settling for an obviously inadequate explanation, especially when there are such far-reaching implications involved in assuming that Paul thought that the Hebrew Bible commands women to be quiet in the presence of men! Do we really think that Paul is saying simply, "Women should be quiet . . . because the Torah says so?" That simply cannot be. That is not the way the apostle Paul used the Torah. No, there must be a better explanation.

My best proposal—and that's all I can offer—is that Paul is referring to some aspect of the Law that creates an ordered community. As New Testament scholar Alan Padgett writes,

> Nowhere in the Old Testament are women called to be silent,
> nor are they called to submit to their husbands. Yet there is

---

8. This is a strange and oft-ignored story. But I think it is profoundly important for our understanding of the Exodus saga, and especially the meaning of the Passover.

excellent evidence for biblical and broadly Jewish concern for silence in worship before God or the Word of God, or while learning from the rabbis (e.g., Deut. 27:9–10; Job 33:31–33; Isa. 66:2; Hab. 2:20).[9]

In view of Paul's overall purpose in 1 Corinthians 14 of encouraging orderliness in the church, this is a much more promising, if underdeveloped, explanation.

The situation is different, however, in 1 Timothy 2:11–14, because there Paul *does* provide a clue about precisely what passage of the Torah he has in mind: Genesis 2. We examined Genesis 2 previously. Not only did we find no hints to point us toward a created hierarchy in that chapter, we also found clear affirmations of male-female mutuality and complementarity (the kind *without* hierarchy). We saw that man's having been created before woman did *not* signify man's superior status or higher rank. We also saw the same view of humanity portrayed in Genesis 1.

At least one question still remains: Why didn't Paul want these women to ask questions in church? I have a (hopefully educated) conjecture, which I'll share shortly, but admittedly this is a difficult question to answer. After all, 1 Corinthians is a letter, which means we only have one side of the conversation. Furthermore, it is one of a series of letters. Paul had written to the Corinthians previously at least once, and they had written to him as well. We are jumping into an ongoing conversation when we read 1 Corinthians. (This fact becomes especially important in "Explanation B," to come.) Thus, I'll share what I think the answer could be, but it is important first to note that the interpretation I gave above does *not* depend on my ability to answer this follow-up question. My main point is that introducing an ideology of gender roles to an interpretation of this text runs contrary to the more natural and more plausible available readings of it. In other words, my argument does not depend on a reconstruction of the cultural context behind this passage; it depends on what the text explicitly says, printed in black and white, on the open page.

Regardless, we still want to know why Paul might have told women to stop asking questions during the worship service. What could have been disruptive or disorderly about question-asking? The most plausible answer that I've been able to find is the one given by the late Kenneth Bailey in his fascinating cultural commentary on 1 Corinthians, *Paul through Mediterranean Eyes.* Dr. Bailey was not only a stellar New Testament

9. Padgett, *As Christ Submits,* 74.

scholar; he also spent his whole childhood and adult ministry life in West Asia[10] and North Africa. This cultural milieu facilitated interpretive insights in his inquisitive mind that are often missed by other commentators who cannot draw from firsthand experience living in cultures similar to those into which the New Testament was written. In a nutshell, Bailey suggests that Paul was addressing a problem in the churches of the first century that Bailey personally experienced in his own ministry. What was the problem? The women were chatting during the worship services. Here is some of what Bailey writes:

> I have preached in village churches in Egypt where the women were seated on one side of the church and the men on the other. There was a wooden partition about six feet high separating the two sections. I preached in simple colloquial Arabic, but the women were often illiterate and the preacher was expected to preach for at least an hour—and we had problems. The women quickly passed the limit of their attention span. The children were seated with them and chatting inevitably broke out among the women. The chatting would at times become so loud that no one could hear the preacher. (These villages had no electricity and no sound amplification.) One of the senior elders would stand up and in a desperate voice shout, "Let the women be silent in the church!" and we would proceed. After about ten minutes the scene would repeat.[11]

Dr. Bailey's host wanted the women to be quiet so that they could learn, not because female voices are intrinsically unsafe. He knew that their society had not encouraged women to seek education, and that this had, tragically, stunted their development as learners. They had not been raised to sit quietly and submit to a teacher. (Also, notice that the children in the church Dr. Bailey was visiting were considered the sole responsibility of the women during the church service—a factor that should not be overlooked!) Bailey thinks something similar was happening in the church at Corinth.

John Chrysostom, a Greek-speaking preacher of the late fourth and early fifth centuries, described a nearly identical problem in the church at Antioch. Here is what he wrote at that time:

10. By West Asia, I refer to what is often called The Middle East. I prefer to call the region West Asia because that way I don't have to assume that my readers are located in Europe or the Western Hemisphere.

11. Bailey, *Paul through Mediterranean Eyes*, 560.

Then indeed the women, from such teaching keep silence; but now there is apt to be great noise among them, much clamor and talking ... Thus all is confusion, and they seem not to understand, that unless they are quiet, they cannot learn anything that is useful. For when our discourse [sermon] strains against the talking, and no one minds what is said, what good can it do them?[12]

Notice how similar this sounds to the problem Dr. Bailey witnessed in the rural Egyptian church, and how similar the solution Chrysostom suggests accords with the one that we have suggested Paul is giving in 1 Corinthians 14:34–35. If the women are to learn, they must be quiet—and the women *must learn*!

Many modern readers of the Bible live in areas of the world where literacy rates are high and where most people have access to schools. Because of this, we assume that everyone knows how to take on a student's role because we assume that nearly everyone has *been* a student at one time or another. But the truth is, this is not the case in many places. Further, it was *definitely* not the case in the times and places in which the Bible was written. In the relatively rare circumstances in which academic opportunities were available in the first century, men were consistently and systematically prioritized over women, more often than not to women's complete exclusion. There were exceptions to this, but they were few and far between.

Of course, we are all aware that education has improved all over the world since biblical times, not only for women but also for men. We know that not many people were well educated in New Testament times like they are today, and we know that women were heavily repressed in many ways. Yet, we often stop short of considering how this would have affected the dynamics of a church gathering. Bailey's description helps us see what the situation may have been like. When children never have the opportunity to go to school, they miss out on more than academic knowledge; they also miss out on acquiring basic learning skills like the ability to sit still, follow directions, and pay attention—all skills that are essential for learning in a church context just as they are anywhere else. We can be certain that the vast majority of women in the Corinthian church, as well as of those in all the churches of the first-century world, would have been, by modern standards at least, woefully uneducated. That is, women were not accustomed to sitting under teaching like some

---

12. Westfall, *Paul and Gender*, 239.

of the men were. Again, there were certainly exceptions, but they were just that—exceptions to the general rule.

This is why I think Bailey's observations might be able to aid our understanding of this passage. They show that, even today, there are situations in which it might be necessary to silence the women of a church. But, the silence is not intended to be permanent, and the reason for it is not because the voices of women are intrinsically unsafe for the church to hear. We should not fear female voices; but we *should* be worried when worship services become too disorganized to be edifying to a local church body. The silence for which Paul advocated had a goal. There is *no* evidence in 1 Corinthians 14, or in this entire epistle, that Paul thought women should be permanently silent, *much less because they were women.* Using this text to silence women who minister in orderly and edifying ways today misses the point entirely, and with devastating effect on the health of the church as whole. The church needs the gifts that the Spirit gives it, and many of those gifts come through women. When we fail to welcome women's voices freely, the church bypasses a crucial opportunity to receive, certainly not all, but far too many of those gifts.

Incidentally, I had more occasion as a church youth director to silence the boys in my youth group than I did the girls. I can say the same about my experience as a high school religious education teacher. I loved the boys under my care every bit as much as I did the girls. But, I must say, when it comes to making lots of noise, the boys take home the prize. In some contexts, this passage could be well-suited to addressing the *men* of a church. In fact, just a few weeks ago as I write this, the pastor of the church I now attend in Istanbul had to ask a few men to be quiet because they were chatting aloud with each other at the back of the sanctuary during the sermon—and, it wasn't the first time our pastor has had to do that!

What is most important to see in all this is that Paul clearly *wanted* the women in the church at Corinth to learn. It is truly concerning, in light of this fact, that the number of opportunities for women to learn continue to lag behind the number given to men in today's world. Of course, the problem is much more pronounced in some areas of the world than in others. But even in my home country, the United States, there are still some Christian seminaries that do not admit women students into some of their educational programs. This is not right. Women should have access to as much learning as possible—not because they are women, but because they are human beings made in God's image. This should be especially true of institutions that exist to serve the church, because the church is supposed to represent God's new humanity—the body of Christ. Today's complementarians have rightly forsaken the old notion, held by many of the church's theologians in the past, that women are spiritually and intellectually inferior to men. Yet, educational opportunities afforded to women within many Christian colleges and seminaries that ascribe to complementarianism continue to be fewer than those afforded to men. This is not to mention the much greater disparity between teaching opportunities afforded men *vis-à-vis* women in such educational institutions. A prominent complementarian theologian opines, "Mixed-gender theology classes should be taught by men. It is illogical to say a woman should train men to be Bible teachers and pastors when she shouldn't be one herself. If women shouldn't be pastors or elders in churches, then they should also not have that role in other contexts."[13] What is perhaps most concerning about this way of thinking is that, over the past few decades, as so-called complementarianism has become a popular ideology, some Christian institutions have *narrowed* instead of broadened the purview of their women teachers and faculty. This is a deeply disturbing trend, for it moves adversely to the trend Jesus set in his ministry.

In the above I tried to show that, when one considers the elements within and around 1 Corinthians 14:34–38 itself, there is no evidence that Paul was trying to push an ideology of gender roles on the Corinthian Christians. I have suggested instead that Paul is trying to correct a disorderly practice in the Corinthian church, and have tried to show that reading the text this way goes much further in making sense of what the text actually says. I argued that it is a superior interpretation to hierarchicalist alternatives because it fits better within the context of the whole chapter, the letter, and the words and phrases in verses 34 and 35.

However, even though the interpretation I offered above is much better than a hierarchicalist reading, it still has its weaknesses, and it still leaves some questions unanswered. For that reason, some of my gracious readers will wonder if there is another plausible interpretation of these verses. Here I will offer another interpretation which I think is also plausible—and I think better—than the interpretation I've just offered. I've been on the fence in the past between these two interpretations, but if I had to choose today I would go with Explanation B below.

---

13. As quoted in Moon, "Should Christian Colleges?," para. 7.

Explanation B: Paul Is Correcting a Corinthian Idea[14]

Every once in a while one encounters Paul speaking in ways that might offend the sensibilities of the more refined among us. Consider, for example, a comment he makes in Titus 1:12–13. He writes, "One of Crete's own prophets has said it: 'The Cretans are always liars, evil brutes, lazy gluttons.' This saying is true. Therefore rebuke them sharply, so that they will be sound in the faith." I suppose Paul had good intentions. But I can't help but think, "Really, Paul? *All* the Cretans are lazy gluttons?! *The whole entire island?!* And you're calling them animals! Didn't your parents teach you anything about good manners?!" For another example, consider what he says in Galatians 5:12. In reference to some who were teaching that circumcision was necessary for church membership, he writes, "As for those agitators, I wish they would go the whole way and emasculate themselves!" I'm not sure if Paul's original readers would have taken this comedically, offensively, or in some other way. But if I were a betting man, I'd wager that none of my gentle readers were ever assigned Galatians 5:12 as a memory verse in Sunday school. Paul's speech was, to put it generously, a little rough sometimes.

Whatever our opinion of it, this is just how Paul talked. Paul was highly educated, but at times he doesn't seem very worried about being polite or sounding refined. My readers will have noticed that I apologize at several points in my explanation above for the abrupt way 1 Corinthians 14:34–35 seems to silence women. While I am utterly convinced that Paul would have had a good reason for doing so (the reason outlined above) I cannot help but wonder if he could have done it more politely. I see enough of this kind of abruptness elsewhere in Paul's writings to persuade me, however, that Paul *could have* said something like this to the women at Corinth. It doesn't seem out of character to me.

Nevertheless, there are actually reasons apart from our (possible) discomfort with Paul's directness to suggest that, perhaps, the ideas in 1 Corinthians 14:34–35 are not from Paul's mind. New Testament scholar Lucy Peppiatt has recently made a thorough, scholarly case for this reading in her well-argued book, *Women and Worship at Corinth*.

The first thing to note is that 1 Corinthians is only one of several letters in an ongoing correspondence between Paul and the Christians at Corinth. Paul has written to them at least once before, and they to

14. For a summary of "Explanation B" of 1 Cor 14:34–38, see Table 4.2 in the appendix.

him (see 5:9 and 7:1). Paul has also received a report about them from some people who were sent to him by a woman named Chloe, who was probably one of the leaders in the Corinthian church (see 1:11). In 1 Corinthians, Paul seems at times to quote from the letter that the Corinthians had previously written him. All scholars agree about this. However, it can be difficult to discern exactly when Paul is doing this and when he is not. There is a simple reason for this: there are no quotation marks in the written Greek of Paul's day!

Now of course, as the writers of their own letter, the Corinthian Christians would have known exactly when Paul was quoting them. This wouldn't have presented any interpretive challenge for *them*. But for *us* (and for the scores of generations of Christians who have read 1 Corinthians before us as well), Paul's habit of suddenly quoting the Corinthians and then responding to them sometimes creates a puzzle. As an example, consider how 1 Corinthians 7:1 appears in the New International Version:

> Now for the matters you wrote about: "It is not good for a man
> to have sexual relations with a woman."

The translators of the NIV were sufficiently confident that Paul is quoting the Corinthians' letter here that they were willing to add quotation marks to their translation. If they are right, the following verse is Paul's *correction* of this statement. The following verse says, "But since sexual immorality is occurring, each man should have sexual relations with his own wife, and each woman with her own husband." If we are reading the NIV, we will think that verse 1 is a *wrong* idea with which Paul disagrees, while verse 2 is Paul's correction of that incorrect idea.

It seems that the translators of the New American Standard Bible, however, were not quite so persuaded. Here is their translation of the same verse:

> Now concerning the things about which you wrote, it is good for
> a man not to touch a woman.

The punctuation in this translation leaves the reader with the impression that the statement, "It is good for a man not to touch a woman," is a teaching from Paul himself. If we are reading the NASB, we will think that *both* verses 1 *and* 2 are Paul's teaching.

Here are some other examples from the same epistle. Notice how in each case the NIV translators felt confident enough to insert quotation marks, and sometimes even add, "you say," to make it even more clear that they are persuaded Paul was quoting the Corinthians in these instances. Notice also how, after the quotations, Paul offers a corrective comment.

> Now about food sacrificed to idols: We know that "We all possess knowledge." But knowledge puffs up while love builds up. (1 Cor 8:1)

> "I have the right to do anything," you say—but not everything is beneficial. "I have the right to do anything"—but not everything is constructive. (1 Cor 10:23)[15]

If we were to read these passages in the NASB or KJV, we would find no quotation marks. We would come away thinking that the entire verse in each case represents Paul's own thinking. That makes a big difference for a person who wants to understand what Paul was trying to teach!

With regard to these three examples, most scholars agree with the NIV translators that the phrases in quotation marks were things the Corinthian Christians had said and that Paul is trying to correct their wrong—or partially wrong—ideas. Perhaps Paul is quoting their letter. Perhaps he is responding to something that Chloe's messengers had reported to him. In any case, interpreters have determined from the context and grammar of the text that these are, in fact, quotations—or summarizations—of Corinthian ideas, and therefore should appear as such in English translations.

The question before us is whether or not 1 Corinthians 14:34–35 is likewise one of these quotations. If it is, it means that Paul's corrective is in verses 36 to 38. Is such a conclusion plausible? Does it make sense, even after a careful examination of the text?

Before taking a close look at the grammar of the passage itself, we need to make three observations from a bird's-eye view. The first thing we should notice is that the church at Corinth was one of the most problematic churches to make an appearance in the New Testament. Furthermore, if we bracket out the passage under discussion for a moment, the problems that the Corinthian church was experiencing seem to have been coming overwhelmingly from the men in the church, not the women. Chapters 1–4 deal repeatedly with arrogance and divisions. While Paul does not specify that the problem is *only* with the men, it is difficult to imagine that this wasn't the case. Paul was not shy about pointing out problems that women specifically could cause, as we will see later when

---

15. See also 6:12.

we examine 1 Timothy. In 1 Corinthians 5, Paul has to address a situation in which a man is engaging in an illicit sexual relationship with his stepmother. The primary issue is not that this happened in the church, but that instead of confronting and rebuking this man, the church as a whole had become arrogant and boastful about his behavior. This seems to be a situation, again, for which the men were primarily responsible. In chapter 6, Paul has to address certain of the Corinthian Christians who were taking one another to court. In a time and place in which women did not have the legal right to do such a thing, this situation had to have been created by the men. It appears also in the same chapter that some of the Corinthian men were having sexual relations with prostitutes. This was obviously a problem with the men, not the women. One might argue that the women were the troublemakers regarding head coverings in chapter 11, but I hope to show later that the men were likely the cause of that issue as well. In a church context in which the men were undeniably causing *a lot* of trouble, it seems a bit strange that Paul would choose to silence the women out of the blue in chapter 14.

The second thing we should notice is that Paul continually tries to exalt the lowly and humble the proud in this epistle. Paul expounds repeatedly upon God's wisdom over against the pompous arrogance of those who exalt themselves according to worldly standards. Specifically, this happens in the cross. The cross has become for us today a symbol of redemption and hope. But in Paul's day it was still a symbol of extreme shame. To proclaim a cross-shaped gospel was foolishness in Paul's world (see 1 Cor 1:18—2:16). What is important for our discussion is the effect this had practically on the church. The Corinthian Christians had apparently not embraced this cross-shaped gospel in their social lives. They were still, for example, showing preference for the wealthy in their communal meals (11:17–34), forming competitive factions (ch. 3), ignoring the consciences of "weaker" fellow Christians (ch. 8), and were even suing one another in court (ch. 6). Paul does all he can in this letter, therefore, to recall his listeners to the centrality of the cross. The cross exalts what is seen as utter folly by the world and humbles the wisdom of the worldly wise. Dr. Peppiatt does not embellish when she writes, "Following Christ for Paul means being identified as the lowest of the low, the scum of the earth, the scrapings from the bottom of a shoe (1 Corinthians 4:8–13)."[16] In the context of a letter in which Paul has repeatedly tried

---

16. Peppiatt, *Women and Worship*, 70.

to exalt the lowly and humble the proud, it seems odd that he would abruptly silence the women in chapter 14. After all, in Corinthian society it was the women—at least if one is speaking generally—who were at the bottom rung of the social ladder.

A third problem with understanding 1 Corinthians 14:34–35 as an expression of Paul's own opinion on women's speaking in the church is that it simply does not agree with how Paul talks about shame and shameful (the NIV translates "disgraceful") things elsewhere in his letters. Conscious of the risk of hyperbole, I would even venture to claim that the idea that Paul would consider a woman's speaking in church to be shameful in and of itself runs about as contrary to Paul's overall approach to the concepts of shame and honor as an idea could. For example, Ephesians 5:11–12 says, "Take no part in the unfruitful works of darkness, but instead expose them. For it is *shameful* even *to speak* of the things that they do in secret" (ESV).[17] The words translated "shameful . . . to speak" are the same, and in the same grammatical construction, as the words "shameful . . . to speak" in 1 Corinthians 14:35. But Ephesians 5:12 is concerned with the *content* of what is being said. That is, what brings shame is what is said, *not* the person who is saying it. To corroborate this point, consider what Paul writes in Philippians 1:15–18:

> It is true that some preach Christ out of envy and rivalry, but others out of goodwill . . . The former preach Christ out of selfish ambition, not sincerely, supposing that they can stir up trouble for me while I am in chains. But what does it matter? *The important thing is that in every way, whether from false motives or true, Christ is preached. And because of this I rejoice.*

Here we see Paul rejoicing in the preaching of the gospel for its own sake, even when those who are preaching it are doing so with corrupt motives. In light of this passage, is it really possible to imagine Paul's describing the preaching of the gospel, on the lips of *anyone*, as shameful? For Paul to, in one place, rejoice openly in the preaching of the good news *regardless of who the messengers are,* and, in another place, try to silence people because he is worried about shame, seems unbearably inconsistent. Paul was a careful, self-reflective theologian. I suspect that the problem is not with Paul's thinking, but with the way we are reading what he wrote in 1 Corinthians 14:34–35.

---

17. See also Eph 5:4; Col 3:8; Rom 6:21.

Furthermore, Paul repeatedly uses the word "shame" to speak about how Christians should *not* feel about speaking of Christ. When it comes to the shame that results from speaking truth, Paul taught that Christians should embrace it, wearing it as a badge of honor.[18] It seems, again, very unlike the Paul we know so well from both the book of Acts and his other letters for him to silence people who are speaking of Christ—say, through preaching or teaching—out of a concern about shame or disgrace.

From a bird's-eye view, those are the three main problems with seeing 1 Corinthians 14:34–35 as coming from Paul's mind, instead of seeing these two verses as a summarization of the incorrect thinking of some Corinthian Christian men. But another problem appears when we dive down for a closer look. If verses 34 and 35 actually represent Paul's own opinion, and he is trying to tell disorderly women to be silent in the church, we would naturally assume that verses 36 to 38 should address the women as well. But they don't. The NIV obscures this fact, so I will quote from the ESV instead: "Or was it from you that the word of God came? Or are you the only ones it has reached? If anyone thinks *he* is a prophet, or spiritual, *he* should acknowledge that the things I am writing to you are a command of the Lord" (v. 37 ESV). In Greek, nouns and adjectives are gendered. I've italicized the word "he" to emphasize the fact that the words "prophet" and "spiritual" in this verse are masculine in Greek. This means that Paul, from what we see on the page, is intending to address *men* in these verses, not women. This presents a problem for any interpretation that sees verses 34 and 35 as a correction of the women at Corinth rather than the men.

But if Paul is simply quoting a Corinthian idea in verses 34 and 35, the problem is solved, for in that case Paul would be telling the men in the church at Corinth that they should *not* be silencing the women. Thus, Paul is communicating something like the following: *"You silence the women because you think their speaking is inappropriate in church. But who are you to say whose voices are and are not appropriate? Did the word of God originate with you?! No, it didn't. Stop ignoring what the Spirit says about this, especially if you say you are a prophet. It is the Spirit who speaks the word in the church, not you."* Notice how well this interpretation would fit with the way the Corinthian men are portrayed in the rest of Paul's letter. In a culture not accustomed to acknowledging the intellectual value of women's minds, and by extension the importance of

---

18. See Rom 1:16; 10:11; 1 Cor 1:27; 2 Cor 7:14; Phil 1:20; 2 Tim 1:8, 12, 16; 2:15.

hearing their voices, one can easily imagine a pompous, arrogant group of men trying to keep women in their place. (I am, unfortunately, certain that many of my female readers will have personally experienced such a thing.) Paul is unabashedly countercultural in so much of what he says in his Letter to the Corinthians that it would be no surprise if he were to be so here as well.

To add just one more piece of corroborating evidence, consider an ancient text quoted by a popular Roman historian who lived a few centuries before Paul. His name was Livy, and his writing was popular both during and after Paul's day. In her captivating book, *The Making of Biblical Womanhood,* historian Beth Allison Barr cites a passage from Livy's *History of Rome* that sounds almost exactly like 1 Corinthians 14:35. In response to a women-led protest against a Roman law that severely restricted women's property and inheritance rights, a Roman consul named Cato the Elder allegedly complained that these women—whom we would certainly label feminists today—were "[r]unning around in public, blocking streets, and speaking to other women's husbands! *Could you not have asked your own husbands the same thing at home?*"[19] The echo of the italicized portion of this statement in 1 Corinthians 14:35 is almost word for word! This demonstrates that the notion that women's voices should be confined to the home was an ideal to which at least some in Roman culture held, which in turn means it is at least possible (if not probable) that Paul could have alluded to that notion in a letter, and that his original readers would have known exactly what he was referring to.

It would be like my saying at a dinner table in the United States, "Children should be seen and not heard." Almost anyone who has grown up in American culture would know exactly the ideal that I would be referencing. But anyone who knows *me* (or most parents from my generation) would know immediately that I do *not* hold to that ideal! So, I could say something like, "'Children should be seen and not heard.' *What, like only adults can say things worth hearing?!*" If someone were to take my words at face value, they would think that I don't value the voices of children. Yet, that would be the *opposite* of what I meant! (Sometimes, taking words at face value is the opposite of how they should be taken.) But, anyone who knows about the (outdated) American cultural ideal about children being silent at the dinner table until they finish eating—which a viewing of several episodes of the delightful iconic American TV series,

19. Barr, *Making of Biblical Womanhood,* 59 (emphasis added).

Little House on the Prairie, would exemplify—would know precisely what I meant by my sarcasm.

Have we proven that 1 Corinthians 14:34–35 is an instance of Paul's habit of summarizing an idea that he opposes, and that verses 36–37 are his correction of that idea? I'll let my careful readers decide what the threshold of proof is in this case. But, it seems to me we should all be able to agree that it is at least a possibility. While this way of interpreting this passage may appear bold or even reckless at first, I find it the most compelling of any interpretation I have examined. It seems to agree the best with Paul's way of applying the freedom of the Spirit to Christian life, with his tone and style in the rest of his letters, and with how we observe him behaving toward women in the New Testament generally. Attributing the ideas in a couple of verses within one of Paul's letters to someone other than Paul may sound at first like a way to explain away the text. But if we're serious about trying to understand what Paul was actually trying to communicate, we have no choice but to be open to the possibility that he sometimes quotes his opponents or summarizes their ideas before he refutes them. I think this is probably one of those cases. If this interpretation is correct, 1 Corinthians 14:34–35 *should not* be used to guide the church's practice today—or in any day for that matter. Rather, 1 Corinthians 14:36–38 should be emphasized *over and against* verses 34 and 35. What will be the result? Women will not only be *allowed* but will also be openly *encouraged* to use their speaking gifts in the church, and will even be defended when some come out against it. It will mean mobilizing women in every sphere of the church's ministry. A young woman who has the desire and calling to become a pastor will be provided the same encouragement and support that a young man called to ministry would receive.

Conclusion

Some of my patient readers may remain unpersuaded by either of the interpretations I have offered in this chapter, and may even continue to see 1 Corinthians 14:34–35 as placing a universal limit on the speaking ministry of women in the church for all time. I hope, however, that the idea that biblical egalitarians are simply ignoring the "clear teaching of Scripture" can someday soon be laid to rest. This is simply not true. Most biblical egalitarians are coming to their conclusions through a process of careful study and engagement with what they see on the pages of their open Bibles.

Although 1 Corinthians 14:34–35 and 1 Timothy 2:11–14 are often read in tandem, they are addressing two different situations. Even though we'll want to return to 1 Corinthians again later, let's jump over first and take a close look at 1 Timothy 2:11–15, the second New Testament passage that has often been used to tell women to be silent (or quiet).

5

Christian Quietness

(1 Timothy 2:11–15)

First Timothy 2:11–15, more than any other text of Scripture, was the stickiest for me when I was in the process of converting from a hierarchicalist to an egalitarian position on the question of women in speaking ministries. The stickiness resulted from Paul's reference to the Genesis creation story. He says that women should be silent because "Adam was formed first, then Eve." Paul seemed to me to be providing a basis for his silencing of a woman in the Hebrew Bible itself. "If Paul roots women's silence in the meaning of the biblical creation story," I thought, "it can't be a mere cultural fluke subject to the winds of time." To accept that conclusion would be to deny the ability of Scripture to speak into *every* culture in *every* age of history, and I had a lot of other reasons not to do that. So, I was in a pickle for a while when it came to this passage. Now, however, I actually think 1 Timothy 2:11–15 presents less of a challenge for the egalitarian position than 1 Corinthians 14:34–35 does.

First, I should say that while I believe Christians today should not dismiss Paul's words as *merely* his own culturally conditioned opinion, I also believe his words should be interpreted with their cultural context in view. This may sound like double-talk at first. But actually it's a standard approach practiced by Christian biblical scholars and taught in Bible colleges and seminaries. It was certainly what I was taught to do in both institutions where I studied Bible interpretation. It is known as the grammatical-historical method. There is really nothing controversial about the notion, broadly understood, that the Bible should be interpreted, as much as possible, within its original context. But as they say, the devil's in the details. And, as we have noticed, this debate is a lot about paying close attention to the details. In what follows we are going to have to mention context a lot, because without context we won't be able to understand well, and interpreters on both sides of the argument about whether or not women should serve the church in speaking ministries know this.

I have encountered quite a few Christians who, while believing that Paul's letters are inspired by God, think that when it came to Paul's comments about women speaking in church Paul was basically a man of his times. What they mean is that Paul, unfortunately, harbored a prejudice against women that reflected the biases of his time and a culture that favored men. These Christians see themselves as justified, therefore, to basically set passages like 1 Corinthians 11:2–16, 14:34–35, and 1 Timothy 2:12–15 aside as merely a reflection of Paul's culture-bound perspective. Such passages are, in effect, not for us today. I want to say something about this reaction to Paul before I move on to explaining the details of 1 Timothy 2:11–15.

I can agree with the statement that Paul was a man of his times, but I take issue with what some of my Christian friends seem to imply when they say this. Often, when someone is said to be a man of his time, the setting has to do with a person revered in history, but whose behavior was flawed in some way. For example, historian Fergus M. Bordewich's fascinating book entitled *Bound for Canaan* tells the story of the Underground Railroad, the network of brave abolitionists (most of whom were Euro-American) who helped Black people escape slavery in the United States to freedom in Canada in the first half of the nineteenth century. These abolitionists were heroes by any reasonable definition of the word. They recognized evil when they saw it and risked tremendous peril, sometimes at great cost to themselves and their families, to stand against it. Part of making someone a historical hero is holding that person up as a model of good behavior for future generations, and there is certainly plenty in the character of these abolitionists to aspire to. At the same time, it would be a mistake for us today to emulate every aspect of these people's lives, because the truth is that many white abolitionists, despite their zealous opposition to the evil of slavery, had absorbed and adopted aspects of the racist philosophy of their time and culture. For example, some of them believed it was improper for Black and white people to mix. They could not imagine a society in which Black and white people lived together as one community. Along with this came opposition to interracial marriage, founded ultimately on appallingly bad theological reasoning. There is no getting around the fact that this segregationist thinking was a product of an ideology that upheld whiteness as supreme. Yet, many heroic white abolitionists held to it. Some white abolitionists even opposed granting full citizenship rights to freed Black people. Bordewich mentions a white abolitionist named William Jay, "one of the most eloquent antislavery men in New York, [who] was shocked when some abolitionists began to call for Black suffrage."[1] Charles Finney, the famous abolitionist and evangelist known today as the "Father of American Revivalism," was president of Oberlin College in Ohio, my home state, when it became the first university in America to integrate Black and white students in the classroom. Nevertheless, he defended racial segregation in the church, as manifest in some churches' practice of having Black people sit behind white people during church services, treating it as if it were a morally neutral matter.[2]

I am not saying that "we today" are superior to those courageous people. For me, the abolitionists are overwhelmingly inspiring, and better human beings than I. But they, like me, were also human beings, which means that they had moral and intellectual shortcomings as well as imaginations shaped by their contemporary society. We could say, then, that even though we revere these abolitionists as heroes, we acknowledge that they were men and women of their times, and therefore seek to follow their example advisedly.

The question before us here is whether or not we should take the same approach with Paul when we read what he said about women. Was Paul a true hero who, despite his world-changing vision, nevertheless could not imagine the voices of women being ultimately essential to the upbuilding of the church? To be honest, in light of the way many in the church have used Paul's words over the past two millennia, I can definitely see why some people see Paul this way. Nevertheless, I think my Christian brothers and sisters who do so are missing Paul's point. I'm going to say something bold: I think that, even by standards on our side of the modern feminist movement, Paul was not biased against the voices of women. I have no doubt that, simply by virtue of being a man, Paul had a lot to learn about the experience of women. I'm also open to the possibility that Paul could have worded what he said a bit more tactfully (though

---

1. Bordewich, *Bound for Canaan*, 139.
2. Jones, *White Too Long*, 91–92.

this is not a hill I'm going to die on). I further assume that Paul had a lot to learn (as we all do) about what the priesthood of all believers in Christ implies practically, especially with respect to male and female equality as such in Christ. But, I do not see evidence in the New Testament that Paul was against the voices of women being heard in the church, even in a teaching capacity. Certainly, Paul had biases that he had absorbed from his culture (after all, he was a finite human being just like the rest of us), but Paul's vision for the church was countercultural in a variety of ways, and his vision for women's voices is an example of this.

As we noted in the last chapter, there is such a thing as silencing people in certain contexts for a finite period in order to cultivate an environment in which their voices can grow to be used more freely. We saw how Paul finds an orderly worship service to be good for the building up of the church body, and that this included the ordering of when and how the church members used their voices. Let's develop this a bit more.

I am writing this during an election year in the United States. One of the many candidates who wanted to be president was a wealthy businessman and former mayor of New York City named Michael Bloomberg. His candidacy sparked some controversy, because while most of the other candidates were obliged to call on millions of donors to support their campaigns, Mayor Bloomberg only needed *one* donor: himself. Those who found this unsettling asked, "Why should a person's ideas for how to govern a country be given a voice just because he has a lot of money?" For such people, it seemed wrong that wealth should determine whose voice is heard and whose isn't. The realistic among Mayor Bloomberg's critics would admit that not *everyone's* voice can be heard in a presidential race. Indeed, they would agree that relatively few people should even consider running for president. Their argument is not that everybody's voice should have equal air time; their argument is merely that wealth should not be the determining factor that allows a person's voice to be heard. They want *some other* criteria to be the arbiter for that. We are not talking about campaign finance right now, but Mayor Bloomberg's indignant critics help point us to two basic questions that are germane to our topic: What makes a voice worthy of being heard in the church? What criteria should be used to choose between the individual voices?

There are many ways to think about this. Let's just start with Sunday morning. In most churches there is a sermon at that time. Depending on the church, the length of that sermon could range from under fifteen minutes to an hour long. The voice of that preacher during that time is arguably the most powerful in the church community. Other powerful voices are those of elders, deacons, directors of ministries, Sunday school teachers, etc. But in most Protestant churches (less so in Catholic and Orthodox churches), the words that are spoken in the Sunday sermon from behind the pulpit are considered the most important of all those spoken throughout the week within the congregation. This is why many pastors carefully craft their sermons during the week, praying, thinking, writing, rewriting, praying again—all because they know that what they say will be taken seriously by those listening. Indeed, people go to church to hear a message from God! It's an astonishingly weighty matter when a preacher stands up and opens his (or her) mouth to deliver a word from God to the gathered people of God.

I studied for four years at a Presbyterian seminary. Before every sermon in many Presbyterian churches the text for the sermon is read aloud. After reading, the reader will say, "The word of the Lord," and the congregation will say, "Thanks be to God." In seminary chapel services we also did this. I grew to appreciate this little ritual because it brought a certain gravity to what was about to happen. Though we at the seminary were not a church, we represented the universal body of Christ as a group of people gathered to hear a word, not only from the preacher, but from God. And yet, the preacher was necessary. We couldn't hear God's word without a preacher.

Due to the importance of the Sunday sermon in Protestant churches the debate about women in speaking ministries has often been framed as a debate about women's ordination to become pastors. As I mentioned before, I grew up in a church tradition in which we didn't have church pastors. When I was part of the Plymouth Brethren I spoke disparagingly of churches that had ordination requirements. "The requirement for preaching the word of God," I thought, "is that a person be saved by Jesus. There is no ordination in the Bible, the apostles themselves didn't require it, so why should we add to what the Bible says?" New Testament scholar Scot McKnight recounts an interaction he had some time ago with the late F. F. Bruce, who was one of the most eminent evangelical biblical scholars of the twentieth century. McKnight asked Professor Bruce, "[W]hat do you think of women's ordination?" Professor Bruce replied, "I don't think the New Testament talks about ordination."[3] Indeed! Professor Bruce's comment is not surprising—he was also active in the Plymouth Brethren,

---

3. McKnight, *Blue Parakeet*, 207.

and (I only learned this later) he publicly defended women in speaking ministries in the church! He didn't defend women's ordination, however, because he didn't believe in ordination in the first place.

But while in seminary I grew more sympathetic to the idea of ordination after learning something about what it means in the older Protestant denominations. An ordained person is someone who has demonstrated not only a calling to ministry and a gift for pastoring, but who has also gone through a rigorous—even strenuous—process of preparation. Ordination is a formalized way of arbitrating whose voices are heard most prominently in the church.

On the face of it, that may sound arrogant or even elitist. Unfortunately, arrogance and elitism can and sometimes do creep into church politics, including the process of ordination. Nevertheless, the idea of discriminating between this or that voice's gaining a hearing in a church (with the Sunday morning sermon usually being the quintessence of that) is absolutely necessary. As I looked back on my experience with the Plymouth Brethren, I realized that even they had a system of discriminating between voices. It was just a lot less formalized than the one used by the older Protestant denominations I encountered in seminary. The fact is, *every* denomination and *every* church must decide which voices will be heard and to what degree. There is no getting around it. The question is, again, what should be the determining factors when making those decisions?

Here, in a nutshell, is the way virtually every church and denomination thinks about this question. They all find one way or another to ensure that the voices most heard in the church are those of people who are (1) called, (2) gifted, and (3) prepared. I know those three categories need a lot of fleshing out before they can be applied in real situations. But virtually all churches and denominations use those three criteria in one way or another.

Now we can finally get back around to our topic. Can a woman be (1) called, (2) gifted, and (3) prepared for church ministries that involve speaking? Here is where the hierarchicalists and egalitarians part ways. A hierarchicalist will reply immediately, "Yes, of course a woman can be called, gifted, and prepared. But, she still has to minister within her God-given role as a woman." The consequence of this way of thinking, however, is that the voice of a woman will *never* be the most prominent within a church or denomination. Her voice must always be less prominent than some man's, whoever that man may be.

I have a plethora of concerns with this kind of thinking. One of them is what it implies (or is in danger of implying) about the meaning of a sermon. In this way of thinking, that sacred moment when a preacher opens the Bible and delivers a word of God to the people of God begins to become not so much about the word being delivered itself, but about the person delivering it. This seems to me logically inescapable. *Every* Christian should be careful not to accept uncritically the words of a preacher, no matter how qualified and prepared that preacher is. We must gauge our acceptance of this or that preacher's words by a constant practice of spiritual discernment. Preachers can be dangerous! But, in order for God's people to receive God's word through preaching, they must come with open hearts and minds. No one should come *completely* open. Still, a generous measure of openness in a listener is essential to the process of receiving God's word through preaching.

Yet, the hierarchicalist asks Christians not only to gauge the words— that is, the claims, arguments, assertions, exhortations, encouragements, commandments, etc.—within sermons, he also requires them to consider the gender of the preacher in that critical consideration. *If the preacher is a woman, no matter what she says, she should not be saying it in the context of a sermon.* Period. That is not an exaggeration of the so-called complementarian position.

Here is the logical fallout. This means that, compared to men, women who preach are going to be held quite literally to an impossible standard of critical scrutiny. Hierarchicalists orient people to respond to the words of women with a higher level of suspicion and a lower level of charity compared to how they respond to the words of men. In other words, if a man is deemed unqualified to be that prominent voice in a church, it will be due to something having to do with his calling, his gifting, or his preparation. But if a woman is deemed unqualified, she might be called, gifted, and prepared; her gender is the only thing muffling her voice.

Is this what Paul had in mind in 1 Timothy 2:11–14? Is he saying that God's word through a female's voice should be heard differently—or not heard at all—simply because of her gender? Unfortunately, many Christians have read Paul this way, which has led to two very different reactions. On the one hand, some Christians have doubled down. Driven by a desire to be faithful to Scripture, they obey what (they think) it says and silence the women in their churches, or other institutions. That is what the church of my childhood years did. Others react quite differently. They reject Paul's words as inapplicable for today, excusing them as an unfortunate example of Paul's culture-bound perspective. "He was a man of his times," they say. But there is a better way to read this text.

Quiet, Not Silent (verses 11 and 12)[4]

As all good interpreters do, let's begin with the context of the passage we're examining. If we look at the first two verses of 1 Timothy 2, we see that Paul encourages the people under Timothy's care to pray for all people, specifically for those in positions of authority. This will contribute to a goal common to all believers: namely, that of living a "peaceful and quiet [life]." The adjective translated "quiet" in verse 2 is *hēsychios*. My readers will recall that the verb *sigáō*—the word translated "to be silent" in 1 Corinthians 14:34–35—means being silent in the sense of not making noise. The word, *hēsychios,* on the other hand, describes a state of tranquility or restfulness. "Quietness" is the right English word here. One can't live a *silent* life, really, but one can certainly live a *quiet* life. A quiet life is a peaceful, harmonious one. Such a life may, of course, include noise—like conversation, music, the sounds of animals or machinery, cheering and applause at a concert or recital, etc. When one is talking about being "quiet" in this sense, the amount of noise isn't the primary concern. This word has more to do with the ebb and flow of a person's soul than it does with soundwaves.

In fact, the verb form of this word is used elsewhere in the New Testament to describe people who are in the act of speaking, but who do so calmly. For example, Acts 11 tells the story of how Peter persuaded the new believers at Jerusalem that the gentiles should be welcomed into the church. At first, these Christians confronted Peter because they had heard that Peter had eaten with gentiles (see Acts 11:2, 3), and according to their understanding of Jewish tradition Peter should not have done that. But after Peter explained that the Spirit had taught him otherwise, the text says, "When they heard these things *they fell silent.* And they glorified God, saying, 'Then to the gentiles also God has granted repentance that leads to life'" (ESV). The words "they fell silent" in this verse come from the verb form of the word translated "silent" in 1 Timothy 2:2. In this setting in Acts the people who are described as having fallen silent are actually speaking! The idea here is obviously that the people calmed

---

4. For a summary of this explanation of 1 Tim 2:11–12, see Table 5.1 in the appendix.

down and acknowledged what Peter was saying. They stopped confronting Peter and instead responded with a peaceful, welcoming, expectant spirit. Actually, I suspect they were making a lot of noise. But with regard to this word, the noise isn't the point because it refers to a different kind of quietness. It's the kind of quietness that comes along with peace, harmony, satisfaction, and trust. Paul uses this same word in 1 Thessalonians 4:11 to encourage all believers—both men and women—to "aspire to live *quietly.*" In other words, *this* kind of quietness is *clearly good for everybody whether male or female,* at least in Paul's view!

Now, let's jump to 1 Timothy 2:11. There we encounter the same word again (this time as a noun). Paul writes, "A woman should learn in quietness (*en hēsychia*) and full submission." Remember, Paul has already used the word "quiet" as an adjective describing the Christian life in verse 2. In the context, it is undeniable that Paul sees quietness as a virtue for both men and women. Paul's command to women (or, more accurately, "a woman") in verse 11 should be read with this in mind. Even though it is directed specifically at women, Paul is by no means saying that quietness is exclusively good for women. One would have to ignore Paul's normal use of the word *hēsychios* elsewhere in his writings to draw such a conclusion. If anyone wants to learn, she *or he* must be in a state of quietness. Note how well this agrees with what we saw in Acts 11. There, the brothers and sisters at the church in Jerusalem had to calm down—that is, be quiet—so they could receive Peter's message. They are the perfect example of the benefits of learning in quietness. This is, undoubtedly, what Paul has in mind for women in 1 Timothy 2:11.

Unfortunately, hierarchicalist interpreters often think that Paul's addressing the women specifically implies his instruction is for them exclusively. But, *specificity does not entail exclusivity* (this principle will become especially important when we look at Paul's instructions to husbands and wives in Ephesians 5). In verse 8, Paul begins to address men and women separately. In each case one can readily see that all the instructions given to the genders separately would be good in application to both together. Thus, Paul says about the men: "Therefore I want the men everywhere to pray, lifting up holy hands without anger or disputing." Of course, by telling men to lift their hands and pray Paul is *not* saying women should refrain from lifting their hands or from praying. Furthermore, even though Paul tells the men specifically to stave off anger and quarreling, it does not follow that women are permitted to be angry and quarrelsome! Why? Because even though Paul is giving these commands to the genders separately, the principle on which they are grounded is the example of Christ. Therefore, they apply to all Christians.

The same can be observed in verses 9 and 10, which address the women: "I also want the women to dress modestly, with decency and propriety, adorning themselves, not with elaborate hairstyles or gold pearls or expensive clothes, but with good deeds, appropriate for women who profess to worship God." Even though Paul is talking specifically to women, he would certainly have forbidden men from dressing ostentatiously or immodestly if he had seen the need. Modesty and humility are virtues to be cultivated by all followers of Jesus, both men and women.

If it is clear that all of Paul's instructions in verses 8 to 10 can be equally applied to both genders because they are all based on core principles of Christian conduct, could we say the same of verses 11 and 12?

Let's look at verse 11 first. Paul tells women (actually it's "a woman"—we'll touch on this later) to "learn in quietness and full submission." Right away we can see that this is good advice for any learner. Any experienced teacher would agree that rowdiness, loudness, or rebelliousness make a student very difficult to teach! But Paul's command to women here is not based only in general advice for students. As it turns out, "quietness" and "submissiveness" are actually Christian virtues in themselves as well. As we noted before, Paul uses the word here translated "quiet" to describe the Christian life generally in verse 2. The same generalization can be made of the command to be "submissive." Paul tells all Christians to "submit to one another" in Ephesians 5:21. In the same spirit, Galatians 2:4 says, "[T]hrough love serve one another." The word Paul uses for "serve" in Galatians 2:4 is *douleuō*, which means literally "to be a slave."[5] The idea of Christians' becoming mutual servants of one another permeates the entire New Testament. Like quietness, submissiveness is also a *Christian* value, and not one that is meant for women only. Therefore, the most consistent way to understand verse 11 is by observing the pattern of Paul's thought in the preceding context. Paul is no more trying to enforce a male-female hierarchy in verse 11 than he was in verses 1 to 10.

But what about verse 12? There, Paul says that he is not permitting "a women to teach or assume authority over a man." Is Paul alluding to a gender hierarchy in verse 12, and then defending it in verses 13 and 14? Hierarchicalist interpreters think so. They argue that Paul's reference to Adam and Eve in verses 13 and 14 is an allusion to a created order in

---

5. BDAG, s.v. "δουλεύω." See also John 13:14.

which God made the man to be an authority over the woman at creation. There are at least three fatal flaws in this interpretation.

First, in our examination of the creation story in Genesis we could find no evidence of such disparity of authority between the man and the woman. In addition, we found good evidence for gender equality.

Second, an interpretation of this text based on gender-role ideology runs contrary to human experience. Granted, on the one hand, experience cannot give us the final word on a faithful interpretation of Scripture. But it cannot be ignored on the other hand. Here is the problem: Those who read verse 12 as an instruction based in an ideology of gender roles consistently cite verses 13 and 14, which refer to the deception of Eve. In such a view, the reason Eve was deceived was because she stepped out of her divinely ordained role as a woman. Rather than submit to Adam's leadership, she became the leader. Likewise, Adam, instead of leading, followed his wife and thereby stepped out of his divinely ordained role of authority in the relationship. Elizabeth Elliot, who was a prominent voice in the complementarian movement, summarizes this view thus,

> The first woman was made specifically for the first man, a helper, to meet, respond to, surrender to, and complement him . . . Eve, in her refusal to accept the will of God, refused her femininity. Adam, in his capitulation to her suggestion, abdicated his masculine responsibility for her. It was the first instance of what we would recognize now as "role reversal." This defiant disobedience ruined the original pattern and things have been in an awful mess ever since.[6]

In this reading, the first sin was a reversal of God-ordained gender roles. The application that follows is that a woman in leadership—or in a teaching role—exposes those who sit under her to deception in a way that a man in a leadership or teaching role does not. This is not because of such a woman's lack of education, gifting, or ability as compared to a man's. Rather, *the woman's femininity in and of itself renders her more needy of leadership relative to the man.* She is more vulnerable to deception than the man if she is not under his leadership. Likewise, the man becomes more vulnerable to deception if he allows himself to be led by a woman.

The problem is, the vast majority of heretics and cult leaders that have emerged in the history of the church over the past 2,000 years have been men, not to mention the vast majority of world history's dictators

---

6. Elliot, "Essence of Femininity," 465.

and tyrants. To make the point even more poignant, especially in our day, we should mention the appalling number of male church leaders who use their power to take sexual advantage of those under their care. This fact would lead one to doubt men's superior discernment abilities and women's inherent vulnerability to deception. Of course, there are plenty of deceitful and gullible women in the world. But on balance, men are ahead both in the business of deceiving and of being deceived. This is probably due less to men's intrinsic gullibility than to the fact that societies all over the world tend to give men's voices more authority than they do to those of women. That is, people are more inclined to follow men than they are women, which causes them to let their guard down more readily before male leaders. I'm not trying to argue that women are intrinsically more discerning than men, but that *both men and women alike* are vulnerable to deception and error as finite human beings. We are not safer with men in authority just because they are men! In fact, that notion itself is dangerous.

There is an even more serious experience-related problem with the "women are more deceivable" understanding of this text. In relation to men, women are disproportionately more involved in the Christian education of children in the church throughout the world. If it is true that women are naturally more vulnerable to deception than men, it would be nonsensical and even reckless for churches to recruit women to teach children in Sunday school because children are especially impressionable. Further, women are routinely appointed as leaders of women's ministries in churches all over the world. If women are more vulnerable to deception than men, this arrangement does not make sense.

A third flaw in the hierarchicalist interpretation of this passage is that it requires an awkward break from the previous context. As we have noted, all of Paul's instructions to men and women in the previous verses are based not in a gender-role ideology but on generally encouraged Christian virtues. They are addressed to men and women separately, but nevertheless apply to both in a general sense. If Paul is introducing a gender-role ideology in verse 12, this would constitute an abrupt departure from this pattern. Of course, it is possible for Paul to break such a pattern, even in an abrupt or awkward manner. But before drawing such a conclusion, interpreters should see if there is a way to read verse 12 that harmonizes better with the context. There is, as we will see shortly.

The hierarchicalist interpretation of this passage is clearly fraught with problems, and that needs to be the first observation we make before moving on to a closer examination of verse 12, and to drawing out more plausible alternative readings. We are not playing it safe by just accepting the hierarchicalist interpretation because it claims to take the text at face value or to enjoy a longer history. There is no good reason for the hierarchicalist interpretations to be the default way of reading this passage. The truth is, a hierarchicalist reading neither takes adequate account of the context surrounding verses 11 to 14 nor are its conclusions practically viable. Once again, it interprets *against* the grain of the text instead of with it.

Let's take a close look at verse 12 now, which is *the only verse in the Bible in which a woman's teaching is discouraged* (remember, 1 Cor 14:34–35 doesn't mention teaching, as such). Suppose verse 12 is like the verses preceding it. Suppose that the principle behind what Paul tells women in verse 12 could equally be applied to men. If this is so, Paul is not encouraging conformity to a gender-role ideology but to a common, universally beneficial Christian virtue. We found this to be true of verses 8 to 11, so it is reasonable to explore the possibility that it is also true of verse 12. The first thing to notice is that the word translated "exercise authority over" is not the normal word for "exercise authority" in the New Testament. The normal word for "exercise authority" in the New Testament is *exousiazō*. It means something like, "have control of"—basically it is what modern English speakers mean when they say "exercise authority." The reason this is so important is that Paul uses *exousiazō* in the context of one of his most important passages about marriage in the New Testament, a passage that is key to understanding Paul's thinking about authority in male-female relationships.

In 1 Corinthians 7:4, Paul makes an assertion that would have been shocking in his time and culture and that continued to be a point of confusion for his interpreters afterward. First he says, "The wife does not have authority (*exousiazō*) over her own body, but yields it to her husband." *That* statement would have been totally normal and acceptable in Paul's day. "Of course the husband has power over his wife's body," people would think, "because the husband is his wife's superior and legal authority." But then Paul adds, "*In the same way,* the husband does not have authority (*exousiazō*) over his own body but yields it to his wife." This would have been utterly revolutionary to Paul's original audience. Indeed, it is still a revolutionary thing to assert in most of today's societies—including those that have been heavily influenced by Christianity. We see here that Paul explicitly sees authority within a marriage relationship as a mutual, two-way dynamic. Here is the clincher: this is *the only place in the entire Bible where a man is clearly said to have authority over his wife.* Yet, Paul speaks of the authority a woman has over her husband in precisely the same way. He even says, "in the same way" to be sure his point isn't missed!

But when we flip back over to 1 Timothy 2:12 we encounter a different Greek word for "exercise authority." Here, Paul uses the verb *authenteō.* Unlike *exousiazō,* which like our English word "authority" can be *either* a positive *or* a negative word, *authenteō* tends to have a negative connotation, especially in contexts in which one person (for example, "a woman") is doing this action toward another person (for example, "a man").[7] The only time this word appears in the New Testament is here in 1 Timothy 2:12. If one goes by its dictionary definition, the word refers to a person who acts on his or her *own* authority (and probably for personal advantage). It is from this word, in fact, that we get our English word "autocrat," a person who assumes an independent and illegitimate stance of authority over others. The noun form of this word, in fact, meant "murderer" in its most ancient uses in Greek literature. This particular meaning softened over time to refer to a person who had the authority to execute another.[8] (We should note that, even though execution is not technically murder, it is still a negative thing to experience, and thus our contention that this is a negative word still stands.)

It seems clear enough that anyone who exercises authority over another person in *this* way is not taking into account the teachings and example of Jesus concerning what true power looks like in the reign of God. In the Gospels of Mark and Matthew, Jesus contrasts greatness under God's reign with how it is defined by the world's system. He says,

> You know that those who are regarded as rulers of the Gentiles lord it over them, and their high officials exercise authority over them. Not so with you. Instead, whoever wants to become great among you must be your servant, and whoever wants to be first must be slave of all. (Mark 10:42–44)

This way of exercising authority is probably close to what we should have in mind when we read 1 Timothy 2:12.

Let's add another important point to our case. When a person uses a unique word—one that she only rarely employs—it is because she is

---

7. See Westfall, "Meaning of Αὐθεντέω."

8. Spencer, *Beyond the Curse,* 86.

trying to say something specific, something she wants to make sure her listeners understand is *not the same* as another more commonly used word that might be easily confused with it. For example, in colloquial English usage, the word "attack" can be used to refer to anything from an attempt to inflict physical harm to a nasty comment on a social media page. Because of the broad ways common words like that can be used, legal professionals develop specific terms (assault and battery, libel) to be sure it is clear what the offense in question involved. I'm sure my readers can think of myriad examples like this. The point is, the more rare, specialized, or uncommon a term is, the more likely it is that Paul—or any author—is intentionally trying to say something that could otherwise too easily be confused with more popular or vernacular understandings of related concepts. As New Testament scholar Jamin Hübner explains,

> [I]f Paul, in 1 Tim 2:12, was attempting to communicate (for example) a general sense of exercising authority, there is little question about what words could . . . have been used. Within [New Testament] data alone, the options are as follows. (1) "Have authority" ([*echei exousian*], used 21 times). (2) "Exercise power/authority," "have the right of control," or "reign" ([*exousiazō*], used 4 times). (3) "Exercise authority" or "rule" ([*kyrieuō*], used 7 times). (4) "To exercise a position of leadership," "rule," or "lead" ([*proistēmi*], used 8 times). The author of 1 Timothy chose none of these in 2:12.[9]

The fact that other ways of speaking about authority are so common in the New Testament shows that Paul wanted to be very careful in 1 Timothy 2:12 to communicate that he was *not* referring to the normal, common understanding of exercising authority, but to something more specific. Paul is carefully specifying that he wants to refer to a *negative* way of exercising authority in 1 Timothy 2:12.

Bible interpreters today can only do their best to imagine accurately what might have been happening in Ephesus that prompted Paul to direct this comment to "a woman" in this verse. But whatever it was, it was something that men shouldn't do either. Unfortunately, most Bible translations fail to capture the negative nuance of the word *authenteō*. Readers of their English Bibles know that exercising authority in and of itself is not wrong; it depends on who does it, and how and why it is done. But the kind of authority that Paul says he does not allow a woman to exercise in

---

9. Hübner, "Revisiting αὐθεντέω in 1 Timothy 2:12," 47.

1 Timothy 2:12 is not a neutral kind of authority. It would be inappropriate for anyone in the church, not just a woman, to assume authority over someone else, man or woman, in this way. The phrase should probably be translated something like "dictate," "domineer," or "be the master of" for that reason. Those are the English terms that would guide readers to the right field of meaning for understanding what Paul is worried about in this passage.

Because this is the only time this word appears in the New Testament, an extrabiblical example might help to clarify the point we are making here. In a part of one of his sermons, the Greek-speaking church father John Chrysostom expounded on Colossians 3:18–19, which is a short passage directed to husbands and wives. In his exposition, Chrysostom uses the same word that is translated "assume authority" in 1 Timothy 2:12—*authenteō*. If we look at the context, it is clear that Chrysostom thought this was a negative word. I've italicized the phrase "act the despot" because it is what translates the word *authenteō*.

> Do not therefore, because thy wife is subject to thee, *act the despot*; nor because thy husband loveth thee, be thou puffed up. Let neither the husband's love elate the wife, nor the wife's subjection puff up the husband. For this cause hath He subjected her to thee, that she may be loved the more.[10]

Notice that, even though Chrysostom obviously thought husbands were their wives' legitimate authorities, he uses the word *authenteō* to describe an abuse of that authority. Thus, while I cannot, unfortunately, claim Chrysostom as a comrade in my cause, I can use this quotation from him as evidence that the word Paul uses in 1 Timothy 2:12 for "assume authority" refers to a misguided kind of authority, not authority *per se*. Obviously, I disagree with what Chrysostom says about the man being his wife's authority. Nevertheless, his comment gives a context that aids our understanding of what the word *authenteō* really means. According to Chrysostom, no Christian person, not even a husband, should behave this way. If Chrysostom, as a Greek-speaking Christian who also read the New Testament in Greek, thought the meaning of the word *authenteō* was negative, it seems likely Paul did too.

Someone could object to this argument because, after all, Chrysostom lived a few centuries after Paul, and the meaning of a word can change over time. This is true. But, in the case of *authenteō*, the meaning

10. Chrysostom, *Homilies*, NPNF 1/13, 305.

of the word actually *softened* over time. That is, the word became less and less negative as time went on. This fact seems to corroborate the point that it was also negative for Paul. If the word still carried negative overtones by the fourth century when Chrysostom was writing, it is all the more likely that it did so in the first century when Paul was writing.

Here is the point: Paul's statement that he does not permit a woman to assume authority over a man has nothing to do with a woman's subservient role. Rather, the reason Paul doesn't want her to do this is because it is an inherently negative and harmful thing to do. It is inherently bad for male-female and husband-wife relationships, regardless of whether it is the man or the woman who is doing it.

Thus, we can think of Paul's desire that women not be the master of men in the same way we might think of anger and quarreling in verse 8. There we noted that, even though Paul tells the *men* not to be angry and quarrelsome, godly women should follow the same instruction and not be angry and quarrelsome either. Likewise, here, even though Paul says he does not permit a woman to be the master of a man, we can assume that godly men shouldn't do this either, whether in relation to women or to other men. In Roman society one might expect a husband to think of himself as the master of his wife because that was his legal status in relation to her. But a Christian husband should think differently. Paul is not drawing a contrast here between two legitimate gender roles but between good and bad behaviors. We will observe later that it is likely Paul has a husband-wife relationship in view here, and the context is probably the home, not the church. More on that later.

But wait. Paul also says that he does not permit a woman to *teach* a man in 1 Timothy 2:12. Teaching, unlike dominating, is not a negative thing to do. Doesn't this prove that Paul is talking about gender roles in this passage?

No, not necessarily. Paul often uses "neither . . . nor" (*ouk . . . oude*) statements in his writing to group two words or terms together to form a single idea. Here are some examples.[11]

> A person is *not* a Jew who is one only outwardly, *nor* is circumcision outward and physical. (Rom 2:2)

> The mind governed by the flesh is hostile to God; it does *not* submit to God's law, *nor* can it do so. (Rom 8:7)

---

11. I've italicized the words that translate *ouk* ("neither") and *oude* ("nor").

[F]lesh and blood can*not* inherit the kingdom of God, *nor* does
the perishable inherit the imperishable. (1 Cor 15:50)

You are all children of the light and children of the day. We do *not*
belong to the night *or* to the darkness. (1 Thess 5:5)[12]

I suspect this is what Paul is doing in 1 Timothy 2:12. When he
writes, "I permit a woman *neither* to teach *nor* to dominate a man," he is
not referring to two separate actions—that is, teaching and dominating.
Instead, he is saying that he does not permit a woman to teach a man *in
a dominating manner*. That is, the negative word "dominate" is meant to
limit or specify what he means by the neutral word "teach." The fact that
the word *authenteō* ("dominate") is so clearly a *negative* term supports
this hunch.[13]

But even if we really are supposed to think of teach and dominate
as two separate actions—the one being positive in nature and the other
negative—the fact remains that the only imperative in verses 11 and 12
is, "Let a woman learn." For Paul, women's learning is not optional; he
actually commands them to learn. Yet, he does not use a command form
when he says, "I do not permit a woman to teach . . ." Instead, he uses
the present tense. Thus, even *if* Paul's comment about a woman teaching
a man is intended to be understood neutrally or positively as opposed
to negatively, we could still argue that Paul is here describing his own
practice in a specific context, and that his practice in that context does
not necessarily constitute a command to be applied for all times and in
every situation.

An important factor that we have not mentioned is that Paul appears
especially concerned about false teaching in his letter to Timothy. In fact,
in 1:3–4 Paul states that false teaching was the reason Paul left Timothy in
Ephesus. When coupled with the negative word *authenteō*, it is likely that
Paul has *false* teaching in mind here rather than teaching in general. The
fact that he was forbidding a woman from teaching a man *at all* shows
how serious the problem of false teaching had apparently become. Paul's
letters to Timothy contain several warnings about false teaching, at least
one of which has women specifically in mind.[14] New Testament scholar
Linda Belleville notes, "Women receive a great deal of attention in 1

12. See also Rom 9:16; Gal 1:1; 4:14; Phil 2:16; 1 Thess 2:3.

13. See Hübner, "Revisiting αὐθεντέω in 1 Timothy 2:12," 50–51 for a thorough
explanation.

14. See 1 Tim 1:3–7; 2 Tim 2:14–19; 3:6; 4:1–10.

Timothy. Indeed there is no New Testament letter in which they figure so prominently."[15] While not all of Paul's comments about women in this letter are corrective, a few are. In 5:11–15, Paul tells Timothy that younger widows should get married because then they won't spend their time going house to house "gossiping." This gossiping apparently included the spreading of false teaching. Belleville writes, "That something more than nosiness or gossiping is involved is clear from Paul's evaluation that 'some have in fact already turned away to follow Satan.'"[16] There was something truly dangerous happening among the women at Ephesus, and Paul is trying to equip Timothy to correct the problem.

Some hierarchicalists argue that, actually, the problem was that the women were teaching men, regardless of *what* they were teaching, and women shouldn't be teaching men because it is not their role in life. But notice that, apart from the passage we are discussing, Paul's concerns throughout the letter have to do with the *content* of the teaching, not with the gender of the person doing it. Paul is not worried about women teaching *good doctrine* in the letter, but about *anyone* who is teaching *bad doctrine.*

That Paul is dealing with an issue specific to the women at the Ephesian church—as opposed to women generally—is shown through his advice about younger widows in 5:14. He tells them to marry. This is striking because in 1 Corinthians 7:6–8 Paul clearly says that, at least from his point of view, it is generally better for widows to remain single so they can focus on serving Christ. But because the problem with the widows at Ephesus has become so dire he gives *different advice about them* to Timothy. We don't know all the features of the false teaching that was happening in Ephesus. But at least part of it involved forbidding marriage (see 4:3). Historians have shed further light on what was happening in Ephesus, as we will mention posthaste. But there is enough in the words of this letter itself for us to see that there was an anti-marriage (and probably anti-man) faction developing in the Ephesian congregation. Paul is completely opposed to this. He knows that marriage is good and he doesn't want to affirm the teaching of anyone who says otherwise.

While Paul does seem to be especially concerned about the women at Ephesus, there were also problems among the men. In fact, *all* of Paul's instructions in chapter 2 seem to be corrective in one way or another. Immediately before chapter 2 opens, Paul tells Timothy about two men who

15. Belleville, "Teaching and Usurping Authority," 206.
16. Belleville, "Teaching and Usurping Authority," 207.

had fallen away from the faith, apparently having become false teachers, and whom Paul "handed over to Satan to be taught not to blaspheme" (see 1:20). In 2:1, immediately following this comment, Paul begins laying out the exhortations we discussed above. He begins with, "I urge, *then* . . ." The word "then" (or, "therefore") shows that what he says in chapter 2 is meant as a corrective or safeguard. Paul's comments about women in verses 11 to 14, therefore, should be understood in light of that context. When they are, it becomes clear that Paul's purpose in saying that a woman should be in quietness was in order to respond directly to the problem of false teaching.

But suppose we were to ignore this context for a moment and assume that "teach" in verse 12 refers to teaching generally, not just teaching error. Would there be a legitimate reason, apart from gender roles, for Paul to prohibit women from teaching? We can begin to answer this question by looking at verses 13 and 14. Interpreters who believe this text is about gender roles think that Paul's reference to Adam and Eve there is his way of pointing to a created hierarchy between the genders. However, there are much more natural ways to understand Paul's reference to Adam and Eve here.

I am going to now provide what I think are the three most plausible ways of understanding Paul's reference to Adam and Eve in verses 13 and 14. The first two depend solely on the wording of the text, as opposed to leaning heavily on historical and cultural context. However, I chose to include a third interpretation that *does* lean heavily on a reconstruction of the historical and cultural context of these verses because, in this case particularly, doing so is exceptionally illuminating. Once again, my purpose is not to establish once and for all *the* authoritative interpretation. Instead, I am trying to show that, whatever ends up being the best interpretation, *it must be an interpretation that tries to be coherent and consistent with the passage and epistle as a whole.* The fact is, hierarchicalists have repeatedly failed to propose interpretations that do this better than egalitarian interpreters have. This is because they are trying to force an ideology of gender roles into the text where it doesn't fit. My only goal in what follows is to provide alternative interpretations that are *more consistent and coherent* and, therefore, more plausible than hierarchicalist approaches. In this case, I am of the opinion that Explanation C below is a little more promising than Explanation A and Explanation B. However, I want to provide all three explanations so that my readers will have a basis for further exploration.

Explanation A (verses 13 and 14): Eve Didn't Learn and Was Vulnerable as a Result[17]

If we look back at Genesis 2, we find that God gave the instruction about the tree of the knowledge of good and evil to Adam before Eve was created. This meant that Adam was expected to relay this instruction to Eve who, presumably, was also responsible to learn it from Adam in quietness and full submission. But if we read the dialogue between Eve and the serpent in Genesis 3, it appears that Eve has not learned well because she inaccurately repeats God's instructions regarding the tree (see Gen 3:3). Hence, one can conclude both that Adam did not teach Eve well *and* that Eve did not learn well from Adam. New Testament scholar Craig Keener notes that, while most blamed Eve entirely for being deceived, some Jewish rabbis taught that Adam was partly to blame. "He had added to God's words when he relayed God's commandment to Eve; this was why she told the serpent that God had forbidden her not only to eat of the tree, but also to *touch* it."[18] It could be that Paul is worried that the women in the church at Ephesus could fall into the same trap as Eve did. Eve, unlike Adam, was *deceived* by the serpent. This had nothing to do with Eve's being a woman. Rather, it had to do with a combination of Eve's failure to learn and Adam's failure to teach her. Adam ate the fruit with his eyes wide open. His failure, unlike Eve's, had nothing to do with deception—after all, he received his instructions directly from God! He knew exactly what he was doing. He sinned deliberately and knowingly. Eve, on the other hand, was deceived by the serpent. Adam's sin had nothing to do with lack of education, while Eve's sin might have been avoided had she learned properly, and this is why Paul uses her as an example instead of Adam—because she is an example of a person whose sin might have been avoided had the proper learning taken place.

At this point someone might object, "Isn't it obvious, though, that Paul picked Eve as his example because he was talking about women? Doesn't this show that women are, after all, innately more vulnerable to deception than men are?" One way to answer that question is to see if Paul mentions Eve's deception anywhere else in his writings. Does Paul, elsewhere, tend to use Eve as a stand-in for women in general? Or, does

---

17. For a summary of "Explanation A" of 1 Tim 2:13–14, see Table 5.2 in the appendix.

18. Keener, *Paul, Women & Wives*, 115 (emphasis original).

he use Eve as an example of a person—whether male or female—who is vulnerable to deception?

As divine providence would have it, there is indeed one other place where Paul mentions Eve's being deceived by the serpent. But, it is worth noting first that if Paul's purpose was to point out the intrinsic differences between men and women by using Eve as a special example of female weakness, one would expect him to use Adam as a special example of male weakness, whether here or somewhere else in his writings. Yet, Paul neither here nor in any of his writings warns *men* specifically *as males* against the dangers of being like Adam. Instead, Adam is the symbol of a fallen human being who represents the brokenness of *all* people—the one in whose place we *all* stand as sinners in need of God's salvation.[19]

As we mentioned, Paul uses Eve as an example of the dangers of deception in another place in his letters. In 2 Corinthians 11:3, Paul is addressing the entire congregation of both men and women. He writes, "But I am afraid that just as Eve was deceived by the serpent's cunning, your minds may somehow be led astray from your sincere and pure devotion to Christ." Therefore, there is good reason to assume, given all that we have observed about the context of 1 Timothy 2, that it was not Eve's femaleness that made her vulnerable to deception. If that were the case, how could Paul meaningfully point to her as a warning for the women *and* the men in the church at Corinth? The fact is, Eve is simply a good example from the Hebrew Scriptures of a person who was deceived. Deception is a danger for all people, regardless of their gender. The fact that Eve was a woman had nothing to do with it. And besides, Adam ate the fruit too! Adam's fault was different from Eve's because he was not deceived. But that observation doesn't work in favor of Adam's superior qualities of discernment for the obvious reason that he, for whatever reason, ended up disobeying God as well.

Thus, Paul's reference to Eve is explainable by the immediate context of the passage. First, everyone *must* learn. Here, women specifically ought to. Failure to do so leaves a person open to deception. And second, no one should teach until he or she has learned. Paul is not prohibiting women from teaching simply because they are women. Nevertheless, he *did* expect them to learn first *before* becoming teachers. For the time being, therefore, he was not permitting women to teach. It would be truly strange for anyone to command another person to learn but then

19. See especially Rom 5:12–21 and 1 Cor 15:20–22.

prohibit her from teaching. In fact, this seems to go against the normal pattern encouraged in the New Testament, which elsewhere seems to *expect* people who learn to later become teachers. For example, Hebrews 5:12 says, "In fact, though by this time you ought to be teachers, you need someone to teach you the elementary truths of God's word all over again." In the same vein, 2 Timothy 2:2 says, "And the things you have heard me say in the presence of many witnesses entrust to reliable people who will also be qualified to teach others." We can be sure that Paul did not make an exception to this general pattern in 1 Timothy 2:11–15.

Explanation B (verses 13 and 14): Eve Failed to Learn and Became Adam's False Teacher[20]

When we were discussing 1 Corinthians 14:34–35, I gave two mutually exclusive explanations. In that case, what I called Explanation A assumed the verses under discussion were Paul's own exhortation, while Explanation B saw them as Paul's summary of a mistaken Corinthian idea. For the passage we are discussing now, however, the contrast between explanations A and B will not be so stark (though Explanation C will present more of a contrast). In fact, most of what we observed regarding the context of 1 Timothy 2:12–14 in Explanation A above remains applicable here.

In Explanation A, I placed a great deal of importance on the fact that the woman was created *after* the man, chronologically. I found this important because of the educational purpose Paul seems to have in 1 Timothy 2:12–14. With that purpose in mind, I noted that *it seems* that Paul was thinking that Adam had been responsible to teach Eve about the tree of the knowledge of good and evil. I cited Genesis 3:3 as evidence, noting that Eve inaccurately repeats the command that God had given to Adam. I observed that Eve's sin was different from Adam's because, whereas she was deceived—seemingly due in part to lack of understanding (that is, education)—Adam sinned knowingly, having gained first-hand knowledge of God's instruction about the tree.

Admittedly, my interpretation involved imaginatively filling in the gaps of the story. I don't apologize for that, but I do acknowledge it to be true. Some interpreters, however, see the interpretation I offered to

20. For a summary of "Explanation B" of 1 Tim 2:13–14, see Table 5.3 in the appendix.

be a bit too ambitious. That is, they think my Explanation A is carrying the analogy Paul is drawing between the Adam and Eve story and the situation of a woman and a man in the church of Ephesus too far. These cautious readers might say I am taking a relatively simple analogy and drawing it out into an allegory, or something too close to it. Even though I'm ready to defend the position, I wouldn't die on this hill. I could indeed be taking the analogy too far in Explanation A.

This brings us to what I am offering as Explanation B of verses 13 and 14. In her fascinating book, *Beyond the Curse,* New Testament scholar Aida Besançon Spencer also notes that Paul's comment about Eve in this passage is meant to be an analogy to the Christian women at Ephesus. She agrees that Paul's note about Adam's having been created first does not imply his superiority over Eve. On these two points, Spencer corroborates the interpretation we considered above. However, when it comes to the *significance* of that chronology, she offers a different interpretation:

> The women of Ephesus were reminiscent of the woman (Eve) in Eden. The Ephesian women were learning and teaching a body of heretical beliefs to others in an authoritative manner, while submitting themselves to unorthodox teachers. Eve too had in her time been deceived into believing certain false teachings . . . Eve authoritatively taught these teachings to Adam. Unfortunately he learned. The entire state of humanity and nature was affected by their actions, enslaved to sin and death. Paul wants to break a similar sequence of events at Ephesus. The church at Ephesus could destroy itself just as Adam and Eve destroyed themselves in Eden.[21]

The strength of this interpretation is that it assumes less about Adam's responsibility to teach Eve in Eden. Rather than focusing on Eve's need to learn, this interpretation focuses on Eve's mistake in becoming Adam's teacher after having sat under the false teachings of the serpent. Thus, this interpretation relies more heavily on the evidence preserved in the epistle of 1 Timothy itself that women really were the primary targets of false teaching at the Ephesian church, and that too many of them had already been influenced by it.

A possible weakness in this interpretation is that it does not explain why Paul says a woman should not teach a man in particular. False teaching should not be spread among men *or* women, so why would Paul specify that a woman should not teach a man specifically? This is why I

21. Spencer, *Beyond the Curse,* 91.

think Explanation A is a bit stronger. It takes into account the need for education of women generally, not just women who have already been deceived, and emphasizes the vulnerability of the women at Ephesus rather than their victimization. I think the education Paul is encouraging is not only reactive, but also preemptive. Paul's primary concern is to equip the women at Ephesus, while the remedial motive is secondary. Most women in Ephesus would have been less educated than the men were. For that reason, I think Paul's temporary prohibition on women's teaching of men makes sense—it was because the women were particularly needy of theological education (even though their religious environment in Ephesus did not emphasize this need).

Despite their differences, Explanations A and B share two essential characteristics: (1) they both try to explain the text in its context, without appealing to extrabiblical gender ideologies, and (2) they both see the text as Paul's temporary correction of a situation that Timothy was dealing with in Ephesus during the first century. In other words, Paul's prohibition on women's teaching men is not universally applicable. Paul himself did not teach it as a universal principle. As Keener points out, it is significant that Paul has to tell Timothy in this letter that he was not allowing women to teach.[22] Timothy had already spent between five and ten years traveling, proclaiming the gospel, planting, and building up churches with Paul. There is perhaps no one who had more firsthand experience of Paul's ministry practices than Timothy had. If forbidding women from teaching men had been Paul's ordinary, run-of-the-mill practice, surely Timothy would have known that already! It makes much more sense to see 1 Timothy 2:12 as a passage in which Paul is employing a temporary solution to a specific problem. Paul has to *inform* Timothy of what he himself is doing about this problem because it would have been new to Timothy. It seems that it had not occurred to Timothy that stopping the women from teaching was one of his options as a pastor.

While I find both these explanations plausible, I have saved, in my opinion, the best for last. Explanation C, which I have been eagerly waiting to share, takes into account the cultural context of ancient Ephesus, where Timothy was a pastor, and the result is exceptionally illuminating. Here, then, is Explanation C.

---

22. Keener, *Paul, Women & Wives*, 112.

Explanation C (verses 13–15): Paul Is Countering the Influences of the Artemis Cult[23]

Over the past several years I created a few videos in which I tried to suc-cinctly explain some of the passages that we are studying in this book. In my video on 1 Timothy 2:12–14, I offered a summary of Explanation A above. Since I made that video, however, I have learned more about the worship practices associated with the Greek goddess Artemis. Drawing on recent archaeological discoveries, Bible scholars have now shown that the worship of Artemis is clearly in the background in Paul's letters to Timothy. My learning has pushed me to prefer what I'm designating here as Explanation C over other interpretations I've encountered, including the one I espoused in my video.

Let's begin with verse 15, which we have not yet addressed. This verse used to puzzle me immensely. "What on earth could it mean that a woman would be saved through childbearing?!" I wondered. And I wasn't the only one puzzled by this passage. While not always the case, sometimes knowing something about the culture behind a biblical pas-sage can serve to virtually clear up all questions regarding what it means. If this is true of any passage of Scripture, it is of 1 Timothy 2:15.

Ephesus was the location of the Temple of Artemis, a building so magnificent that the celebrated Jewish philosopher Philo numbered it among the "Seven Wonders of the Ancient World," along with such mar-vels as the Great Pyramids of Egypt and the Hanging Gardens of Babylon. (To get an idea of how important the goddess Artemis was to the Ephe-sian citizens of the first century, read Acts 19:23–41.) How magnificent her temple was is not as important for our purposes, however, as know-ing what Artemis's role was as a goddess in the religious consciousness of her worshippers.

In the past, the importance of Artemis worship for understanding 1 Timothy 2:15 was debated among Bible scholars because she had for centuries been misunderstood. For a long time, scholars perpetuated the incorrect notion that Artemis was a fertility goddess, and that temple prostitution was part-and-parcel to her worship. However, more than enough archaeological evidence has now been collected to show that, in fact, something nearly the opposite was true. Far from being a goddess who promoted sexual license, Artemis was a virgin deity who promoted a

---

23. For a summary of "Explanation C" of 1 Tim 2:13–15, see Table 5.3 in the appendix.

celibate lifestyle among her devotees. Her male priests were eunuchs, and her priestesses were virgins. New Testament scholar Sandra Glahn has shown that a great deal of Paul's letter to Timothy seems to be addressing, almost directly, ideas and teachings associated with the religion of Artemis at Ephesus.[24] Recall, for example, the false teaching that prohibited marriage, mentioned in 1 Timothy 4:3. But the connection between what Timothy was addressing in the church at Ephesus—particularly among the women—and Artemis worship is most clear in 2:15.

According to myth, Artemis was the twin sister of Apollo. When their mother Leto gave birth to Artemis, Artemis turned around and served as her mother's midwife in the birth of her twin brother! With this myth in mind, Artemis's women devotees called on her for safety during childbirth—and they had to appease her as well, for she had the power to kill a woman in labor if she saw fit.[25] Furthermore, one of Artemis's titles was "savior."[26] That is, she was invoked by Ephesian women to *save them during childbirth*. Of course, this would not be obvious without the light of archaeological research. But with it, it is virtually without question that Paul had the worship of Artemis in mind when he wrote 1 Timothy 2:15.

In our day, at least in what has come to be called the developed world, the rate of maternal mortality has been pushed low enough by advancements in medical knowledge and technology that fear has become a secondary sentiment associated with pregnancy. When a woman conceives a child, the mood among family and friends tends to be joyful, celebratory, and expectant. Of course, pregnancy and childbirth are still arduous and dangerous, and always will be (and this is probably an understatement . . . as a man I will never be able to fully understand). But historians calculate that, in the first-century world, childbirth was the number one cause of death among women.[27] For women who had children, it was the most imminent danger they faced in their lifetimes. What battle was to men, childbirth was to women. At the same time, married women were under tremendous pressure to have many children in order to maintain local populations.[28] In verse 15, therefore, Paul seems to be telling the women at Ephesus that God is the one they should trust with these fears, not

---

24. See Glahn, "Identity of Artemis," and Glahn, "First-Century Ephesian Artemis."
25. *DDD*, s.v. "Artemis."
26. Glahn, "Identity of Artemis," 330.
27. Glahn, "First-Century Ephesian Artemis," 451.
28. Glahn, "First-Century Ephesian Artemis," 451.

Artemis the midwife goddess. Paul is clearly trying, through his mentee Timothy, to shepherd the Ephesian Christians toward a more mature and established faith. As is always the case, for the Ephesians this meant difficult growing pains involving audacious transfers of trust and allegiance from things like wealth, prestige, power, nationalism, and various gods and goddesses, to Jesus.

Artemis worship can also illuminate Paul's comments in verse 13. In the myth about Artemis's origin, she is born first, and then turns to help her mother give birth to her younger twin brother. Glahn explains why this is important.

> To Jews, the Adam-and-Eve narrative was the old, familiar creation story. But for gentiles—the focus of Paul's ministry—the Genesis narrative was new. The non-Jewish members of Timothy's spiritual community were well versed in a far different creation story. They had a special pride of place about this story, because they believed its events [i.e. the birth of Artemis and Apollo]—known throughout the empire—took place near their city. In these gentiles' creation narrative, the woman came first, and that gave her preeminence as the first twin. Competition persisted between cities that worshiped one or the other of the twins, with Artemis's followers insisting she was superior because she was born first. So in Timothy's context, the creation story from Genesis contrasts completely with the local story and would have served as a logical corrective.[29]

The point Dr. Glahn is making is not that Paul wanted men *as opposed to women* to take pride of place in the life of the Ephesian Christians. Instead, Paul was *counterbalancing* the worldview of the dominant religious culture in Ephesus that set the woman over against the man as his competitor rather than his companion. Glahn continues, "If Timothy's charges in Ephesus were unduly influenced by the Artemis cult and its over-exalting of woman, the Genesis story provided needed balance."[30]

Given what we observed regarding Paul's prohibition about a woman being dominant over a man in verse 12, it is worth noting that the goddess Artemis didn't get along well with men, to understate the matter. In myths about her she is repeatedly found killing male gods who offend her (though I should add, she's ready to kill goddesses too if she sees the need). While this bit of cultural background knowledge is not absolutely

29. Glahn, "First-Century Ephesian Artemis," 463.
30. Glahn, "First-Century Ephesian Artemis," 464.

necessary for interpreting the passage, it helps us imagine what Paul and Timothy might have been up against as they strove to establish a Christ-honoring church in the midst of a city whose predominant religious influence was profoundly un-Christlike. From our perspective, it may be difficult to appreciate the need for Paul's insistence that women be tutored before they teach others. But, if we try to imagine ourselves in Paul's shoes, I think we would find plenty of room for empathy. Surrounded by an anti-marriage and possibly anti-man religious context, the women in the church at Ephesus were experiencing special temptations that many of us today might struggle to comprehend.

It is important also for us to think carefully about another contextual aspect of this passage. Nearly every commentator I have read or preacher I have heard teach on this passage has assumed it applies to what women and men should do or not do in a church setting. But Westfall rightly argues that the text itself provides little warrant for that assumption. On the face of it, 1 Timothy is a *personal* letter, not a letter intended for public reading in a church. It absolutely has relevance for the church as a whole, but it should not be read in the same way as, for instance, Romans, Galatians, or Ephesians, which are addressed to "the saints who are at . . ." or "the church which is in . . ."[31] In 1 Timothy, Paul is interested in equipping a young servant of the church with good pastoral advice not only for church members *when they are gathered together*, but also for when they are at home and out and about in society. Note, for example, that in Paul's day birth happened in the home. Paul's mention of childbirth in verse 15, as well as his use of the singular references to "a woman" and "a man" instead of the plural "women" and "men" leads the interpreter more naturally to the conclusion that Paul has a home setting in mind here rather than a gathered church setting. Paul is worried about marriages, and about how a culture saturated with Artemis-esque thinking is affecting Christian marriages negatively. Note that the "they" in verse 15 seems to refer to *both* the woman *and* the man. They *both* need to "continue in faith and love and holiness." Paul is trying here to turn the male-female relationship back to its created design, one in which each part serves the other and participates mutually in the stewardship of creation. The vision taught in Genesis 1 and 2 is never far back in Paul's mind. It all fits together beautifully.

---

31. See Westfall, *Paul and Gender,* 286–90.

Conclusion

I will let Dr. Glahn conclude:

> Seeing the reference to Eve's creation order in 1 Timothy 2:13 as an all-time prohibition against females imparting spiritual content to males has created far more textual difficulties than it has resolved. But seeing it as an apologetic against false teaching in Ephesus fits the context and allows interpreters to better synthesize the whole counsel of God.[32]

---

32. Glahn, "First-Century Ephesian Artemis," 463.

6

Christian Submission

(Ephesians 5:21–33 & 1 Peter 3:1–7)

UNTIL THIS POINT, WE have discussed the only texts in the New Testament that directly relate to the silencing or quieting of women. I have tried to show that, when interpreted properly, we can see that factors besides an ideology of gender roles lie behind them, and that they do not limit women who are called, gifted, and prepared in their service to the church. Now we turn to texts that are often used to support the notion that men were made to lead and women to follow.

The most-often-discussed passage having to do with submission in this debate is Ephesians 5:21–33, because it is the place where Paul develops his teaching about man and woman in marriage most fully. In the space of thirteen verses, Paul twice tells wives specifically to submit to their husbands. Paul says the same in Colossians 3:18, and the apostle Peter also gives this instruction in 1 Peter 3:1. A godly woman is described by Paul in Titus 2:5 and by Peter in 1 Peter 3:5 as someone who submits to her husband. In all, that's four times in the New Testament that wives are directly told to be subject to their husbands, and two additional times that they are indirectly—but clearly—told the same. That's six submission passages directed at women! Of course, for those who see the Bible—and particularly the New Testament—as revealing God's will and plan, one time would be enough. Still, it's impressive that this command is repeated this often. Before we get any further, however, we should make two observations.

First, wives are never told to *obey* their husbands in the New Testament. Peter comes close to saying they should in 1 Peter 3:6, but stops short of actually doing so. I hope to explain why I think this is important hereafter.

Second, wives aren't the only group of people who are told to submit themselves to another group in the New Testament. Romans 13:1, 5, Titus 3:1, and 1 Peter 2:13 all command submission to governing authorities. That's four times. Slaves are told to submit to their masters in Titus 2:9 and 1 Peter 2:18, and, unlike wives, are even told to obey their masters in Ephesians 6:5 and Colossians 3:22. In addition to these more prominent examples of the command to submit, Paul also commands submission to every "fellow worker and laborer" in 1 Corinthians 16:16. Whoever wrote the Epistle to the Hebrews also tells his (or her?) readers to submit to and also obey their leaders (13:17). Finally, Peter tells young people to submit to older people (1 Pet 5:5). It's clear that the command to submit is ubiquitous in the New Testament! So, what does this mean, exactly, for the debate about women in speaking ministries in the church? What does it mean for married Christians? A lot.

Hierarchicalists consistently argue that a woman's silence, to whatever degree, is directly related to her role as a person subject to male authority. They hold that wives are subject specifically to their husband's God-given leadership, and all women should at least symbolically represent their submissive role by deferring to men when it comes to certain speaking ministries in the church, and, of course, when it comes to leadership roles in the church. I worded that vaguely on purpose. I can't get much more specific than that because, as we noted before, there is tremendous variety among hierarchicalist churches in their practice of what they call complementarianism. The reason behind limiting the role of women is virtually always the same, nonetheless. In every case, women need to be submitting to at least one male's authority, and this should be reflected *somehow* in the church's practice.

For some, the fact that the New Testament commands wives to submit to their husbands several times is enough to resolve the debate. "How could anyone argue," someone might ask, "that women do not need to submit to men when the Bible says it so clearly?!" Indeed, how could they?

This was another sticky point for me when I began revisiting this issue shortly before graduating from college. I had been told repeatedly throughout my life that affirming women in speaking ministries was a slippery slope toward denying biblical authority. "If women do not have to obey the biblical mandate to submit, what commands will we choose to throw out next?" It sounded like a strong argument against the egalitarian position. Well, I was in for a surprise!

It turns out the argument commits a logical fallacy known as the straw man fallacy. A straw man is flimsy and light. You can easily push him over because he's not a real man. When I commit the straw man fallacy, I argue against a caricature of an idea that doesn't *really* represent the idea of my opponent accurately. I push over a straw man, which is just a parody of my opponent's argument, instead of attacking the real argument that she is presenting. The fact is, no biblical egalitarian argues that women should ignore the Bible's commands to submit to their husbands! That's right. They just never say that. Biblical egalitarians consistently teach that women *should* submit to their husbands. Submission is not a problem at all for the egalitarian position. In fact, it is not an exaggeration to claim that egalitarians emphasize submission *more than hierarchicalists* do. Let me explain.

One of the basic rules of Bible interpretation is that one has to consider first what the words on the page actually say before developing theology beyond what they say. Only after establishing what the words on the page mean (to the best of one's ability) should one begin asking theological questions of the text. Sometimes we bring questions to the text that the original author was not trying to answer. This, of course, is completely understandable and normal, and is by no means wrong. But, the careful interpreter will think, "Okay, I have this question. But, what is the question that *this particular text* was answering for its original readers? Is it the same as mine, or different? Can this text answer my question too, or not? And if so, to what extent? What are the limitations of this text for answering my question?"

To give an example of how this can affect the interpretation of a biblical text, let's consider Jesus' comments on divorce and remarriage. Here are the passages:

> But I say to you that everyone who divorces his wife, except on the ground of sexual immorality, makes her commit adultery, and whoever marries a divorced woman commits adultery. (Matt 5:32 ESV)

> And I say to you: whoever divorces his wife, except for sexual immorality, and marries another, commits adultery. (Matt 19:9 ESV)

> Whoever divorces his wife and marries another commits adultery against her, and if she divorces her husband and marries another, she commits adultery. (Mark 10:11–12 ESV)

> Everyone who divorces his wife and marries another commits adultery, and he who marries a woman divorced from her husband commits adultery. (Luke 16:18 ESV)

I have read several helpful books and many articles by Bible scholars and pastors about the topic of divorce and remarriage. One of the primary questions that one would like to have answered with regard to this topic is: Under what circumstances, if ever, is it appropriate for a Christian to remarry after a divorce? This is an extremely important question. And on the surface of it, one might assume that the passages above are the right place to find the answer. But notice two things.

- First, only two of these passages (Matt 5:32 and 19:9) suggest a possible circumstance in which a person's divorcing a spouse might be appropriate—that is, when the spouse commits adultery. This is known as the exception clause. But notice that these passages only mention a scenario in which a husband is divorcing his wife, *not* one in which a wife is divorcing her husband. That is, these passages only address men. The fact is, these passages only provide the exception clause for a man whose wife has committed adultery, not for a woman whose husband has done so.

- Second, while Matthew *does* provide an exception for divorce in the case of adultery, none of the passages above permit the remarriage of a woman who has been divorced by her husband, *even if he divorced her for some other reason*! In other words, there is no indication in the passages above that a woman could remarry at all, even if her first husband had divorced her for some unjustifiable reason.

What should we do with this? Every modern Christian book that I have read on the topic of divorce and remarriage assumes that, *if* remarriage is ever appropriate for Christians under any circumstance, the norm should be the same for men and women. For example, if it is permissible for a man to divorce an adulterous wife, it is also permissible for a woman to divorce an adulterous husband. Likewise, if it is permissible for a man to remarry after his wife leaves him, it is also permissible for a woman to do the same if her husband leaves her. The logic, in our modern mindset, is always that men and women should be held to the same standards. They should be treated equally, as it were.

But, is that what we see in the passages above? Actually, it's not—at least if we limit ourselves only to what is actually written in the text. In the words on the page, Jesus only allows an exception for husbands seeking to divorce their wives (or to remarry), not vice versa. If the exception clause applies to wives in the same situation, Jesus does not say so.

These observations may seem a bit nitpicky to a modern reader. However, modern readers, who live on this side of massive, far-reaching feminist movements, come to the text with assumptions about male-female equality that earlier interpreters did not. Look at what Basil of Caesarea, a fourth-century Christian theologian, wrote about the church's teaching in his day regarding remarriage after divorce (note: I suggest reading this a couple of times):

> The decree of the Lord that it is forbidden to withdraw from marriage except in the case of fornication [cf. Matt 5:32; 19:9] applies equally to men and to women, at least according to the logic of the idea . . . But custom requires wives to keep their husbands, even if the husband commit adultery and fornication. Therefore, I do not know if a woman who lives with a man who has been divorced by his wife can be called an adulteress. The blame in this case falls upon the woman who divorced her husband and depends on the reason why she withdrew from the marriage. If she was being beaten and would not endure the blows, it would have been better for her to tolerate her husband than to separate from him. If she would not endure the loss of money, that is not an acceptable reason. But if her motivation was the man's living in fornication, this is not the customary observance of the church. Rather, a wife is instructed not to separate from an unbelieving husband, but to remain because it is uncertain what will result. For how do you know, wife, whether you will save your husband? For this reason a woman who leaves her husband is an adulteress if she goes to another man. But the man who has been abandoned may be pardoned, and the woman who lives with such a man is not condemned. If a man who has left his wife goes to another, however, he is an adulterer because he makes the woman commit adultery. The woman who lives with him is an adulteress because she has taken another woman's husband to herself.[1]

---

1. Hunter, *Marriage and Sexuality*, 238–39.

Basil's reasoning (rightly) probably strikes most of my readers as profoundly unjust. However, it is important for us not to allow our righteous indignation to prevent us from seeing how carefully Basil—and the churches whose thinking he represents—has read the biblical text. As we noted, according to what Jesus (and Paul—see 1 Cor 7:10–11) says *specifically* about men and women respectively in the passages to which Basil alludes, his conclusion that the stipulations for permitting divorce and remarriage are more strict for women than they are for men fits. To summarize, Basil reasoned that Jesus' so-called exception clause about men and remarriage applied to men *only*.

Incidentally, I believe that the norms for marriage, divorce, and remarriage *are* the same for Christian men and women. I think men and women *should* be treated equally in this regard. But, it would not be possible for me to conclude this simply by reading the words of Jesus as they are recorded in the Gospels. We can only arrive at a fair and equal understanding of Christian norms for divorce and remarriage by doing some extrabiblical theological reasoning. In these passages' context, Jesus is responding to *men* who had asked him a question about when it was permissible for a *man* to divorce his wife. And, Jesus responds to *that* question. We wonder if a woman ever asked Jesus a question like this. If that ever happened, we have no record of the conversation. But we modern readers, most of whom live in societies in which women have the legal right to get a divorce, would like to know what Scripture says to *both* Christian men *and* Christian women on this topic. Thus, to fill in the gaps, we simply assume that men and women should be held to the same standard, and therefore assume that any circumstance that would permit divorce and remarriage for a Christian of one gender would be the same for the other. Even though I understand why Basil interpreted the above passages as he did, I think he was wrong to hold women and men to separate standards. I assume most, if not all, of my readers will agree. Nevertheless, Basil's reasoning *is undeniably* biblical, in the strictest sense of the term.

Now, we can relate this example to our present topic. If Basil were alive now, some of us might want to say to him, "Yes, Jesus didn't mention an exception clause *specifically* in relation to women. But because we know that God holds all parties to the same standards of sexual exclusivity and fidelity in marriage, we can *assume* that Jesus would teach the same standard for divorce and remarriage to both genders." In other words, we would be saying that a biblical instruction directed *specifically to* one gender is not necessarily *exclusively for* that gender only.

This is the basic idea that allows for my reading of Paul's commands regarding wives' submission to their husbands. Just because Paul tells wives *specifically* to submit to their marriage partners, this does not mean that submission is *exclusively for* wives. We have a record of Jesus answering a male-oriented question for a male audience because, in his context, men had nearly exclusive legal control of their marriages. When it happened, it was the men who did the divorcing, not the women. Thus, Jesus answered the question he was asked within the context in which he was asked it. I think we should read Ephesians 5:22 and other passages that tell wives to submit to their husbands in a similar way. Yes, Paul told women *specifically* to submit to their husbands. But this does not mean the standard for men in marriage is different. Just like we modern Christians apply the logic of Jesus' comments regarding men and divorce and remarriage to *both* men and women, we should also apply Paul and Peter's comments about submission in marriage to both men and women, even though they directed the instruction specifically to married Christian women in their time and context.

Many people come to the "wives submit" passages in Paul's New Testament letters with the question, "Who is in charge?" But, there is ample reason to conclude that the original readers of these letters were asking an entirely different kind of question. Paul's readers weren't wondering who was in charge; they knew who was in charge in their society already. Instead, they wanted to know how to live as faithful Christians within their social context. No New Testament letter *ever tells anyone to actively take charge over another person.* To make this particularly relevant for our discussion, I'll note more pointedly that husbands are *nowhere* in the New Testament commanded to take a place of rule, authority, or even leadership in relation to their wives. No New Testament writer saw the need to tell men to take a place of leadership or to take on a headship role in the home. In fact, I hasten to point out that the word "headship" itself is absent from Scripture. The Bible teaches that man *is* the head of woman, not that he possesses headship, as if it's a badge men can carry around in their pockets—a badge they can lose if they're not careful. The Bible never describes men as being more or less faithful to their role of headship. In other words, if we just read what is written—which is what we should do first—we will find a lot about submission in marriage, one-sided though it be, but *nothing* about taking up or clinging to authority in marriage. Yes, wives are told to submit, but husbands are *never told to be their wives' leaders.* Never. Not even once.

If women should think of their role as one of submission "because the Bible says so," how should men think of their role? The Bible is not against leadership in and of itself; on the contrary, the Bible seems to assume the importance of good leadership for the health of a church, and for society in general. But when it comes to marriage, the Bible stops short of telling husbands that they should actively take a leadership role in relation to their wives. This fact may be difficult to swallow for some because of the scores of Christian men's conferences, sermons, and books for men (and women, for that matter) that have taught otherwise. Nevertheless, the call for men to be leaders of their wives, whether it is practically expedient or not, cannot be found in the Bible. The question remains, then: What should a Christian husband try to be for his wife? Does the Bible have anything to say about how husbands should think about themselves in relation to their wives?

It most certainly does! In the Gospels, Jesus repeatedly demonstrated that his way of ruling as the Sovereign and Savior of humanity was by becoming its servant. And, anyone who wants to participate in Jesus' reign must also become a servant of others. Not only must all followers of Jesus become servants, they must serve "the least of these" (Matt 25:40). Jesus *never* talks about his followers becoming leaders. On the few occasions when his disciples seem to be trying to set themselves up as leaders within Jesus' movement, they end up looking like fools.[2] With this in mind, how is a Christian husband supposed to see himself in relation to his wife and family?

His wife has been told already over and over again in the New Testament to submit to him. Her role is, therefore, clear enough: she is to be his servant. To our ears, that probably sounds harsh, or even wrong. But in light of what Jesus teaches in the Gospels it is not in the least surprising. Paul and Peter were merely telling women, as wives, what it would mean for them to be followers of Jesus within their marriages. There is no evidence that Paul and Peter met with any resistance to this idea. As we noted, the Christian women listening to Peter and Paul's Epistles knew exactly who was in charge according to the laws and customs under which they lived. Their question wasn't, "Who's in charge here?" It wasn't within their power to make a difference with respect to that anyway.

---

2. See, for example, Mark 9:33–37; Luke 9:46–48; 22:24–27.

Rather, they wanted to know, "How can I live as a Christian in my situation?" Suppose the men who were listening to Paul and Peter's Epistles were asking the same question. Would the answer be, "Husbands should consider themselves their wives' masters?"

Tragically, the conclusion that the Bible teaches the right of husbands' mastery over their wives has been reached, to the detriment of women's (and men's, I would argue) well-being, with egregious frequency in the church. Many women have the physical and emotional scars to prove it. In response to this fact, complementarians usually respond by introducing a hyphenated term: "servant-leadership." "Husbands should serve their wives," they say, "*by leading them in a Christlike way.*" To their credit, most complementarian leaders speak against men's abuse of their power over their wives. They emphasize repeatedly that husbands should *not* use their God-given authority to advance their own interests, much less to mistreat their wives. Instead, they should use their God-given authority to the benefit of their wives and families. Without a doubt, this emphasis on servant-leadership is an improvement on the older, more unqualified and unnuanced version of male authority over women. But, it begs the question about biblical support. The term "servant-leader" does not appear in the Bible.

I acknowledge that leaders can serve those they lead, and I also think the idea of servant-leadership is invaluable for society today. Indeed, servant-leadership is at the heart of what makes successful representative, democratic governments work. But, in a discussion like this one, in which all parties are trying to base their arguments on what Scripture says, we need to go back and look at the words written in our Bibles. Servant-leadership is a modern concept created to accommodate the Christian principle of serving others to a democratic society's sensibilities. But in Jesus' original teaching, as it has been passed down to us in the Gospels, there are no hyphens. Jesus just said, "Be a servant." Full stop.

Egalitarians, by contrast, see Paul and Peter as merely instructing specific people about how they should follow Jesus within their particular circumstances. Once we locate Paul and Peter's submission command within the basic teaching of Jesus for *all* his followers, it becomes more difficult to think of it as a command exclusively for women. The fact is, if any husband wants to follow Jesus, he is going to have to see himself as a servant of his wife. Whether or not he is a leader is irrelevant with respect to who he is as a follower of Jesus. The submission will become mutual, two-sided. He will begin to see her as his equal, corresponding partner instead of as his underling.

We have come full circle, then, back to God's design for the male-female relationship portrayed in the Genesis creation story. It's kind of like an algebra equation. We know that the equation equals "a Christ-centered marriage," so here is what our equation might look like:

$$X + Y = \text{a Christ-centered marriage}$$

Christ came to restore God's fallen creation back to God. So, we know that a good, Christ-centered marriage looks, at minimum, like what we find in Genesis 1 and 2. We know that the role of a wife in marriage is that of a servant because of the explicit commands in the New Testament, "Wives, submit to your husbands." Thus, let X equal "a wife who serves her husband." So far, so good. Now, if we can solve for Y, we've solved the equation. Of course, Y stands for the husband's role. If the equation equals what we found in Genesis 1 and 2—that is, "a good, Christ-centered marriage"—then Y must be a role that is equal and opposite to role X, because this is how Genesis portrays the husband and wife's complementarity in God's original design. Therefore, Y *must* correspond to the role of the wife. So, let Y be equally in an opposite and corresponding way, "a husband who serves his wife." There it is. Now we've solved the equation:

$$\frac{\text{a wife who serves her husband}}{+ \text{ a husband who serves his wife}}$$
$$\text{a Christ-centered marriage}$$

Both Paul and Peter come very close to stating that Christian husbands and wives should see each other as partners in mutual service. Right before Paul tells wives to submit to their husbands in Ephesians 5:22, he writes, "submitting to one another out of reverence to Christ" (5:21). Actually, in most English translations the word "submit" has been added in verse 22. In the Greek text, the word "submit" only appears in verse 21, and it is clear that verse 21 applies to all Christians in the church. It is like a subcommand under "be filled with the Spirit" (Eph 5:18). In other words, submission *to one another* is one of the outcomes of being filled with the Spirit. Similarly, when Peter addresses husbands in 1 Peter 3:7, he says that wives are "heirs together with you of the grace of life." This is another clear affirmation of the mutuality of their relationship. In

Christ, what the wife is to the husband, the husband also is to the wife, at least in terms of authority. Quoting 1 Corinthians 7:4 again might serve to reinforce this point: "The wife does not have authority over her own body but yields it to her husband. In the same way, the husband does not have authority over his own body but yields it to his wife."

Submission, therefore, is not necessarily unidirectional. It *can* be done mutually and is, in the New Testament view of things, not only for hierarchical relationships. It should be noted that the New Testament is utterly unique in this regard. According to experts, no other Greek text from the time of the New Testament speaks about mutual submission. Outside the New Testament, a command to submit always assumes a hierarchical relationship.[3] Indeed, the same is often assumed today, even after 2,000 years of gospel influence on the world! But in the upside-down way of doing things in Jesus' kingdom, the king himself comes as a lowly servant. That glorious passage in Paul's Letter to the Philippians (2:3–8) is probably already popping into some of my readers' minds:

> Do nothing out of selfish ambition or vain conceit. Rather, in humility value others above yourselves, not looking to your own interests but each of you to the interests of others. In your relationships with one another, have the same mindset as Christ Jesus: Who, being in very nature God, did not consider equality with God something to be used to his own advantage; rather, he made himself nothing by taking on the very nature of a servant, being made in human likeness. And being found in appearance as a man, he humbled himself by becoming obedient to death— even death on a cross!

If a husband and wife apply what Paul teaches in this celebrated passage, they will find themselves submitting to each other out of reverence to Christ.

To summarize what we've observed up until now, we have seen that Paul and Peter's commands that women submit to their husbands need to be read within the context of the New Testament's teaching as a whole about servanthood—particularly Jesus' teaching in the Gospels. Those who are great in God's kingdom are those who serve. Thus, there is no reason to limit submission in Christian marriage to wives only. All Christians are commanded to submit. On that basis alone we could conclude

---

3. See Grudem, "Myth of Mutual Submission."

that Christian husbands should submit to their wives. However, Paul and Peter both have more to say about this. Let's start with Paul.

Ephesians 5:21–33: Participating in the Victory of Christ[4]

In his letter to the church at Ephesus, Paul uses two mysterious and profound metaphors for Christ's relationship to the church. Paul likens Christ to a head, and the church to Christ's body. In the following I will argue that these two metaphors are meant to be understood together. If we only focus on the single metaphor of a head, we will fall short of comprehending what Paul is trying to teach both about Christ's relationship to the church and, as a result, about a husband's relationship to his wife in Christian marriage.

To begin, let's review the overall salvation story the Bible tells. We need to keep this story in mind as we begin reading Paul's letter to the Ephesians because part of what Paul wants to do in this letter is explain the church's place in that story. As we read, one of the questions we should be asking is, "How do Christ and his work relate to the church and the church's work?" In bullet-point form, here is a summary of the story:

- God created a good world and designated humanity as God's representative within it.

- Humanity disobeyed God and thereby fell into sin, becoming subject to decay, death, and enmity with God, along with all of creation. But God promised to restore this good creation.

- God came into the world, identified with humanity, and became subject to humanity's death in the person of Jesus. But Jesus rose from the dead, thereby providing hope for the salvation of fallen humanity.

- Jesus' death and resurrection is a sign that all of creation is being restored to the goodness that God intended in the beginning.

- Redeemed human beings also will be restored to take the place that God intended for them.

God is the main actor and hero of this story. But notice that whatever God is doing Christ is also doing. Jesus is at the center of the whole project, and is, in fact, God in the flesh working out God's redemptive plan.

---

4. For a summary of this explanation of Eph 5:21–33, see Table 6.1 in the appendix.

In Ephesians 1, Paul explains that God's plan from the very start was to unite all created things in Christ. The soaring theology in this chapter is some of the most profound and mysterious in the whole Bible. In verses 18 to 23, Paul describes Christ as a conqueror who crushes his enemies under his feet. If we didn't know *how* Jesus did this, we would have cause to associate Jesus with some domineering, imperialistic, vengeful power. But we know that Christ conquered through weakness, by giving himself up to evil's worst designs and, finally, coming out the other side victoriously alive. God raised him from the dead. Therefore, the enemy was defeated because the enemy's ultimate weapon, death, failed to overcome Jesus. As a result, Christ's enemies were vanquished. To express this, Paul imagines Jesus as an earthly conqueror seated somehow on top of all earthly powers and kingdoms and authorities. The striking part comes in verses 22 and 23, which say, "And God placed all things under his feet and appointed him to be head over everything for the church, which is his body, the fullness of him who fills everything in every way." It is here that Paul first employs the metaphor of a head in this epistle to describe Christ, and it is here that we must begin if we want to understand how Paul uses the metaphor later in chapter 5.

On the one hand, Paul is obviously talking in this passage about how Christ is victorious and, therefore, an authority over the whole universe. But something interesting happens in Ephesians 1:23 when Paul mentions Christ's relationship to the church, as singled out from the rest of creation. Whereas Christ is head over all *other* things, he is head for the church. This means Christ's headship (if my gracious readers will forgive the use of an extrabiblical term) in relation to the powers of the world means a crushing, conquering, vanquishing force. But in relation to the church, Christ's being head means something quite different. Christ is *against* the powers of evil, but he is *for* the church.

This may seem like a subtle distinction between the two relationships, but the next distinction is not so subtle. Paul continues by saying that Christ is the head of the church, "which is his body, the fullness of him who fills everything in every way." Here, Paul introduces a *second* metaphor: body. While Paul used only one metaphor—head—to describe Christ's relationship to the powers of the world, he uses *two* metaphors—head *and* body—to describe Christ's special relationship to the church. This is extremely important, and here is why: when it comes to a living human being, the head and the body must remain connected in order for the organism as a whole to thrive, or live at all. The head and the body can only live interdependently, and their mutual separation leads inevitably to their mutual demise. They are—to borrow a key phrase from Genesis 2—"*one flesh.*"

Because head and body are so inextricably connected in every living person, whatever the head does the body also does, and whatever the body does the head also does. If the church is Christ's body, therefore, this means that the church integrally *participates in* Christ's victory. As a result, the church's relationship with Christ is not one of enmity such that we should fear him as a conqueror, but one of unity such that we should see ourselves as having died and risen *with* him. In Christ *we also* have conquered.[5] We find our completeness in our connection with him as our head and, remarkably, he with us. The New Testament even says that Christ's church will reign *with him* (2 Tim 2:12)! No New Testament text makes this truth more explicit than Ephesians 2:4–6, where Paul writes, "But because of his great love for us, God, who is rich in mercy, made us alive with Christ even when we were dead in transgressions—it is by grace you have been saved. And God raised us up *with Christ* and seated us *with him* in the heavenly realms *in Christ Jesus.*"

We often pass over this passage too quickly in a rush to get to verse 8. But let's pause long enough to appreciate what Paul is claiming here. He is saying that, because the church is in Christ, it is united with Christ in his death, resurrection, and reign. Thus, Jesus' headship means for the church something entirely different than it does for his vanquished enemies. For the church, the fact that Jesus has been made the "head over all things" means we participate with him in his victory over all things, because we are his body. If the head is victorious, it follows that the body is also victorious.

In Genesis, God created humanity as God's image in the world, to preside over nature and to steward it as God's representative. The creation has fallen under sin, but in Christ that creation is being restored. In fact, Paul even speaks about this in the perfect tense—he talks as if creation *has already* been restored. What is more, he says that the church, in Christ, is already seated with him on his royal throne in heaven, reigning over the redeemed creation. This is Pauline theology at its highest. Christ is head *over* creation, but in Christ the church participates with, and shares in, that rule. The last line of the praise chorus "All Hail King Jesus," by Dave

---

5. See also Rom 6:4 and Col 2:12; 3:1–4.

Moody, encapsulates and personalizes this truth. Addressing Christ, worshippers proclaim, "And I'll reign *with you* throughout eternity!"

Paul spends the next few chapters in Ephesians expanding on this mysterious relationship. Paul's main practical concern in Ephesians, as well as in most of his writings, is the integration of gentile followers of Jesus into the fledgling community of faith—a faith essentially Jewish in its provenance and character. In Christ, however, the gentiles also become a part of the story of Israel. The primary metaphor Paul uses to expound upon the unity of Jew and gentile is that of a body. We use the term, "body of Christ" so frequently in the church today that, oftentimes, I suspect we forget that it was coined to teach a very practical lesson about the church's mission in the world. For Paul, all of the things that formerly signified a wall of separation between Jew and gentile—and, therefore, between other nationalities, ethnic groups, etc.—have, in Christ, become obsolete. Now, Jew and gentile are part of one body of Christ. In Ephesians 3:4–6 Paul writes, "In reading this, then, you will be able to understand my insight into the mystery of Christ, . . . This mystery is that through the gospel the Gentiles are heirs together with Israel, members together of one body, and sharers together in the promise of Christ Jesus." The reasoning can be summarized in this short dialogue:

> Q: *What is Christ to the church?*
>
> A: *He is its head.*
>
> Q: *What is the church to Christ?*
>
> A: *It is his body.*
>
> Q: *How many bodies does Christ have?*
>
> A: *One—and this is why Jew and gentile are one in Christ.*

The head, as a metaphor, appears again in 4:15–16. This whole passage is worth quoting:

> Rather, speaking the truth in love, we are to grow up in every way into him who is the head, into Christ, from whom the whole body joined and held together by every joint with which it is equipped, when each part is working properly, makes the body grow so that it builds itself up in love. (ESV)

Notice in this passage how the church is described as a body that somehow simultaneously grows both *into* and *from* its head. Paul says something similar in Colossians 2:19. There, Christ is the "head, from whom the whole body, supported and held together by its ligaments and sinews, grows as God causes it to grow." Thus, head as a metaphor seems to mean for Paul both the source and the culmination of something. A thing's head is that from which the thing came and that *for which* the thing exists. Simply saying that head means "source" is probably not generous enough a definition to include all that Paul wants to say with this metaphor. The idea of source is included, but it also carries the notion of ongoing dependence and nurture.

Some of my readers might be concerned about something at this point. "If we say that Christ's being the church's head does *not* entail his being the church's authority, are we arguing that Christ is not actually Lord of the church?" No, that is not what I am saying. Christ certainly *is* Lord of the church. How could he not be, since he is Lord of all things?! However, the fact that Christ is Lord does not mean that every metaphor that we use to describe Christ's relationship to the church automatically refers to his lordship. Think of all the metaphors that Jesus used to describe himself in the Gospels. He called himself "the gate" (John 10:9), "the light of the world" (John 8:12), "the vine" (John 15:1), "the good shepherd" (John 10:11–14), "the bread of life" (John 6:35), "servant" (Luke 22:27), and "the way" (or "path"—John 14:6). Paul and the writer to the Hebrews also liken Jesus to a "brother" (Heb 2:11; Rom 8:29). Each of these metaphors teaches something different than the others about who Jesus is to us. But notice that most of them do not emphasize Jesus' lordship. Of course, that doesn't mean Jesus isn't Lord; it just means that not all metaphors used in the Bible for Jesus are meant to teach us about his being so.

At the risk of oversimplifying a piece of complex theology, I thought it might be helpful to summarize in bullet-point form what we have discussed above before we get any further:

- By becoming a servant of all, Christ has accomplished victory over the powers of sin and death.
- When a conquerer is victorious, his whole body is victorious.
- Christ is the head of the church, and the church is the body of Christ.
- If the church is the body of Christ, the church participates fully in the victory of Christ over sin and death.
- The church, therefore, reigns *with* Christ.

- If the church is the body of Christ, the church should serve as Christ served.

Once again, this does *not* mean that Christ is not the church's Lord, boss, or leader. He certainly is. The point is, rather, that the head-and-body metaphor doesn't highlight this particular aspect of who Christ is in relation to the church, at least in Paul's writings. Paul never portrays Christ the head as someone who gives commands, makes decisions, or even leads the church.

This is crucial for understanding how Paul later uses the same metaphor for husbands and wives in Ephesians 5. Just like Christ has, through his self-giving death and victorious resurrection, exalted the church to share in his rule, so Christ-following husbands are to, through their self-giving service, *exalt their wives* to a place of shared status with them as co-representatives of God in a world God has now begun to renew. The picture we should have in mind is the one painted in Genesis 1 and 2, where male and female are portrayed as different yet equal stewards of God's creation. But I'm getting ahead of myself.

Now that we have traced Paul's use of the head-and-body metaphor through Ephesians 1–4, we are in a good position to discuss 5:23, where the metaphor shows up once again in the context of Paul's comments about marriage. In English we speak of the headwaters of a river as the river's source. We also sometimes say that a conflict came to a head, meaning it reached a climax. We also use head as a verb to talk about movement in a certain direction as in, for example, "The geese are heading south for the winter." But we are most accustomed to using head as a metaphor for a person in leadership or authority. A CEO is the head of a company. A president is the head of an organization or university. In the school where I teach at the time I am writing this, there is even a position officially called, "Head of School." As a result, we (English speakers anyway) instinctively plug "leader" or "boss" into the places where we see "head" in Paul's letters. That seems to work fine in 5:23, especially since wives are told to submit in verses 22 and 24. So, if we just read "head" as meaning "boss," it would simply be, "For the husband is the [boss] of the wife as Christ is the [boss] of the church, his body, of which he is the Savior. Now as the church submits to Christ [its boss], so also wives should submit to their husbands [their bosses] in everything." That makes sense on the surface: bosses and leaders are people to whom their underlings submit. Thus, if wives should submit to their husbands, it makes sense that husbands are like their leaders or bosses.

But reading the text in this simplistic manner ignores the complexity—and beauty—of the head-and-body metaphor that Paul has already developed in the first four chapters of Ephesians. If we were to go back and simply plug a word like "leader" or "boss" into the other places in Ephesians where Paul uses "head" as a metaphor, we would ruin his entire theological argument! As we have observed, when Paul speaks of party A using the metaphor head in relation to party B, its body, it is the unity of A and B that he is emphasizing, not the leadership of A or the subordination of B.

Of course, head *could* mean something like boss or leader. As a metaphor, the word head *can* carry that meaning. But as we saw before, every time Paul uses head to describe Christ's relationship to the church in his letter to the Ephesians, he always speaks of the church as Christ's body. Again, these *two* metaphors have to go together. And, when we think of them together, the idea that head means "boss" or "leader" quickly breaks down.

Consider this: while it is true that a CEO is the head of her company, would anyone refer to the company as the CEO's body? Of course not! Likewise, even though someone could say, "He's a good student—he's the head of his class," it would be nonsensical to say, "He's a good student—the rest of the class is his body." Surprisingly, the fact that Paul uses two metaphors—not one—for Christ and the church is often overlooked in debates between biblical scholars surrounding the use of "head" in this passage. But if we don't keep them together, we're doomed to miss Paul's meaning, no matter how thoroughly we study the word "head" on its own.

If we go back and look at how Paul relates Christ as head to the church as his body, it becomes quite clear that, by employing these metaphors, Paul is trying to show the nurturing, caring, serving posture that Christ adopts toward the church. While it may seem counterintuitive to us, Paul calling Christ the church's head does *not* emphasize Christ's lordship over the church. Instead, it emphasizes Christ's mysterious oneness and intimacy with the church—an intimacy and oneness accomplished through Christ's self-giving service. This is markedly different from Christ's relationship to his vanquished enemies who persist in rebellion against him. Yes, Christ is head *over* his enemies—but Paul does *not speak of them as Christ's body,* and this makes a tremendous amount of difference! When it comes to Christ and his foes, we have a single metaphor;

but when it comes to Christ and his church, a second metaphor is added. Instead of a conquerer-and-conquered relationship, there is participation—the church *with* Christ sharing in his victory over sin and death.

This is why, when he turns to speak directly to husbands in Ephesians 5:25–33, Paul holds up the nurturing, cherishing, caring, cleansing, saving action of Christ as the appropriate example for a Christian husband to model. It is also the reason why Paul *never* tells Christian husbands to be their wives' leaders—not even servant-leaders. It's because the head-and-body metaphor is not about authority. There is a complete absence of anything like, "husbands, be sure to take leadership in your home" or, "husbands, keep your wives under your authority." Indeed, there isn't even something like, "Husbands, be merciful, gentle authorities in your homes." *Paul seems completely uninterested in maintaining a Christian husband's authority over his wife.* All he cares about is pointing husbands toward Christ's example of loving, self-giving service. It is truly unfortunate that, instead of reading Paul's words for what they are, many pastors and Bible teachers today choose to fixate on the one word—head—and proceed to admonish men on that basis toward being leaders and authorities of their wives, as if this were a Christian husband's primary calling. This is not Paul's message. Paul had ample opportunity to call men to take a place of leadership over their wives, but he never did so.

Now, we should pause here to note that in Paul's context men *were* their wives' legal authorities. Roman law recognized a man's authority over his wife, much as it did his authority over his children and slaves. That being the case, Paul's instructions about wives' submitting to their husbands would have been understandable in his time for, as we observed, Paul also tells citizens to submit to their governments, slaves to their masters, and children to their parents. Being a husband, no less than being a father, master, or governor, was a legally recognized position of authority for Paul's readers.

This fact stresses the importance of reading what Paul says to wives in the light of what he says to husbands immediately afterward. Paul tells wives to submit to their husbands as the church submits to Christ. But then (almost as if he expects husbands to be listening in) he immediately begins reminding husbands about what Christ, *specifically as the church's head,* did for the church. Christ is the servant of the church. Christ gave himself up for the church, nurtures the church, cares for the church, lifts the church up, and shares *everything, including his right to reign and rule,* with the church. There is nothing in what Paul says to men about their having the liberty to give their wives orders, being their leaders or, well, doing *anything* other than serving them. This may not be an explicit declaration of husband-wife equality, but as New Testament scholar I. Howard Marshall puts it, "We have, then, in the New Testament the beginnings of the development of a different understanding of marriage in which a wife is not her husband's chattel, but they are mutually responsible partners."[6]

In Paul's theology, participation in Christ is his primary argument for social change in the Christian community. Christ's body is the principle image Paul employs to illustrate the importance of mutual love, service, care, and even tolerance elsewhere in his letters.[7] A good example of how being in Christ causes social change can be found in Paul's short letter to Philemon. In this letter, Paul asks his friend to welcome back a slave named Onesimus. While we don't know exactly what had happened, it seems Onesimus had run away from Philemon, and may have taken something from him on his way out. Paul says something striking in verses 15 and 16: "Perhaps the reason [Onesimus] was separated from you for a little while was that you might have him back forever—no longer as a slave, but better than a slave, as a dear brother. He is very dear to me but even dearer to you, both as a fellow man and as a brother *in the Lord*." Notice that the basis on which Paul is asking Philemon to welcome Onesimus as his brother rather than as his slave is the fact that they are both "in the Lord." For Paul, participation in the death and resurrection life of Christ has practical implications for our earthly relationships. Paul's vision for the unity of Jew and gentile in the church in Romans, Galatians, and Ephesians is also founded on our mutual participation in Christ. Though it is only one example of many, Galatians 3:28 says, "There is neither Jew nor gentile, neither slave nor free, nor is there male and female, for you are all one *in Christ Jesus*."

Once we find ourselves in the Messiah, we discover a new reality spread out in front of us. And, in this new reality, worldly systems' ways of ordering human beings over and under one another is radically subverted. The question we are asking here, of course, is whether or not this new reality challenges humanity's nearly universal assumption about male authority. New Testament scholar Lucy Peppiatt thinks it does. She writes, "What can be claimed for the radically new relations of Jew and

---

6. Marshall, "Mutual Love and Submission," 191.

7. See Rom 7:4; 1 Cor 12:4–31; Eph 4:12; Col 3:15.

gentile and slave and free can, *mutatis mutandis*, be claimed for man and woman. The status of being 'in Christ' or 'in the Lord' shapes a new worshipping humanity where all come together as one before God."[8]

The church's participation in Christ is the driving theological idea behind Paul's instructions to Christian husbands in Ephesians 5. Notice how beautifully he connects this theology to the overall narrative of the Bible. He carefully selects a specific passage from the Genesis creation story to support his instruction that husbands give themselves to their wives as Christ did to the church. Ephesians 5:31 is a direct quotation of Genesis 2:24. This is not a general throwback to a created hierarchical order as some interpreters argue. Instead, Paul is saying, *"Look how God, in the beginning, prescribed that a man would leave his family—his life, his interests—and cling to his wife. Now in Christ, you husbands are to participate in that restored purpose of God for your marriage. You too should leave aside your own interests and serve your wife in the same way that Christ gave his life to serve the church."*

If my gracious readers read beyond this book they will encounter heated and, at times, caustic material on this subject. They also may be overwhelmed by the sheer amount of scholarly work that has been done on this passage in particular. It is easy in the face of such a hostile and information-flooded environment to simply shrug one's shoulders and leave it up to others—the educated people—to decide. If I may, I'd like to encourage my gentle readers directly to not give in to that impulse. Instead, set this book down and simply read Ephesians 5:21–33 for yourself. Look at exactly what it says *to* wives and exactly what it says *to* husbands. For those of you who are married, create two lists: a wife list and a husband list. Then, for one whole day, follow the lists. If you're a husband, do what Paul says in Ephesians 5:25–33. If you're a wife, do what Paul says in verses 22 to 24. Then, the next day, switch lists. If you're a husband, follow the wife's list; if you're a wife, follow the husband's list. See what difference it makes. The one rule is that you cannot amend any commands to the lists that aren't there. I think you will find that, in practice, Paul's teachings are actually just Jesus' teaching about being a servant of others applied specifically to wives *vis-à-vis* their husbands and vice versa.

---

8. Peppiatt, *Women and Worship*, 134.

Table 6.2—Paul and Peter's Commands and Prohibitions to Husbands and Wives

	Husbands	Wives
Ephesians 5:21–33	Love wives (3x)	Submit to husbands (2x) Respect husbands
Colossians 3:18–19	Love wives Do not be harsh with wives	Submit to husbands
1 Peter 3:1–7	Live with wives in understanding Honor wives	Submit to husbands Avoid elaborate dress Adorn inward beauty
1 Corinthians 7:3, 10–11	Give to wife sexual rights Do not deprive spouse sexually (except for a time of fasting) Do not divorce wife	Give to husband sexual rights Do not deprive spouse sexually (except for a time of fasting) Do not leave husband

Contrary to popular commentary on this passage, Paul does *not* depart here from the theological center of Jesus' example to set up a paradigm for the Christian home. Hierarchicalists tend to posit modern feminism as the force behind the mutual submission interpretation of 5:21. One claims, for example, that "people didn't see mutual submission in Ephesians 5:21 until feminist pressures in our culture led people to look for a way to avoid the force of Ephesians 5:22."[9] That claim is debatable, to put it liberally. But does it really matter whether or not theologians of the past recognized the biblical call to mutual submission or not? It is important to respect and listen to theologians of the past. But they shouldn't have the final word. As is often pointed out, the institution of slavery was defended (and is still defended by some) based on Ephesians 6:5–9. Truly, that myriad white American Christian theologians and pastors used the Bible to defend their enslavement of Black people is an indelible blot on Christian history.

But, Paul never endorsed slavery as an institution. Rather, he instructed Christian slaves and masters about how to show the character

---

9. Grudem, *Biblical Foundations*, 225. Oddly enough, George W. Knight, a bastion of complementarianism, contradicts Grudem on this in a book which Grudem himself co-edited (see Knight, "Husbands and Wives," 217).

of Jesus *within the broken institutions of their context.* Similarly, Paul instructs wives to submit, as the convention (and the law) expected, to their husbands. But above, beyond, and sovereign over submission within these man-made institutions is the mighty reign of Christ, a reign whose power is meted out through self-sacrificial, self-subordinating love. This is the same submission to "one another" that shows the "fear of Christ" (5:21). Craig Keener summarizes this point masterfully,

> It is clear that the submission of verse 22 ["wives, *be subject . . .*"] cannot be other than the submission of verse 21 from the simple fact that the word "submitting" does not even appear in the Greek text of verse 22: is has to be borrowed from verse 21. It is perfectly legitimate to read verse 22, "Wives, submitting to your husbands," as long as we understand that we must take verse 22 as an *example* of verse 21's mutual submission. Indeed, one commentator points out that verse 22 might be translated, "for example, wives to your husbands," and this is no doubt its force. *Wives should submit to their husbands because Christians should submit to one another.*[10]

Paul's careful application of the gospel to wives does not justify Christian husbands' seeing themselves as their wives' authorities.

If this sounds like feminism, so be it! Whether or not this teaching fits within this or that modern social movement is not the point. The point is, calling men to take a place of leadership over their wives is adding to the Bible. Instead of doing that, let's simply stop where Paul stops. Paul is speaking into a culture different from ours, for sure. But, if we can avoid corrupting his words by adding our own commands, the Spirit can instruct us today just as the Spirit instructed Paul's original readers. We might come to Ephesians asking, "So, who's in charge in a marriage?" But the first readers already knew who was in charge—the laws of their day made that crystal clear. They knew who could give commands, and who couldn't. *Their* question was, "Now that I know that all earthly authorities have been subjected to King Jesus, how should I live within my context in light of that reality?" They had the better question. We should be asking the same.

Now, let's see if Peter agrees with Paul.

---

10. Keener, *Paul, Women & Wives,* 169 (emphasis added).

1 Peter 3:1–7: Participating in the Suffering Christ[11]

In an argument against the call to mutual submission egalitarians see in Ephesians 5:21, one theologian comments on a possible reason Paul used "be subject to" instead of the stronger word, "obey" in Ephesians 5:22 (though, as noted above, the word translated "be subject to" does not occur in verse 22). He writes,

> For a wife to be submissive to her husband will probably not often involve obeying actual commands or directives (though it will sometimes include this), for a husband may rather give requests and seek advice and discussion about the course of action to be followed (compare Phlm. 8–9). This is probably why Paul used the broader term "be subject to" when speaking to wives, rather than the specific word "obey" (*hypakouō*), which he used for children (6:1) and for servants (6:5).[12]

No doubt, this reasoning is meant to temper the authoritative power given husbands in a hierarchicalist scheme of marriage. I can understand why this scholar would want to do this. However, 1 Peter 3:6 presents Sarah as a model for Christian women, specifically insofar as she "obeyed" Abraham and called him "lord." Is Peter telling Christian husbands to see themselves as lords of their wives, and to expect obedience from them?

Peter's letter is to Christians who have been scattered by persecution. They exist as "aliens" in the world (1:1). His exhortation in 2:11 seems to be a reference to the exile of the Israelites from the promised land, which they had been experiencing in various forms for over seven centuries. Peter is inviting gentile Christians (see 2:9–10) to identify themselves with Israel as the chosen people of God—not only the chosen people as they experience God's salvation, as in the Exodus story, but also as they suffer under the oppression of foreign, imperial powers in the Exile. Peter encourages them that their present suffering is not in vain, but that they stand in the legacy of the prophets (1:10) who predicted the sufferings of Christ in which they were partaking (1:11). Not only were they to think of themselves as aliens due to their having been forced out of their ancestral lands, but due also to their sanctification in Christ. They were to be set apart for a purpose (1:13–15) in light of the priceless cost of their salvation (1:17–21). Because they received such a salvation, God promised that they would persevere to the end (1:22–25).

11. For a summary of this explanation of 1 Pet 3:1–7, see Table 6.3 in the appendix.

12. Grudem, "Myth of Mutual Submission," 1.

In 2:1–10, Peter tells these Christians to continually "grow up in your salvation" (2:2). The marvel is that, though they were once "not a people," they have now been made "the people of God" (2:10). This is some of the greatest theology in the Christian faith. Like Paul, Peter was a man of action; he always applies the theology he expounds to practical life. "Beloved," he writes, "I urge you as aliens and exiles to abstain from the desires of the flesh which wage war against the soul" (2:11 NRSV). Peter is calling for a people who are distinct, separate from the world in which they live—not geographically, but in their thinking and living. Doubtless, Jesus' teaching in the Sermon on the Mount (Matt 5–7) was not far from Peter's mind as he wrote this letter. God's people should be noticeably different from the world in which they live. They are strangers in it until heaven and earth, now broken away from each other by sin, finally come back together again. But Peter also wants to encourage his readers because he knows they are enduring great suffering. In order to do this, he always points to the example of Jesus. As he suffered, so Christians are called to suffer as well.

All Christian behavior for which Peter advocates in his epistles is for a purpose: to bear testimony to Christ before the world. Peter writes, "Conduct yourselves honorably among the gentiles, so that, though they malign you as evildoers, they may see your honorable deeds and glorify God when he comes to judge" (2:12 NRSV). Perhaps the most counterintuitive characteristic of Christian testimony that Peter encourages is submission. Peter says that to submit—even to the point of suffering abuse from others—is an act of sharing in the sufferings of Christ. He writes in 1:13–15,

> Submit yourselves for the Lord's sake to every human authority: whether to the emperor, as the supreme authority, or to governors, who are sent by him to punish those who do wrong and to commend those who do right. For it is God's will that by doing good you should silence the ignorant talk of foolish people.

This instruction is not an arbitrary expression of piety. The purpose, as Peter introduces it in 2:12, is so that watching gentiles (here the word signifies non-Christians, particularly non-Christians who actively oppose the faith) will glorify God for having seen Christ's presence embodied humbly in God's elect people. "By doing right" in this way, they would "silence the ignorant talk of foolish people" (2:15).

Similarly to Paul's pattern in Ephesians, Peter turns next to specific applications of this general instruction. His first specific instruction is to slaves. "Slaves, in reverent fear of God submit yourselves to your masters, not only to those who are good and considerate, but also to those who are harsh" (2:18). Notice that Peter is *not* providing a masterplan for the ideal society. Far from it! Peter openly acknowledges the abuse and oppression that many of his readers suffer. He even compares these Christians' suffering with what Christ endured on the cross. Instead, Peter is encouraging people living *within unjust power systems* about how to live as followers of their crucified and risen Servant-King, Jesus. He writes, "For it is commendable if someone bears up under unjust suffering because they are conscious of God" (2:19). Patient endurance in the face of unjust suffering is an evidence of, or testimony to, God's grace. Why? "To this you were called, because Christ suffered for you, leaving you an example, that you should follow in his steps" (2:21). Peter's message is this: *Christ suffered unjustly for your salvation. Therefore, you should bear up under unjust suffering for the salvation of your oppressors—because you participate in the redemptive suffering and new life of Christ as his elect people.* If this message is hard to accept, it is not because it is unclear. The message is crystal clear. It is its clarity that makes it difficult to embrace.

Then we come to chapter 3. There, Peter applies this same theology to a second specific group: wives. Verse 1 begins with, "in the same way." This, of course, refers to what Peter said to slaves in the previous chapter. Just as slaves were to bear up under unjust suffering in light of Jesus' example, so wives are to do the same. This immediately clues the modern reader into the addressees' identity in this verse. At least some, and perhaps many, of the wives Peter has in mind are suffering *unjustly* under the rule of their husbands. These husbands are not, as Peter says, just the good and gentle to whom it is easy to submit, but even those who "are disobedient to the word" (3:1). Why should wives submit and even obey husbands like this? For the same reason that slaves were to submit to unjust masters—that "they [husbands] may be won without words by the behavior of their wives, when they see the purity and reverence of your lives" (3:1–2; see also 1 Cor 7:15). For Peter, the purpose of submission is to bear public testimony to the suffering of Christ, with the hope of winning the disobedient to faith in him. That is Peter's message as it applies to wives and it agrees seamlessly with the theme of his letter as a whole. Again, the message is clear. It is not hard to understand what Peter is asking these women to do, though it may be hard to accept it.

Notice again that Peter is not laying out a set of guidelines for what a Christian household should look like. Instead, he is addressing women who are trying to follow Jesus in households ruled by non-Christian husbands—husbands that are *not* submitting to the lordship of Christ within a system of rulership that has yet to be transformed by the Spirit of Jesus.

Because this passage has been used so often in recent times to bind women to physically, emotionally, and spiritually abusive men, it is crucial that we emphasize what Peter is not teaching. Peter is not teaching that women should allow themselves to be abused, even when they have recourse to escape. This is one of those cases in which ignorance about the historical context of a biblical text can have devastating consequences. Peter was speaking into a culture in which the status of most women was often little better, and sometimes worse, than that of slaves. Granted, the experience of many slaves in the Greco-Roman culture of the time was considerably better than it was for slaves in European colonies in more recent history. Nevertheless, when compared to their counterparts in most Westernized societies today, free adult males wielded a stunning amount of legally protected power over members of their households in the first-century Mediterranean world, including their wives. Why is this so important for our goal of understanding Peter's message? It is important because, like the Christian slaves he addresses in the same letter, Peter is writing to women who are suffering in *circumstances from which they quite literally had no escape.*

In a conversation about this book, my friend Marisa used the word "persecution" instead of "abuse" to describe Peter's perspective on these Christian wives. That seems accurate. Peter is telling these women that, through their suffering, they are participating in Christ's passion. Not only does this have the effect of comforting these women in their pain, it also increases the gravity of their abusers' crime. Just as the earthly powers who crucified Jesus, moving as they were in collusion with their demonic spiritual cohorts, were setting themselves up against a holy and all-good God, so those who use their authority within an earthly society to take advantage of, or mistreat, people under them are doing the same. Abuse of any vulnerable person is tantamount to participating in the crucifixion of God incarnate—Peter is implying nothing less than this in this passage.

If I may take on a pastoral tone for a moment, if a Christian woman—or man, for that matter—is experiencing abuse from someone, including a marriage partner, it is important that she or he seek refuge as soon as possible. In many parts of the world, Christians are persecuted for their faith. They are imprisoned, tortured, and sometimes killed. However, these Christians do not intentionally seek out persecution. Rather, they bear up under suffering, a suffering that they cannot escape without denying Christ. This is the situation Peter was addressing in his letter. Christian women whose husbands are abusive should not simply tolerate such abuse, and they should *certainly not do so* because of a commitment to some extrabiblical gender-role ideology. Allowing an abuser to continue hurting others without confrontation is dangerous for the abuser's own soul. We need to remember that those who persecute or abuse others are not only harming the victims but themselves as well. God wants to redeem and transform their lives too. Further, pastors, friends, and others should do everything they can to help the abused and persecuted find refuge and healing. The teaching of 1 Peter is not opposed to this—not in the least! Many women and men reading this book live in societies in which avenues of escape from persecution and abuse exist. If there is a way to escape abuse, that way should be taken. This is the best way to stop the abuse from continuing unchecked. Notice Peter's concern not only for the salvation of the abused, but also the abuser. Seeking refuge from an abuser is a way of confronting the abuser, not to seek his harm but to show him his need for deliverance.

Peter does not leave out the Christian husbands in his audience. In 3:7 he again says, "in the same way," and proceeds to address them. Peter tells these husbands, "[B]e considerate as you live with your wives" (3:7). While this would have been a respectable instruction according to moralists of Peter's day, what follows would have been countercultural. He adds, "showing honor to the woman as the weaker vessel, since they are heirs with you of the grace of life, so that your prayers may not be hindered" (ESV).

Too often, Peter's comment about wives' being the "weaker" vessel is understood as a pronouncement on women's constitution as human beings. That is, many of us have mistakenly read Peter as saying that women are less intelligent, more weak-willed, or simply physically weaker than men. Of course, a majority of men can build more muscle than a majority of women. But, in its context, this does not seem to be what Peter is talking about. As Stackhouse observes,

> [I]t is not clear that Peter is asserting something universal about
> women, something essential about them, as if all women every-
> where and always are "weaker" than all men. Indeed, that seems

to be obvious nonsense, so let us look for an alternative interpretation! What is not nonsensical, sadly, is that in a patriarchal
society, Peter is telling the simple truth: economically, politi-
cally, legally, educationally—when it comes to most dimensions
of social power, women are weaker than men.[13]

Instead of telling them to step into a place of headship or exercise
authority over their wives, Peter emphasizes husbands' equal status
with their wives before God as "fellow heirs" of grace. In view of *that*
truth, Christian husbands ought to dwell with their wives. Given the legal and social reality into which he was writing, Peter would have been
hard-pressed to emphasize male-female equality more clearly to these
husbands. Peter does not go so far as to tell husbands to submit to their
wives. But, we have to remember that, according to Roman law, husbands
were their wives' legal masters. Peter is addressing people who live in a
culture that has yet to be transformed by the gospel. Peter takes a bottom-
up approach. Christian husbands should behave toward their wives in ac-
cordance with Jesus' example as a suffering servant, *not* according to their
status as legal authorities over them. Once again, the text says nothing
about an intrinsic leader-follower or master-servant relationship between
husband and wife. To a couple in a Christian marriage, in which both
spouses follow Jesus, Peter only has one thing to offer: Christ's example.
He says, *Be like Jesus to one another. Serve one another. Dwell with one
another as fellow-heirs of God's grace.* That's it. Peter has nothing to say
about working through a static hierarchical structure in the household.

If my readers are following along with their Bibles open, they have
no doubt been waiting for me to get around to explaining verses 5 and 6,
which say,

> For this is the way the holy women of the past who put their
> hope in God used to adorn themselves. They submitted them-
> selves to their own husbands, like Sarah, who obeyed Abraham
> and called him lord. You are her daughters if you do what is
> right and do not give way to fear.

Here we encounter one of those texts whose meaning is far more
obscure to modern readers than it must have been for its original readers.
The issue is not the meanings of the words. That much is straightforward
enough. Instead, the issue regards how Peter is using the Hebrew Scriptures. Here is the problem:

13. Stackhouse, *Partners in Christ*, 77.

Peter says that Sarah (1) obeyed Abraham while (2) calling him "lord." But in all of Genesis, Sarah only once refers to Abraham as "lord" and, in that instance, she is *not* obeying him! Furthermore, she is arguably in rebellion against God in that particular situation. The passage is Genesis 18:12. It reads, "So Sarah laughed to herself as she thought, 'After I am worn out and, my *lord* [Abraham] is old, will I have this pleasure?'" Furthermore, there are very few, if any, examples in Genesis in which Sarah is encountered obeying her husband. The exception—and that is what it would be—is when she obeys Abraham and lies about her being Abraham's wife to the pharaoh in Egypt (Gen 12:11–13; see also 20:2). In other words, the only time we encounter Sarah obeying Abraham is when she is conspiring with him in a lie, thereby putting herself in grave danger. In fact, it is likely that Sarah actually became a part of Pharaoh's harem in that story, which means she may have had sexual intercourse with him. In any case, after all that Peter has to say in his letters about the importance of Christian holiness, it is simply unfathomable that Peter would be encouraging women to obey their husbands in *exactly* the same way we find Sarah obeying Abraham in Genesis.

Hierarchicalists and egalitarians alike struggle to understand why Peter mentions Sarah at this point. And, while I am aware that this may disappoint my readers, I confess that I am not quite sure about what to do with these two verses. This is one of those instances, therefore, in which I will play my comparison card. That is, while I cannot say that I have personally landed on the single *best* interpretation, I *can* say that the hierarchicalist approach is inferior to alternative approaches. After all, the goal of this book is not to provide final, authoritative interpretations of these texts, but to show that biblical egalitarian approaches to interpreting them are the more plausible and promising. Biblical egalitarian interpretations, I am arguing, flow with the grain of the text, in agreement with the themes of the gospel, and make more sense of the relevant Scripture passages within their surrounding contexts. If this makes it seem like I am being evasive, I apologize. This is the best I can do.

Let's begin by looking at how hierarchicalists typically read these two verses. According to their view, Peter is asking Christian women to follow Sarah's *biblical* example of submission. But as we noted, there is almost no biblical record of Sarah submitting to Abraham at all, let alone in a Christlike way. At best, Peter's audience would have been confused—as are many who take this view today; at worst, Peter does not seem to know his Bible—a view that is tantamount to giving up, and which neither side of this debate would be eager to entertain. I'm not ready to give up yet, and I'm guessing my forbearing readers aren't either. Let's keep the question open.

So, if Peter is not referring to how the Bible portrays Sarah, the alternative is to see if there is any *extrabiblical* literature that would have been known to Peter's audience that does, in fact, portray Sarah as an ideal, obedient wife. It just so happens that such literature *did* exist in Peter's day. New Testament scholar Peter H. Davids cites some of this literature in a chapter on this passage. It is worth quoting him at length here:

> But we do find Sarah frequently using *kyrios* ["lord"] when referring to, or addressing, Abraham in extracanonical Jewish works such as the *Testament of Abraham* (roughly contemporary with I Peter). In this work especially, *kyrios* is used by Sarah to address Abraham (usually "my *kyrios* Abraham"), although only in casual or solemn discourse, not in contexts of "obedience." This reinterpretation of Genesis accords with other Hellenistic Jewish literature from this period. For instance, Philo "indicates Sarah's obedience to Abraham (or vice versa) was a matter of some discussion among biblical commentators in the first century." Philo looks on instances where men listened to their wives as bringing a curse, using Genesis 3:7 as his prototype. Josephus argues in one place, "A women is inferior to her husband in all things. Let her, therefore, be obedient to him; not so that he should abuse her, but that she may acknowledge her duty to her husband; for God has given the authority to the husband." Influenced by this culture, these authors developed creative ways of dealing with texts in which women (Sarah in particular) gave instructions that their husbands heeded. They might allegorize the woman so that the man would be heeding virtue rather than a woman, or minimize the woman's (Sarah's) role together, or alter the passage by inserting elements on which the text is silent.[14]

It seems that Peter was speaking into a culture that, for whatever reason, viewed Sarah as a model wife—one who respected and obeyed her husband. There is no doubt that the sources Davids cites in the above quotation would be labeled misogynistic by just about anyone reading this book. I would agree. But this only serves to drive home the point that Peter is making. He is asking his readers to follow the example of Christ *even in a culture that is thoroughly un-Christlike.*

---

14. Davids, "Silent Witness," 232.

To be honest, because I am aware of how often this passage has been used in Christian churches to permit or even enable abusive husbands to continue hurting their wives, I cannot help but be disquieted by it. It is even uncomfortable to talk about this text—which may be one of the reasons why so much of the debate about this issue focuses on Paul instead of Peter's Epistles. But even in admitting that, I once again want to point out that Peter in no way even hints that Christian men should demand obedience of their wives, much less lift a finger or level a harsh word against them. He doesn't even hint that Christian men should think of themselves as their wives' authorities, which is probably the most important observation to be made for our present discussion. Peter could have easily pointed Christian men to Abraham as *their* example of an ideal husband. He could have said, "Husbands, be like Abraham, who was a leader to his wife." But he didn't. The only person that Peter holds up to husbands as a model for their behavior—as a person whose example is worthy of following—is Jesus himself.

Conclusion

In my opinion, the debate that is raging about the role of women in ministry and marriage actually has more radical implications for men than it does for women. If women truly begin to carry an equal status to men in the church and the home, the ones who will have to do the most changing will almost certainly be the men. Not only would women take roles that were previously reserved only for men, but men would also have to shift their spheres of responsibility. Perhaps no area would be more universally affected than the home lives of married men, especially those who are parents. Seeing marriage as a partnership of equals leads inevitably to the conclusion that the task of child-rearing and homemaking, in all its aspects, is for both parents equally—from diaper-changing and onward. (That might be enough for some readers to toss this book out right now!) If we men are persuaded that we should pursue the equality of women in every sphere of life, there *will* be growing pains along the way. I trust that I have not been guilty of giving my good readers the false impression that a belief in the equality of the sexes will always make life easier. The truth is, such a belief and the choices that follow from it will often introduce difficult challenges that can make the simplicity of gender-based, male authority attractive. Nevertheless, I am persuaded that it is worth the pain. If we as Christian men simply read what Peter and Paul say directly to Christian men—just the words on the page—and follow those words without adding anything else, we are going to find ourselves becoming more and more like Jesus, our Servant-King. In the end, that isn't a sacrifice; that's eternal gain! It will be hard at first and will look strange to outsiders. But by God's grace and through the power of the Spirit, we will experience a deeper knowledge of God's reign both in our churches and in our homes. The effects will ripple out into the world as well, if we let it happen.

7

Authority over Her Own Head

(1 Corinthians 11:2–16, part 1)

To SAY THAT 1 Corinthians 11:2–16 is difficult to interpret is an understatement. This passage has stumped interpreters for centuries and is definitely the most difficult passage that we will discuss in this book. Nothing like a consensus has emerged about what it means. Among the questions to which this passage gives rise are:

- Does Paul teach that women are not made in God's image?
- Does Paul condone the forced head-shaving of women who refuse to cover their hair?
- What do angels have to do with covering women's hair?
- Why does Paul say that long hair on men is unnatural?
- Why is it disgraceful for a woman to uncover her head while praying or prophesying?
- Why is it disgraceful for a man to cover his head while praying or prophesying?

For our purposes in this book, two additional questions are paramount. First, Did Paul encourage the women in the church at Corinth to wear head coverings as a symbol of male authority? Of course, if the answer to this question is yes, it would undermine most of the arguments I've presented in this book. If the answer is no, we will want to know what head coverings *did* mean. The second question we must address has to do with the use of the head as a metaphor in this passage. We have already discussed this metaphor when we studied Ephesians 5. But this passage gives us occasion to return to it. Our question again will be: Does Paul's use of the head as a metaphor for man's relationship to woman imply man's authority over her? Again, if the answer is yes, we will have grounds to doubt the conclusions that we have reached up to this point. If the answer is no, we will want to discover how Paul is using this beautifully multivalent metaphor in this passage. While we may have occasion to touch on others, these are the two questions that we *must* answer if we are to decide whether or not this passage teaches a hierarchical relationship between men and women. We will discuss the importance of head coverings in this chapter, and we will save our discussion of the head metaphor for the next.

Do Head Coverings Symbolize Male Authority?

Head coverings on women have been a part of my environment for most of my life, whether I have lived in Christian-majority or Muslim-majority communities. As I described in chapter 1, I attended a Plymouth Brethren church throughout my childhood and youth. The women in most Plymouth Brethren churches believe the Bible commands them to cover their heads, so they do so. However, they only wear their head coverings during church services. Outside of service times, they wear whatever they want on their heads, or just go bareheaded. About four years ago as I write this, I moved with my family to Istanbul where we live in a neighborhood populated by mostly conservative Muslims. Many of our female Muslim neighbors and friends in Istanbul also cover their heads. In a book like this, we cannot thoroughly discuss all the things that head coverings can mean in various contexts. However, there is one key distinction I've noticed between how my childhood church and my Muslim neighbors practice female head covering. The difference is about hair and symbolism.

The fact is, Muslim women who cover their heads (not all Muslim women do this) do so in order to cover their hair. There is undoubtedly a sense in which a Muslim woman's headscarf is a symbol of her devotion to God. However, to say it that way skips an important part of what she is doing. A Muslim woman covers her head because her hair is for her husband's (or future husband's) eyes only. Thus, she wears the covering out of a sense of pious decency and modesty. The headscarf in and of itself means nothing if not as a sign of her exclusive fidelity to her husband. This, in turn, shows her devotion to God, for fidelity in marriage is extremely important for pious Muslim women.

Women in Plymouth Brethren churches, on the other hand, are not worried at all about whether or not their head coverings actually cover their hair, and they are not worried about whether or not the men around them see their hair either. In fact, their head coverings are usually made of lace fabric. Sometimes, they consist of a small circle of lace just large enough to cover the tops of their heads—about the size of a yarmulke, the small, round head cap that many religious Jewish men wear.

As a young person growing up around this custom, I always wondered why Christians in other churches ignored the Bible's clear command regarding head coverings. However, I don't remember ever asking whether or not it mattered that the women in our church weren't *really* covering their heads. This was because I was taught that head coverings, in and of themselves, don't serve any practical purpose—like the purpose of actually covering something. Rather, they were merely a symbol of male authority. That was all. They were just a symbol. Was my church right? Were the head coverings discussed in 1 Corinthians 11 just symbols?

To answer this question, we will move down to verse 10, where the word "symbol" appears in some English translations. It turns out that my church and I had overlooked a crucial detail—or nondetail—in our reading of 1 Corinthians 11 (one that I'm sad to say I never saw despite the scores of times the elders and preachers in our church taught us about head coverings from 1 Corinthians 11). The problem is that the word "symbol" does not appear in 1 Corinthians 11:10, or in the chapter at all. It's just not there. Yes, it's in some translations of the Bible, and it's certainly in many commentaries about the passage. But it's not in the original Greek text.

Translating the Bible is no easy task and, try as they may to avoid it, translators always leave the mark of their own interpretations on the translations they produce. The way 1 Corinthians 11:10 has been translated in some modern English translations is a case in point. For example, compare how the English Standard Version and the New International Version, two widely used and (generally) dependable, modern English versions, translate this passage:

> That is why a wife ought to have a symbol of authority on her
> head, because of the angels. (ESV)

> It is for this reason that a woman ought to have authority over her own head, because of the angels. (NIV)

Note that the word "symbol" is absent in the NIV and the word "own" is absent in the ESV. Also, the ESV has "wife" where the NIV has "woman." Now, take a look at how two other popular English translations, the King James Version (KJV) and the New American Standard Bible (NASB), translate this verse:

> For this cause ought the woman to have power on her head because of the angels. (KJV)

> Therefore the woman ought to have *a symbol of* authority on her head, because of the angels. (NASB)

Notice that the NASB italicizes the words, "a symbol of." This is because this meticulously mechanical translation of the Bible italicizes words that are absent from the Greek text, but which the translators found necessary to add for the sake of clarifying the text's meaning. The NASB translators were trying their best to produce as literal a translation as possible, and wherever they added words they tried to make this clear to the readers by italicizing them. In this case, the KJV doesn't add anything at all. The KJV is the truest of all four of the translations quoted above to what the Greek text actually says.

Here is what has happened. The translators of the ESV and the NASB seem to have interpreted the word "authority" in this verse as belonging to someone *other than* the woman. By translating the Greek word *gynē* as "wife" instead of "woman" (both of these are legitimate translations), the ESV translators seem to be understanding the text as saying that a woman's head covering is a symbol of *her husband's authority.* If we were to read the ESV without comparing it to other translations, we would likely conclude that this passage is specifically for married women and that it does not apply to single women. The NASB translators seem to take a similar approach, but they italicize the word "symbol" to ensure that readers of the English translation know that they have added a word that isn't present in the Greek text.

The NIV translators, on the other hand, add the word "own" to the English translation. This implies that they interpret "authority" here to be *the woman's own* authority. There is no symbol involved. Instead, the verse says that a woman ought to have authority *itself* over her head. The authority is not someone else's, but "her own." The NIV translators add "own" to be sure readers understand this is what the verse means.

Which is the best translation? I personally prefer the KJV in this case because I like a translation that leaves as much of the interpreting up to its readers as possible (without, of course, compromising the use of good English grammar). But, if I had to choose between just the ESV and the NIV's take on this verse, I'd go with the NIV's. This is because it makes much more sense of Paul's preceding argument, as we will soon see. In the meantime, we should restate two facts about verse 10. First, the word "symbol" does not appear in this verse; the word is not there, and there is no good reason to add it. Second, and most importantly, the authority mentioned in this verse undeniably belongs to the women about whom Paul is speaking, *not their husbands*.

We can support this second claim by looking at other places in the New Testament where the phrase "have authority" appears. These two words in Greek are *echō* ("to have") and *exousia* ("authority"). There is nothing difficult to understand about these words for us English speakers. When we say in English that a person has authority, we mean that the authority belongs to her. We might say, for example, "The president has authority to veto bills." New Testament Greek uses "has authority" in the same way. The meaning of *exousia* is a little broader than just "authority," however. It can also mean "control" or "right." In English, we speak of the right to do this or that, like the right to vote, for example. But, we could replace the word "right" with "authority" and communicate the same idea. The same is true with the word *exousia* in Greek. The point we are making right now is that literally every time the New Testament uses the word "have" (*echō*) with "authority" (*exousia*) as its object, one can tell clearly by the context that the authority being spoken of belongs to the person who has it, *not* someone else. To put it another way, when person A has authority over this or that, that authority always belongs to person A, not person B, C, etc. There are at least twenty-four places in the New Testament where the phrase "has authority" is used,[1] so I will just reference its occurrences in Paul's writings as examples. I've italicized the words that translate *echō* and *exousia*:

---

1. Matt 7:29; 9:6; Mark 1:22; 2:10; 3:15; Luke 5:24; 12:5; 19:17; John 10:18; 19:10–11; Acts 9:14; Rom 9:21; 1 Cor 7:37; 9:4, 5, 6; 11:10; 2 Thess 3:9; Heb 13:10; Rev 9:3; 11:6; 14:18; 16:9; 17:13; 18:1; 20:6.

> Does not the potter *have the right* to make out of the same lump of clay some pottery for special purposes and some for common use? (Rom 9:21)

> But the man who has settled the matter in his own mind, who is under no compulsion but *has control* over his own will, and who has made up his mind not to marry the virgin—this man also does right. (1 Cor 7:37)

> Don't we *have the right* to food and drink? Don't we *have the right* to take a believing wife along with us, as do the other apostles and the Lord's brothers and Cephas? Or is it only I and Barnabas who [do not *have*] *the right* to not work for a living? (1 Cor 9:4–6)

> We do this, not because we do not *have the right* to such help, but in order to offer ourselves as a model for you to imitate. (2 Thess 3:9)

These cross-references show that the most natural reading of 1 Corinthians 11:10 is this: "Because of this a woman ought to have authority over [her] head." The authority is *hers*, Paul is saying. It is not her husband's or someone else's. It seems to me the word *exousia* in this verse should be translated "right" instead of "authority." After all, this is how it is translated in 1 Corinthians 9:4–6. Why not use the same translation in 11:10 as well? The idea is that, according to Paul, a woman has the right to decide what to wear on her head.

My more careful readers might still wonder, "Okay, so the word 'symbol' isn't there, and the phrase 'has authority' normally refers to the person's own authority. But by saying that a woman should have 'authority *on* her head,' couldn't Paul be implying that head coverings are a symbol of her husband's authority?" This is a good question. What if we did another survey of the New Testament, but added the word "on" (*epi*) to the mix? Would we still find that authority (*exousia*) always belongs to the person who has it? Just so we don't get confused, we should mention that the word *epi* can be translated "on" or "over." But in Greek it's the same word. Here are all the places in the New Testament that speak of someone's having authority "on/over" (*epi*) some other thing or person, with emphasis added:

> But I want you to know that the Son of Man *has authority on* earth to forgive sins. (Mark 2:10 and Luke 5:24)

... and they *have power over* the waters to turn them into blood and to strike the earth with every kind of plague. (Rev 11:6)

Still another angel, who *had charge of* the fire, came from the altar and called in a loud voice. (Rev 14:18)

They were seared by the intense heat and they cursed the name of God, who *had control over* these plagues, but they refused to repent and glorify him. (Rev 16:9)

... The second death *has* no *power over* them, but they will be priests of God and of Christ and will reign with him. (Rev 20:6)

One can clearly see that whenever a person "has authority over/on" something or someone, the authority, again, belongs to the person who has it. In 1 Corinthians 11:10, *Paul means exactly what he says*: women should have authority over their own heads.

Understanding that verse 10 does not mention a symbol of male authority helps us narrow down the interpretive possibilities of 1 Corinthians 11:2–16 as a whole. Even before we delve into the overall argument of the passage, it is possible to see what it is *not* saying. Whatever Paul *is* saying in this passage, it *cannot be* that women are supposed to wear a symbol of male authority on themselves. Whatever head coverings meant to the Corinthians, the clear meaning of verse 10 is that women should be the ones who decide what is best for them to wear or not wear over their heads. We will expand on the significance of this later. For now, suffice it to say that we have answered our first question. First Corinthians 11:10 does not teach that head coverings are a symbol of male authority. In fact, the only people who are explicitly said to have authority over anything or anyone in this text are the women.

Having established that head coverings are not a symbol of male authority in 1 Corinthians 11:10, we have now to ask what they *do* mean. What is Paul saying in this passage to the men and women of Corinth, and what is the relevance of what he says for Christians today? A satisfying answer will require a careful look at the arguments of the whole passage. As I did in our discussions of 1 Corinthians 14:34–35 and 1 Timothy 2:8–15, I will provide more than one plausible explanation of what this passage means for the male-female relationship in the Christian life. While these two explanations do not contradict one another on every point, they cannot both be correct in their entirety. There is one crucial claim that they have in common, however, which we should be aware of right at the start. Most interpreters of 1 Corinthians come to

11:2–16 assuming that Paul was addressing a problem that the women were causing. "If the issue is head coverings and women were the ones who were expected to wear them," we suppose, "it must have been the women who were at the root of the problem Paul was trying to address." This is how I viewed this passage my whole Bible-reading life, until very recently. Now, I think my assumption was unfounded, and it confused my understanding of the passage. It is much more likely that Paul is defending the women of Corinth, and that his primary addressees are men.

Now, let's take a look at two possible readings of this text, both of which try to read with the flow of the passage, and examine it in light of its cultural context as much as possible given what scholars have been able to uncover.

Explanation A: Paul Is Defending Women Who Wanted to Cover Their Heads[2]

In her brilliant book, *Paul and Gender,* New Testament scholar Cynthia Long Westfall makes a surprising claim: she says it was the men, not the women, who were making a fuss about head coverings in the Corinthian church. If my readers are like me, they often assume that if anyone in the Corinthian church would have been supportive of Paul's telling the women to cover their heads, it would have been the men. Even though the passage doesn't say anything like that, we make that assumption because most of us are reading the Bible from a modern, postfeminist-movement, Westernized perspective. We assume before we read the passage that veils are a repressive instrument of male-dominated societies. We assume that, if given the chance, most, if not all, women would prefer to go bareheaded like most men do (at least when they're indoors). The reality, however, is that things are much more complicated than that.

Part of the basis for the assumption that the women were the problem behind this passage is the notion that head coverings were a symbol of male authority. We reason that, naturally, men would want to maintain that authority and, in turn, women would naturally want to resist it. But actually, head coverings were not primarily symbolic. They had a very real function—namely, to cover a woman's hair.

2. For a summary of "Explanation A" of 1 Cor 11:2–16, see Table 7.1 in the appendix.

In the West and in many Westernized areas of the world today we associate veiling with Islam. This, in my experience, has complicated the matter of reading 1 Corinthians 11 a great deal. We Westernized people largely think of the veil as a purely religious symbol donned for purely religious reasons (whatever that means).[3] Of course, any Muslim woman who veils *is* making a religious statement. There is no doubt about that. But the question remains: *What* statement is she making? To put it another way, what aspect of the values of Islam is she trying to uphold? In my experience as a Western person talking with my Westernized friends, I've noticed that we tend to assume Muslims understand the veil as basically a symbol of male authority. While the Qur'an does seem to teach that husbands have a degree of authority over their wives,[4] the veil doesn't just symbolize male authority *per se*. Instead, it has the more basic function of protecting a woman's decency. Cultures in which women veil maintain the practice because of a certain perspective on appropriate dress codes. If a woman wants to appear pious, respectable, and upstanding in front of other people in many cultures around the world, she must cover her hair in public.

Even in cultures that have been influenced by highly individualized, Western ways of thinking, we still have a general sense of what are the appropriate ways to dress in various contexts. I used to wear my hair and beard long down to my chest and shoulders. But that was when I was a painter and handyman. When I started working as a church youth director and a high school teacher, I felt the need to keep my hair cut and shave or trim my beard down in order to conform to the expectations those around me had of a person in my vocation. I'm still the same long-haired, bearded guy on the inside. But I feel the need, impressed on me by my society's expectations, to conform to a certain image associated with being a professional.

Other conventions that govern how we dress are modesty and decency. A person's dress is modest if it falls short of ostentation or the flaunting of wealth. It's probably more complex than that, but this is at least a minimal definition of what modesty is in relation to dress. Decency, on the other hand, relates to sexuality. A person who dresses

---

3. The idea that religion can be separated out from the rest of life is itself a modern idea that complicates discussions like this. See Cavanaugh, *Myth of Religious Violence*, 57–122.

4. See An-Nisa (chapter 4), verse 34. I should note that I am reading this verse in translation. I do not have a knowledge of Arabic.

indecently is somehow sending too strong a sexualized message through his or her dress. The standards for this vary radically from culture to culture and place to place. But decency standards exist in some fashion in every culture nonetheless. Usually, if not always, women face much more complex and demanding strictures when it comes to modesty and decency relative to men. This is where the veil comes in. In the time of Paul in the world surrounding the Mediterranean Sea, a woman's hair was (and still is in many places) considered sexually alluring. To be honest, it would be pretty hard to argue that a woman's hair is *not* considered sexually alluring in Westernized contexts as well—five minutes of TV commercials would probably supply enough material to prove the point. The difference between now and then—or here and there—is that in Westernized cultures a woman is not considered indecent or seductive simply for going out bareheaded, and therefore her bare head is not considered shameful. But this was not the case in Paul's day, nor is it the case in many contemporary cultures of the world.

We confuse ourselves when we read 1 Corinthians 11 with modern Islam as a filter because Islam did not invent veiling. Rather, Islam has simply preserved a very old cultural convention of decency by enshrining it in overtly religious teaching. To be accurate, we should note that Muslims disagree about how veiling should be applied. Many Muslim women do not cover their hair at all, noting that veiling is not actually mentioned in the Qur'an. My point is that, for most Muslim women who cover their hair, while veiling *is* a sign of religious devotion to Islam, the *reason* for this is because a woman's hair is simply not something to be displayed in public. A woman's exclusive sexual commitment to her husband is extremely important in Islam, and the veil is directly connected to that commitment.

The dynamics change a bit when Muslim women enter Westernized contexts in which bareheadedness is not considered indecent by the wider culture. In those contexts, the Muslim veil may take on a more exclusively symbolic function. Even though she knows that virtually no one around her will think she is acting inappropriately for letting her hair be seen, a devout Muslim woman might choose to veil to symbolize publicly her devotion to Islam and might do so without consciously considering it a necessity for decency. Nevertheless, *originally*, veiling was a matter of sexual decency and, precisely because of that, a religiously pious woman might naturally have wanted to veil herself when in public in cultures throughout the Mediterranean world in the time of Paul.

Standards of decency that relate to women's dress can be a symptom of male domination. When I was growing up in the early American homeschool movement, my family joined a large, internationally active homeschool organization that taught an exacting dress code of decency for women. Girls and women were expected to wear long, loose-fitting skirts basically all the time, including when they were outside playing soccer or basketball, or even when they were working outdoors. The concern that drove this idea was that, if a boy or man were to see the contours of a female body, this might arouse him sexually. Girls and women, as the argument went, should cover themselves liberally to avoid causing a brother in Christ to stumble. The result of this type of reasoning was repressive for women and girls. Every day when they awoke and chose what to wear for the day, they had to consider carefully what thoughts their garb choices would or would not produce in the minds of the men around them because, as they were told repeatedly, they bore some of the responsibility for those thoughts. Also, there are some activities that are simply impossible to do—or at least to do safely—while wearing a dress or skirt. For example, it is extremely difficult to enjoy a day at the beach, or even to go swimming at all, while conforming to those kinds of strict standards. I remember one day when my sister tried to ride a go-cart with a friend in her required ankle-length skirt. The skirt, which of course was hanging close to the ground as she sat in the cart's low-riding seat, got caught in the cart's front wheel and was immediately torn from her legs. Thankfully, my sister's skirt was loose enough that it was torn off rather than pulling her out of the cart, and she was not hurt (and she also had enough foresight to wear a pair of shorts underneath). But incidents like this illustrate how decency standards can present special burdens for women, even in a Westernized subculture like the one in which I was raised.

The topic of decency standards' effects on the welfare of women in society deserves sustained reflection and critique. For now, I just wanted to acknowledge that decency standards can and often do repress women, and the same could be said of the practice of veiling. When a society expects women to dress in certain ways and penalizes them through shaming or mistreatment—or by simply causing them inconvenience—when they do otherwise, this is a way of oppressing them. It would be better for women if they did not have to worry about how men think about their bodies. In a flipped but related way, women in Western and Westernized cultures who feel compelled to conform to particular norms of beauty—whether it has to do with makeup usage, body type, etc.—may also suffer a similar kind of oppression. Of course, men are also expected to follow certain, often unspoken rules of appearance as well, but these are usually less demanding (and a lot less expensive) than those expected of women. Most teenage girls' fathers do not require them to wear makeup when they go out. In fact, many discourage it. Yet, some societies somehow teach young girls that wearing makeup is expected of them. When a girl chooses to wear makeup, is she acting freely, or is she bowing to the expectations of others? And, when a father gives her the freedom to wear makeup if she wants to, is he colluding with a repressive culture or is he teaching his daughter to think autonomously? I don't have a satisfying answer to those questions, but I know that any thoughtful answer is going to be somewhat complicated.

When it came to veiling, the situation was even more complicated in first-century Corinth. Corinth was a port city known all over the Mediterranean for its sexual licentiousness. In order to clearly distance herself from the sexually promiscuous culture around her, one of the things a pious Corinthian woman might do would be to wear a veil. Such a woman's husband in Corinth may have cared little about his wife's veiling. But, due to the shame that she would feel and experience should she appear in public uncovered, she may have chosen to veil automatically, even without her husband's encouragement.

In addition to concerns about decency, Keener points out that the issue of modesty was also wrapped up in the question of head coverings.[5] While the use of head coverings was ubiquitous throughout the Mediterranean world, there was considerable variety in *how* and *when* women were expected to cover their heads. As 1 Timothy 2:9 and 1 Peter 3:3 make clear, women's hair was not kept from view all the time in the cultures in which the first Christian communities were planted. Some women may have preferred to cover their hair out of a sense of modesty. But at home, they may have displayed elaborate hairstyles. In that context, there was no problem. Still, some women may have preferred to cover their heads to avoid drawing attention to their hair while at the church gathering, especially if they were somehow involved in leading the congregation in worship. In a church that was struggling for unity across socioeconomic lines that would normally keep people separate from one another in social settings, head coverings may have served to reduce tension as well as

5. Keener, *Paul, Women & Wives*, 22.

distraction in worship. If so, the use of head coverings would have had an equalizing effect.

In many Christian denominations today, everyone who is involved in leading worship wears a robe. I used to think this was a way to show off pompous religiosity. But a pastor explained to me that robes serve to mitigate distractions. If everyone in the front of the church is wearing a robe or other nonindividualized garb, the worshippers won't have to worry about what anyone is wearing, and they can more easily focus on worshipping God instead.

Everyone who lives in a society must think about modesty and decency standards. My wife and I both dress differently while living in our religiously conservative neighborhood in Istanbul than we do when we are visiting family and friends in the United States, Canada, and Ecuador. We do this because we want to be accepted by our neighbors. We don't want to put people off, make our neighbors feel uncomfortable, or draw attention to ourselves. I say all this to drive home the point that, if Paul was trying to support women's veiling in Corinth, this does *not* mean that he was forcing them to do so. Even though we might (rightly) judge a society that pressures women to veil as repressive, we can at the same time understand why a woman might choose to veil of her own accord within such a society. When a person feels compelled to follow the conventions of decency in a given culture, one could say that she *is* being treated unfairly. However, perhaps paradoxically, a person who wants to give her as much autonomy as possible—say, her loving father or husband—would doubtless encourage her to wear whatever she deems appropriate for herself. He would say precisely what 1 Corinthians 11:10 says: "Let her have authority over her own head." In other words, for an adult woman, he would leave the decision up to her.

Veiling is not a simple matter. There are a plethora of styles *and* reasons behind the practice. As we have noted, veiling was a practice in West Asia long before the birth of Islam. Both Jewish and Roman women veiled, in various ways, as did men in certain contexts. Ancient Assyrian law even regulated the practice. Interestingly, while most women were required by law to veil in ancient Assyria, prostitutes and slave women were forbidden from doing so. Even though these laws are from a far earlier time than the New Testament, they provide a taste of how engrained the shame and disgrace associated with going bareheaded could become in a society in which veiling is practiced. Veiling is an ancient and enduring practice, and it still continues today, both with and without the encouragement of Islam. We have to remember that the Mediterranean world had been governed by massive empires for centuries before New Testament times. Empires have a tendency to move people around, scrambling and mixing up groups that had formerly been kept separate from each other. Cultural norms in the first century, especially in a port city like Corinth, were in constant flux as a result.

Suppose someone were to ask us, "What is the custom regarding head coverings in Toronto?" Any adequate response would be complicated to say the least! One would have to include Orthodox, Reformed and Conservative Jewish, Orthodox Christian (Russian, Coptic, Syrian, Greek, etc.), Roman Catholic, Sikh, Hindu, Islamic, Amish, and Mennonite customs, and also the Royal Canadian Mounted Police—and that would only be the start! If we would struggle to talk about the norms of head coverings in modern metropolitan centers like Toronto, New York, Istanbul, or London—places that we can go and visit today—we get an idea of how difficult it is for historians to reconstruct the head covering dynamics that were at work in a place like Corinth in the time of Paul! In fact, it is likely that Paul himself didn't understand all the relevant factors, which is probably part of the reason why he leaves it up to the women to decide what to do about it (smart guy, that Paul!).

I would be remiss if I failed to also mention a fact of which many in the United States are ignorant. Most of my fellow Americans know about regimes in Muslim-majority nations, such as Saudi Arabia and Iran, that have forced women to veil. But many of us are ignorant of the fact that many ostensibly secular governments in countries such as France, Turkey (in the past), China, and elsewhere have, at different times and to varying degrees, obliged women to go bareheaded in certain public spaces against their own will. Even the government in Quebec, Canada nearly passed a law that would have restricted certain women's freedom to cover their heads as they chose. Either way, as I am sure my good readers will agree, whether by enforcing veiling or by enforcing bareheadedness, the women affected by these laws are being repressed. They are not being given authority over their own heads. In stark contrast, Paul says that women should make the decision about what to wear on their heads for themselves. Someone might be surprised by how modern Paul's thinking is here. But this is no anomaly in Pauline thought. Paul believed in freedom in Christ, and this is just another example of how that belief works itself out in practice.

The question of head coverings, what they mean, how they relate to women's rights, and how they play a part in the politics of power and control even in modern societies is bewilderingly complex. We can safely assume that the situation was equally complex in the Mediterranean world of the first century. Appreciating how complicated the situation probably was in Corinth is crucial for understanding Paul's comments about head coverings in 1 Corinthians 11. The Corinthian church met in homes. Thus, the boundary between public and private life in the church was no doubt difficult to define. This is one of the possible reasons why the question of head coverings had come up in the Corinthian church.[6] Westernized people tend to assume that it was the women at Corinth who wanted to remove their head coverings. But in reading the text this way we are probably projecting a postfeminist-movement perspective back onto the text. We *assume* that women would have been more concerned about expressing their autonomy than they would have been about maintaining a pious and dignified appearance within their communities. But this is probably not what was happening. It is more likely that it was the *men* in the Corinthian church who were pressuring the women to remove their head coverings, but the women did not want to do this because they were concerned about appearing indecent and improper. The presence of the words "dishonor" (v. 5) and "disgraceful" (v. 6) used in this connection with bareheadedness may point to the idea that norms of decency are the impetus for what is said about head coverings in this passage. Paul is most likely defending women's right to cover their heads as they wished. "They should be able to do this," Paul says, "because they ought to have authority over their own heads to do as they see fit and proper." Notice that Paul isn't worried about women dressing this or that way because of the men's sexual impulses. All he mentions are the angels (I honestly do not know what that means). Again, a lot of this is my imaginative reconstruction of what the situation might have been. But this is all we can do.

What can be said with confidence is that Paul is *not* laying down a new, arbitrary law that would have been in any way special for the Christian churches of his day. Instead, he was merely encouraging the women to follow their culture's conventions of decency and modesty insofar as *they*, as Spirit-filled followers of Jesus, saw necessary, and was leaving the final decision about what that meant up to *them*. Implicit in this encouragement was a view of church gatherings as public rather than private

6. See Westfall, *Paul and Gender*, 31–34.

affairs. Women should behave in the house church gatherings, Paul says, as they would out in public. Paul is supporting these women in their desire to do this.

To support my claim that Paul wants to leave the decision about head coverings up to the women, I would point to verse 16. This verse is often neglected in discussions of this passage as a sort of afterthought. But it actually provides a crucial piece for our reconstruction of Paul's stance toward the whole head covering discussion. The word translated "practice" or "custom" in this verse must refer to the practice of wearing head coverings. It is the only thing that could be called a practice mentioned in the preceding verses. But notice how the word immediately before practice is translated in two popular English translations:

> If anyone wants to be contentious about this, we have no *other* practice—nor do the churches of God. (NIV, *emphasis added*)

> If anyone is inclined to be contentious, we have no *such* practice, nor do the churches of God. (ESV, *emphasis added*)

By the phrasing, "we have no *other* practice," the NIV seems to imply that all the other churches held to the practice of using head coverings. That is, the other churches had no *other* practice except that of veiling. But by the phrasing, "we have no *such* practice," the ESV implies the exact opposite! The ESV leads the reader to think that the other churches did *not* have any such practice as veiling. Which is correct?

This time, the ESV provides a much better translation than the NIV. The word translated "other" by the NIV and "such" by the ESV is *toioutos*. It means "such!" The standard New Testament Greek dictionary defines it as, "of such kind, such as this, like such."[7] Surprisingly, therefore, even after all that Paul has said about veiling, he ends by saying that this should not be a contentious issue in Corinth because this is *not* a universal practice of the churches of Christ. Paul seems to be saying, "Let the women have authority over their own heads—let them veil if they see fit. This is not an issue worth fighting over. Some of the other churches don't even have this custom." Not unlike his approach to the issue of meat offered to idols in the previous chapter, Paul emphasizes freedom, in Christ, to make choices about certain behaviors while at the same time maintaining the need to think about how a given behavior will affect the testimony of the church before the community.

---

7. BDAG, s.v. "τοιοῦτος."

If the interpretation we have just offered is correct, in verses 4 to 7 Paul is exaggerating to make a point. Because the issue behind head coverings is hair, Paul seems to be saying, "Look, the women need to either cover their hair or shave their heads. Which do you think is more reasonable? Of course, it's to cover their hair. So, stop causing a fuss about this! Let them wear their head coverings." Paul would be saying something similar in verses 13 to 15. There, he makes the comment that the woman is the glory of the man, but the woman's hair is her glory. This comment has baffled interpreters for years. (We will look at these verses closely in the next chapter). For the purposes of this book, however, these verses are illuminating because they show that the matter of head coverings really was about hair, and how and where hair should be exposed. In other words, there is no evidence that the issue was about whether or not women were submitting to male authority.

As I see it, the strength of what I have offered here as Explanation A is the way it takes into account the experiences of women today who live in cultures where veiling is practiced. Once we understand that veiling is directly related to decency and modesty in dress, many pieces of the puzzle fall into place. On the flip side, however, one can never be sure that interpreting an ancient text by drawing heavily from contemporary experiences is going to yield accurate results. That is the possible weakness of this explanation and might leave some of my readers wondering if there are plausible alternatives. Further, while this explanation does help account for several of the most important pieces of the puzzle that this chapter asks us to assemble, it leaves other pieces out. Some might wonder if there is an alternative explanation that also strives to read along the grain of the text. For such an alternative, we proceed to Explanation B, which I find to be the most compelling interpretation available.

Explanation B: In Christ, Veiling Is Not Necessary[8]

This explanation of what Paul says about head coverings is going to re-mind readers of our Explanation B of 1 Corinthians 14:34–35. This inter-pretation suggests that much of the argument in 1 Corinthians 11:2–16 is actually not Paul's own teaching. Rather, he is quoting or summarizing things that the Corinthians either have been saying or that they wrote

8. For a summary of "Explanation B" of 1 Cor 11:2–16, see Table 7.2 in the appendix.

about in their letter to Paul. After summarizing and repeating *their* thinking on the matter, Paul corrects them. If we recall from our discussion of 14:34–35, all interpreters agree that Paul does this sometimes in this letter. But it is difficult to know *when* he is doing it. For us reading the letter today, this blurs our vision; it makes Paul's argument *less* clear. But for the Corinthian Christians this would have had the opposite effect. By referring directly to their arguments and then addressing them, Paul would have signaled to the Corinthian Christians exactly what he was talking about. As modern readers, we should remember that while Paul's Epistles are written for our benefit (see 2 Tim 3:16), they were not written *to* us. Paul had his original readers principally in mind when he wrote, so it was considerably easier for them to understand what he was saying than it is for us. Even though the idea that Paul may be summarizing their arguments in parts of his comments about head coverings in 1 Corinthians 11 may seem strained or farfetched to us, we need to remember that, if Paul *is* summarizing mistaken Corinthian ideas in parts of 1 Corinthians 11, any *other way* of interpreting those parts of the chapter is doomed to failure. In this case there are some strong clues in the text that point to the possibility that Paul is, in fact, doing just that. Here are six of them that are readily identifiable:

- In verse 2, Paul praises the Corinthians for holding to the traditions that he had passed down to them. If the women (or the men on their behalf) at Corinth had been disregarding Paul's teaching that they should wear head coverings, why would Paul be commending them?

- Verses 11 and 12 make the opposite point of verses 8 to 10. It's possible that Paul is expressing his own thoughts in dialogue form— something like having his own mental table tennis match. But it also might be that in verses 11 and 12 he is refuting a Corinthian idea expressed in verses 8 to 10.

- In verse 13, Paul tells the Corinthians to judge for themselves regarding whether or not it is proper for a woman to pray with her head uncovered. While we don't know, the answer would seem to be yes! Jesus, in fact, famously accepted a woman's act of devotion involving her unveiled hair when others judged her for her impropriety (see Luke 7:36–49; see also John 12:3). Would Paul's standard for women's hair have been different from that of Jesus? That seems extremely unlikely. Further, as Alan Padgett points out, Greek does not have question marks. It is therefore possible that verse 13 contains no question. It could be translated: "Judge for yourselves: It is proper for a woman to pray to God with her head uncovered."[9]

- The claim in verse 14 that "nature itself" demonstrates long hair on men to be improper is obviously not true. Nature teaches no such thing! Further, it is likely that Paul had long hair when he was in Corinth. It seems that Paul completed a Nazarite vow while he was there, which means his hair would almost certainly have been noticeably long (see Acts 18:18), because this is what fulfilling a Nazarite vow required (see Num 6:5). As a person who was immersed in the study of the Hebrew Scriptures, it is highly unlikely that Paul would have condemned long hair on men categorically as unnatural because he would have been aware of the Bible's approval of the Nazarite custom, which involves a vow by which a person devotes himself to God—the least improper thing for a person to do!

- Verse 7 says that men ought *not* cover their heads because it is disgraceful. But given that Paul was a religious Jew, it seems nearly impossible that Paul would have believed such a thing. The priests in the temple at Jerusalem were required by biblical law to wear head coverings during rituals of worship (see Exod 28:4, 37, 40), and the custom of covering one's head during prayer continues in Jewish communities even today. Furthermore, Moses—whom all Jews of Paul's day revered highly—famously wore a veil, at least for a time (Exod 24:29–35; see also 2 Cor 3:13). Far from being a shameful thing to do, a Jewish man's veiling himself—especially when in prayer—showed reverence and respect. It is possible that Paul himself, being a devout Jew, covered his head while praying. While we are not sure whether or not it was a religious requirement of Jewish men in the first century, the wearing of various kinds of head coverings for men gradually became widely customary among Jewish groups not long afterward. The use of a prayer shawl called a *tallit*, for example, became a standard religious practice for Jewish men within a few centuries, and still continues as such among religious Jews today, as well as the use of yarmulkes.

- In verse 16, Paul, seemingly referring to the custom of wearing head coverings, says that it is not an issue worth fighting over because "the churches of God" don't have that custom. If most of the

9. See Padgett, *As Christ Submits,* 107–8.

churches didn't have the custom of wearing head coverings, why would Paul tell the women at Corinth to wear them? Perhaps he is actually quoting Corinthian arguments about why head coverings are necessary, and then dismissing them in verse 16.

Perhaps none of these six clues on their own is strong enough to persuade us that significant portions of 1 Corinthians 11 are not Paul's teaching. But when taken together, an impressively strong case begins to emerge. Suppose we test this idea and see if the argument flows, and also if it would match with Paul's teaching elsewhere.

If Paul is defending the Corinthian women's right to remove their head coverings, verse 2 makes sense. He is commending the church for holding to his teachings, showing that the use of head coverings was *not* one of them. The only alternative to reading verse 2 this way is to say that Paul was being sarcastic—that is, he was saying, "You've done really well (yeah, right)" while meaning, "You've done really poorly." But if Paul is not using sarcasm in verse 2, this implies that veiling was *not* one of his teachings. This, in turn, would imply that verses 4 through 10 would have to contain a lot of mistaken Corinthian thinking that Paul would then correct. Some of the Corinthians (probably the men—see ch. 4 above) were suggesting that women should cover their heads because their origin (according to Gen 2) is man. Women ought to cover their heads because of who they are to men.

One reason for seeing this section as possibly Corinthian rather than Pauline thinking is the way that Paul contradicts it in verses 11 and 12. Notice that verse 11 begins with, "Nevertheless, in the Lord." The word translated "nevertheless" (*plēn*) here signals a contrast with what has just been said. With that phrase Paul indicates that, in Christ, things are *not* as they are described in verses 4 through 10. Instead, women and men are interdependent and bear the image of God mutually.

Then we get to verse 13. In this interpretation the answer to the question, "Is it proper for a woman to pray to God with her head uncovered?" is "Yes, of course it is!" The answer to the question in verses 14 and 15 is, in turn, "No, nature does not teach us that long hair on men is inappropriate. Long hair grows on men naturally." As noted before, Paul likely had long hair while he lived in Corinth. If that is true, the question in verses 14 and 15 would have been asked facetiously. Perhaps the Corinthian men were reasoning something like this: "Women have long hair as a natural covering. This means that women need a covering. So, we think

women should veil themselves." Perhaps Paul is responding to this con-
voluted thinking by saying, "No, men have long hair too, unless they cut
it—like I did after my Nazarite vow when I was in Corinth. Remember
that? Your reasoning is wrong." In other words, Paul's comments about
long hair on men—comments that have stumped many Bible commentators—are actually sarcasm. That is, *the statement was never supposed to
make sense!* Instead, Paul said it to expose the absurd reasoning of some
of the men at Corinth who were insisting that the women in the church
cover their heads.

If we read the text this way, verse 16 suddenly makes sense. Paul
relativizes the whole head covering issue. He says in effect, "This is not
a custom that any of the other churches practice. Stop being contentious
about this." This sounds *a lot* like what Paul—the apostle famous both
then and now for his teaching on freedom in Christ—would have said! In
Paul's mind, head coverings are in the same category as circumcision, ab-
staining from meat offered to idols, and observance of holy days.[10] Sure, a
Christian can observe those practices. But, in Christ there is liberty. Those
things in and of themselves are simply not required of Christians. What is
required is love of one's neighbor and the unity of the church. If keeping
this or that custom helps to foster the church's unity or to show love to a
weaker brother or sister in Christ, by all means, keep that custom! But
otherwise, the custom is not necessary. This is classic Pauline doctrine.

Someone might object that attributing sarcasm to Paul in this
passage is a copout. After all, when we say, "This is sarcasm," we are essentially saying that its meaning is the *opposite* of what it says! "Is that
really a good way to read the Bible," some of my careful readers might be
wondering? This is a strong objection, which is partly why I have chosen
to include Explanation A above, ready at hand in case this one fails to
persuade. But, it is important to notice that no matter which interpretation we choose, sarcasm *has* to be present at some point in this passage.
It's either in verse 2, or it's in verses 4 to 10, 14 and 15. Paul was certainly
capable of sarcasm, and he uses it fairly frequently in this epistle.[11] The
trouble with sarcasm is that, without context, it is very difficult to detect.
And, when it comes to understanding an ancient letter like 1 Corinthians, context is precisely what we as modern readers do not have—especially when the topic is the elusive meaning of a cultural custom like head

10. See Rom 14; Gal 5–6; 1 Cor 7:17–19; 8; 10:23–33; Col 2:16–18.

11. See for example 1 Cor 1:13; 4:8–10; 11:22. See also Gal 5:12.

coverings. Does Paul use sarcasm in 1 Corinthians 11? Yes, for sure. But, *where* does he use it? That's a more difficult question to answer.

Versions of what I offer here as Explanation B have been advocated recently with care and detail by Lucy Peppiatt and Alan Padgett, whose excellent work has helped me immeasurably to understand this difficult passage better. While these two scholars differ with each other in important details of their arguments, and my argument differs from both of theirs as well, their general approaches are similar to what I have described here, and readers who want to examine more sustained, thorough treatments of this passage by two experienced biblical scholars should read their books.[12] I think this approach goes a long way to solving the interpretational problems we noted above and, I confess, I find it the most persuasive of all the approaches I have seen.

The ostensible weakness of this approach, of course, is that it depends on the idea that relatively large portions of 1 Corinthians 11:2–16 reflect the Corinthians' thinking, rather than Paul's. But, I hasten to reiterate, no such weakness would have been apparent to Paul's original readers. They would have known exactly what Paul was doing. The first job of the Bible interpreter is to try to understand, as best as possible, the text in its original context. In this case, I think the above way of reading this passage is probably how the original readers would have understood it.

When one begins to read the *many* interpretations of this passage that are available, it is easy to despair of ever understanding it. However, when it comes to finding clarity about how we should *apply* this passage to our Christian lives today, I think there is good reason for hope. When we realize that (1) head coverings were *not* symbols of male authority, and (2) the only authority mentioned in the text belongs to women, we discover that the message of the passage serves to elevate the status of women up to equality with men rather than to subordinate them under men. Verses 11 and 12 are clearly the heart of Paul's argument in this section of Scripture. Those two verses are the "in the Lord" statement! *No one* argues that those verses contain sarcasm. Those two verses should be the ones that guide our application of this passage in our Christian lives today, whether in the church, home, or in wider society.

---

12. See Padgett, *As Christ Submits,* and Peppiatt, *Women and Worship.*

Conclusion

In the above we have only touched upon the issues involved in interpreting this difficult biblical text. But a detailed analysis has not been our goal. Our goal has been to make enough solid observations to equip us to discern between plausible and implausible interpretations of the passage. We have observed that, while head coverings in and of themselves can be a symptom of male domination within a culture, Paul's comments about them in 1 Corinthians 11 actually *counter* male domination. He places the authority of women over their own heads in the hands of women themselves.

But we're not finished discussing 1 Corinthians 11 yet. In verse 3, Paul writes, "But I want you to realize that the head of every man is Christ, and the head of the woman is the man, and the head of Christ is God." Does this statement imply a male-female hierarchy at creation? Also, we need to address verse 7. Historically, this verse has been used to deny that women are made equally as men in the image of God. Is that what this verse implies? These are our next big questions, for which we've reserved a chapter of their own.

8

God and Christ; Man and Woman

(1 Corinthians 11:2–16, part 2)

WE WILL NEED TO begin by saying something about how the head metaphor is used in 1 Corinthians 11:3. The passage says (1) the head of every man is Christ, (2) the head of Christ is God, and (3) the head of every woman is man. Hierarchicalists reason that, because Jesus followed the will of God the Father while on earth, and because Christ is clearly every man's authority, it follows that man is woman's authority. Is this what Paul is communicating here? Once again, we find ourselves discussing how Paul is using one of his favorite metaphors.

We have found along the way that one of the most important things we must do to guard against reading extrabiblical ideas into a text is to be sure we distinguish between what it actually says and what we have grown accustomed to *assuming* it says. The first thing to be noted, in this case, is that the supposed roles of authority and submission, which hierarchicalists use as interpretive keys to guide their construction of the meaning of this passage, are nowhere to be found within the text itself. As we've noted, the only time the word "authority" appears in this whole chapter is in reference to women's authority over their own heads. As we noted in our discussion of Ephesians 5, "head" as a metaphor does not necessarily signify a person in authority. It can refer to something's source or place of origin, and also to the end point or goal of something. We noticed that, normally, this is the basic idea from which Paul begins in his development of head as a metaphor elsewhere in his letters. Here, I argue, he is doing the same thing, and this becomes clear in verses 11 and 12, where he writes, "Nevertheless, in the Lord woman is not in-dependent of man nor man of woman; for as woman was made from man, so man is now born of woman. And all things are from God." The phrase "in the Lord," we should remind ourselves, signals that Paul is looking at the situation from the perspective of the new postresurrection reality that Jesus introduced through his work on the cross. It is hard to imagine a more open statement of male-female equality and mutual de-pendence than this! Sometimes, when trying to figure how an argument in the Bible works, it helps to look at the conclusion. That is, sometimes it helps to read an argument *backwards*.[1] In this case, verses 11 and 12 are clearly the conclusion to Paul's argument. Why is Paul talking about where woman and man came from at the conclusion of his argument? Well, it's because that is what his argument was about. If we understand head to mean "source" instead of "authority," Paul's conclusion makes a lot more sense. The fact that woman comes from man in the Genesis creation story—an idea perhaps alluded to in verses 7 and 8—is balanced by Paul's statement in verses 11 and 12.

But questions still remain, the primary one being: Why did Paul say that Christ is the head of every man? Surely Christ is the head of every woman as well, no? I want to remind my patient readers again that there is a wide consensus among New Testament scholars, no matter what their position on women in ministry, that this is one of the most difficult pas-sages in the New Testament to interpret. Once again, we find ourselves at a crossroads. There is no safe option. There is no guarantee that stick-ing with older, more familiar interpretations, just because we've become more accustomed to them or have heard them more often (or from our favorite Bible teachers), is safer than going another way. To be truthful, I may change my mind in the future regarding some of the things that I will say in this chapter. Nevertheless, as living, changing, choice-making beings, we have to continue to live out this Christian life as faithfully as we know how to do. We have to strive to discern what the Spirit is saying to us through Scripture, ever hoping that God will give us grace where we fall short.

---

1. See Padgett, *As Christ Submits*, ch. 5.

Who Is Christ to God, and Who Is Woman to Man?

It is easy to get stuck in 1 Corinthians 11 because of all the elements in it that sound strange to our modern ears. But here is where I'll appeal to an argument I've used a couple of times in this book. We do not need to understand this text comprehensively in order to know what it is *not* saying. As we noted in the last chapter, by inserting the word "symbol" in verse 10, some Bible translators have made an already enigmatic text even more complicated than it needs to be. Further, by not taking into account that "head" in this text most likely signifies something closer to "source" or "origin" rather than "authority," complicated questions about hierarchical structures are far too often imported to the text that muddy the waters even more. But, if one is able to stand back a little bit and see Paul's argument from a birds-eye view, it becomes clear that, whatever else Paul might be saying, he is *not* arguing that women are intrinsically men's subordinates. Verses 11 and 12 are clearly the climax and conclusion of whatever argument he is trying to make in the previous verses. Therefore, the theology of *those* verses should be what drives our application of this passage in our lives as followers of Jesus.

In the meantime, however, we still want to know how Paul is using head as a metaphor in this passage. If we resist the temptation to despair and instead look closely—and do a little concordance work—I think we can move in our reading of this text from frustration to fascination, and hopefully even to worship.

Let's take a close look at verse 3. It says, "But I want you to realize that the head of every man is Christ, the head of the woman is the man, and the head of Christ is God." At first blush, this verse may seem to outline a simple chain of command in which God outranks Christ, Christ outranks man, and man outranks woman. On this first-blush reading, the arrangement could be illustrated by Diagram 8.1. Noting the clear biblical teaching that Jesus submitted himself to the will of God, many hierarchicalists (though certainly not all) teach that Jesus' submission actually reflected God the Son's *eternal* subordination to the higher authority of God the Father. In other words, Jesus' submission to his father's will was not a temporary act that the incarnate Son of God undertook while he was on earth. Rather, for all of eternity the Trinity has existed in a hierarchical relationship, with the Father in authority over the Son and both the Father and the Son in authority over the Spirit. With this theology in mind, these hierarchicalist interpreters see this passage as teaching a chain of command with God on the top, women (or at least wives) on the bottom, and Christ and men (or at least husbands) in between.

Interpreting 1 Corinthians 11:3 in this way requires that "head" be understood as a metaphor for authority. However, as we noted before, Paul's comment regarding the source or origin of man and woman in verses 11 and 12 renders the meaning of "source" or "origin" much more likely. This, along with our observations about how Paul uses the head-and-body metaphor elsewhere in his writings, argues strongly against reading head in this passage as a stand-in for authority. While it is true that head *can* mean authority, the context of the passage should be what guides our interpretation of how Paul is using it here. If we assume from the outset that head means authority, of course we will arrive at the conclusion that 1 Corinthians 11:3 is describing something like a chain of command. But that would not be a sufficiently careful approach to interpreting Scripture.

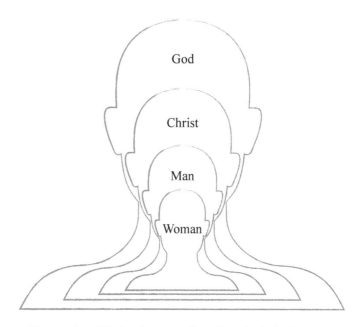

Diagram 8.1—"Chain of command" reading of 1 Corinthians 11:3

Nevertheless, the most serious problem with reading this text as describing a chain of command goes beyond interpretation to theology, for it touches on the heart of the Christian doctrine of God as Trinity—one God existing eternally in three persons. If Christ is God incarnate, as all

Christians believe, Christ cannot possess anything less than full power and authority over all things. Not only does Christ possess this authority, Christ also exercises it. In a monotheistic worldview, there simply is no such thing as God's having the capacity to be subordinated to anything or anyone. I don't say this because of a worry about the morality of subordination as such (though, that is certainly a worry worthy of attention). Rather, I am simply pointing out that it seems philosophically impossible that, in a monotheistic worldview, a person could legitimately be called God and yet possess anything less than full authority over all things that are not God. Saying that the incarnate Son—the man Jesus—submitted to the authoritative will of God as the perfect human being is one thing. Saying that the eternal Son, who was and is one with the Father both in substance and in will, is somehow under the Father's authority eternally is another. How could we say that the Son has all authority if there is a measure of authority that the Son does not possess—a measure that the Father has but the Son does not?

This is a complex and extremely important theological issue which I am not equipped to address at length here. However, the doctrine of the eternal subordination of the Son in the Trinity, for which many hierarchicalists advocate by citing 1 Corinthians 11:3, must be called into question. It cannot serve as a presupposition upon which other theological arguments are based because it is, at best, a questionable doctrine. Hierarchicalist interpreters often use it almost in passing as an argument for the subordination of women, as if it were a doctrine on which all Christians agree. It's not! Not by a long shot. It's a very controversial claim to make. Furthermore, it is based at least in part on a wobbly, first-blush reading of 1 Corinthians 11:3.

The reason we can call the chain-of-command take on 1 Corinthians 11:3 a first-blush reading is that a careful look shows that the text does not set things up that way. If Paul had wanted to describe a chain of command, he would have named the four parties link by link, in order. Instead, what we have in the text is three sets of *parallel* or *analogous* relationships (see Diagram 8.2).

- First, Christ is the head of man.

- Second, the man (or husband) is the head of woman (or wife).

- Third, God is the head of Christ.

Diagram 8.2—Three parallel relationships reading of 1 Corinthians 11:3

The careful reader should take note of the order Paul uses. This is not a mistake. Paul is doing it this way for a calculated reason. Before we dive into a search for that reason, we need to make three foundational observations.

- First, the immediate context—namely verses 8 to 12—shows that the argument Paul is addressing is founded in male and female origins. The head metaphor in this passage clearly includes the idea of origin.

- Second, the three relationship pairs are analogously parallel to each other. That is, there is a sense in which Christ's being the head of man is *like* the man's being the head of the woman, which in turn is *like* God's being the head of Christ. The question before us is: In what sense is each of these three pairings like the others?

- Third, the last pair mentioned—God is the head of Christ—is almost certainly the key to understanding the other two, and particularly the middle pair. Paul places it last for this reason. If we can discern what Paul means by his statement that God is the head of Christ, we will have the key to unlocking what he means when he says man is the head of woman.

The place to start, then, is to find what Paul had already taught the Corinthians about God's relationship to Christ. Paul nowhere else calls God the head of Christ. But, Paul *does* speak of God the Father's relationship to Christ in other terms just a few chapters previous to this one! This is surely the right place to start in our search for a key to unlock the meaning of 1 Corinthians 11:3. Let's go, then, to 1 Corinthians chapter 8.

In 1 Corinthians 8, Paul is emphatic about the oneness of God. Paul was a faithful Jew and would never entertain the idea that there might be more than one God. Yet, seamlessly, in the same breath, he puts Jesus and God on the same level, doing the same work, and worthy of the same worship. This is precisely the kind of theology, present not only in Paul's writing but all over the New Testament, that led to what we now know as the doctrine of the Trinity. Perhaps the most striking example of this is in verse 6 of this chapter. In the midst of a discussion about whether or not Christians should eat meat sacrificed to idols (an important issue for early Christians living in Greco-Roman culture) Paul makes this remarkable declaration, "[Y]et for us there is one God, the Father, from whom are all things and for whom we exist, and one Lord, Jesus Christ, through whom are all things and through whom we exist" (ESV). The wonderfully helpful *Commentary on the New Testament Use of the Old Testament* notes that this verse intentionally alludes to the Shema, a statement from the Torah that came to be Judaism's formal confession of belief in the one God of Israel.[2] The word "shema" means "hear." The Shema appears in Deuteronomy 6:4, which says, "Hear, O Israel: The LORD our God, the LORD is one." New Testament scholar Richard Bauckham hears an echo of the Shema in Zechariah 14:9, which predicts a day when the God of Israel would become king over all the earth.[3] Notice that Paul seems to think this has happened through Jesus' crucifixion and resurrection. For that reason, Paul astonishingly *includes Jesus in the Shema* in 1 Corinthians 8:6! In Paul's theology, what God has done, Jesus has done; and what Jesus has done, God has done. As he says in 2 Corinthians 5:19, "God was in Christ, reconciling the world to himself."

Because 1 Corinthians 8:6 displays Paul's view of the relationship between God the Father and Christ so clearly, and because it appears within the same epistle, it can act for us as a kind of lens through which to read 1 Corinthians 11:8–12. Notice that in 8:6 Paul says that all things are "from" (*ek*) God the Father, and that all things exist "through" (*dia*) Christ. If we place 1 Corinthians 8:6 alongside 1 Corinthians 11:8–12 an illuminating pattern emerges. Notice that the woman comes *from* (*ek*) the man in verse 8, and that she is made *for* or *through* (*dia*) the man in verse 9. In verse 11, Paul repeats that the woman was made *from* (*ek*) the man. However, in verse 11, Paul adds that *just as* the woman was made *from* (*ek*) man, *so also* the man's existence is *through* (*dia*) the woman. Then Paul ends 11:12 with the comment, "But, all things are from God," which even more clearly connects this passage with 8:6. When we see how interrelated these two passages are, we observe that, actually, *the*

2. Carson and Beale, *Commentary on the New Testament Use*, 717.

3. Bauckham, *Jesus and the God of Israel*, 96.

woman in 1 Corinthians 11:12 is analogous to Christ in Paul's revised ver-
sion of the Shema in 8:6. In other words, just as Christ shares the status of
God the Father in 1 Corinthians 8:6, so the woman shares the status of the
man in 11:12. This can be hard to see in an English translation, so I have
created a diagram (Diagram 8.3) to show where the same Greek preposi-
tions are used in each of these two passages. Note that in the ESV (which
I've chosen to use in the diagram) the little preposition *ek* is translated
as "from" sometimes and "made from" sometimes. Also, *dia* is translated
variously as "through," "for," "created for," and "born of." Don't let the
various translations confuse you—these are all the same word in Greek.

1 Corinthians 8:6   1 Corinthians 11:8–9, 11–12

                                                     For man was not made from

[Y]et for us there is one God, the   woman, but woman from man.

Father,   Neither was man created for

from whom are all things and   woman, but woman for man.

for whom we exist,   …

and one Lord, Jesus Christ,   Nevertheless, **in the Lord** woman is

through whom are all things and   not independent of man nor man of

through whom we exist. (ESV)   woman;

                                                     for as woman was made from man,
      ◯ = *ek* ("from," "out of")
      ◯ = *dia* ("through," "via")   so man is now born of woman.

                                                     And all things are from God. (ESV)

Diagram 8.3—Juxtaposition of 1 Corinthians 8:6 with 11:8–9, 11–12

What can we take away from this observation? If Paul's goal in 8:6
was to identify Christ's divinity as being *equal* with God the Father's,
rather than to distinguish Christ's (subordinate) role from God's role, it
would seem to follow that Paul is doing something similar with man and
woman in 1 Corinthians 11:8–12. When we see the analogy he is drawing

between the role of Christ and the role of woman in relation to man, it becomes clear that, actually, Paul is carefully using the head metaphor in this passage to elevate the woman to a new oneness, in Christ, with the man in a shared humanity. Notice again that what mediates the contrast between verses 8 and 9 (where the woman might seem to be *under* the man in some way) and verses 11 and 12 (where the woman is brought back up alongside the man in a mutually dependent and beneficial relationship) is that glorious Pauline phrase, "in the Lord." "In the Lord," men and women can see one another differently than they otherwise would. "In the Lord," Genesis 3:16 does not need to continue, and we can return to the vision of male and female mutuality we find in Genesis 1 and 2.

By the time we get to verse 12, therefore, the chain-of-command reading of verse 3 has become completely untenable. We can summarize the argument this way:

All things come from God and through Christ.

   Man is made by God and through Christ.

      Woman comes through man,

         but, *in the Lord*, we know that . . .

      Man also comes through woman.

   Woman is also made by God and through Christ.

All things come from God and through Christ.

The issue of whether or not the Son is eternally subordinate to the Father is too involved for me to discuss at length in a book like this.[4] But every Christian should be aware that the doctrine of the eternal subordination of the Son is highly problematic, and should not be accepted without careful consideration. In my opinion, it is far too controversial to be used as support for a hierarchical relationship between Christian men and women. As the above illustrates, I think Paul and other New Testament authors see the Father and the Son as equal in authority. What the Son does, the Father does, and the authority of the Father is the authority of the Son. Being equally God implies equality in level of authority. When Christians confess, "Jesus is Lord," we are including everything under his lordship. There is no sense in which Christ possesses anything less than complete and entire authority over all things. Despite the fact that it is often used for arguments to the contrary, it seems to me that 1 Corinthians

---

4. For a sustained, fair, and careful discussion of this issue, see Erickson, *Who's Tampering with the Trinity?*

11, when read in light of Paul's overall teaching about Jesus and especially in light of 1 Corinthians 8:6, teaches just that. Hence, I conclude that man and woman, when analogized to the Father and the Son as they are in the passage we are discussing here, *are also equal in authority with each other.* This conclusion agrees well not only with Paul, but also with the picture of male and female presented in Genesis 1 and 2. Once again, we find that it all fits gloriously together!

Did Paul Teach That Women Are Not Made in God's Image?

What happens if we press this analogy a bit further and take its implications down to 1 Corinthians 11:7? As we noted before, this verse has been used in the past by many theologians to argue that woman is not made in the image of God, or that she is made in God's image in only a secondary sense. One solution to the problem this verse creates is to attribute it to Corinthian thinking. As we saw in Explanation B in the previous chapter, this is one way of resolving the several contradictions in this passage. Because many in the church have pointed to verses 7 through 10 to justify the notion that women are not fully made in God's image as men are, verses 7 to 10 have rightly been subjected to scrutiny, not only because they seem to pose a theological contradiction with Genesis 1:27, but also because of the effect this interpretation has had on the way women have been treated in the church. Could it be that these verses are, yet again, Paul's summarizing of an incorrect Corinthian idea, which he then corrects in in verses 11 and 12?

Given what we've seen regarding Paul's habit of quoting or summarizing Corinthian ideas and then responding to them elsewhere in this letter, it is certainly a possibility. However, while I agree with those who argue that Paul is quoting the Corinthians at length in this chapter, I want to propose that verses 7b through 10 reflect Paul's own thinking, not a summarization of mistaken Corinthian notions. I contend that Paul *did* teach that women were made in God's image, and that his statement that woman is man's glory supports that idea. I arrive at my conclusion by means of a little concordance work.

I begin by asking, "What does Paul mean elsewhere in his writings when he says that person A is the glory of person B?" Once again, the relationship of God the Father with Christ is the key to understanding what Paul means. First, let's look at Romans 1:22 and 23. These verses say, "Although they claimed to be wise, they became fools and *exchanged the glory* of the immortal God *for images* made to look like a mortal human being and birds and animals and reptiles." This may seem irrelevant at first. But look how the word "glory" is parallel to the word "image" in this text. With that in mind, it seems plausible that when Paul says in 1 Corinthians 11:7 that the woman is the glory of man, he is not saying the woman is lesser than the man, but that she is, in fact, his representative image. She is distinct from him, but is nonetheless his equal and opposite reflection.

This point may still seem unrelated to what we are discussing here regarding the God-and-Christ analogy with male-and-female. But let's look at another Pauline passage that parallels the words "glory" and "image." Second Corinthians 4:4–6 says,

> The god of this age has blinded the minds of unbelievers, so that they cannot see the light of the gospel that displays the glory of Christ, *who is the image of God.* For what we preach is not ourselves, but Jesus Christ as Lord, and ourselves as your servants for Jesus' sake. For God, who said, "Let light shine out of darkness," made his light shine in our hearts to give us the light of the knowledge of *God's glory* displayed in the face of Christ.[5]

Here again there is a clear parallel between the words "glory" and "image." This corroborates our above point that Paul's saying that the woman is the man's glory is not likely intended to relegate her to a secondary status relative to the man. But this passage brings out a further point—it shows *both* that Christ is God's glory *and* that Christ is God's image. Once again, we can see a fairly clear analogy between God-and-Christ and male-and-female. But this analogy, far from serving to subordinate women, serves to exalt women to an equal status with men. Just as Paul saw Jesus as the glory of God and concluded that, in fact, Jesus is to be praised as the King of all creation—indeed, as one who is equal with God the Father—so woman, who is the glory of man, should be seen as man's equal in every way. Whenever Paul talks about the relationship of God the Father and Christ, he *always* emphasizes the co-equal status that Christ enjoys with God, and he prays to Christ, worships, praises, and exalts Christ along with God the Father. Whatever status the Father has,

---

5. See also Heb 1:3.

the Son has. The point is, *in the Lord,* man and woman are likewise of equal standing with each other.

There is one more passage we need to mention to bolster this claim. In 2 Corinthians 3:18 Paul mentions in one verse not only the words "glory" and "image," but also a veil! It is surprising that this passage is not mentioned more often in connection with debates about head coverings in 1 Corinthians 11. In 2 Corinthians 3:12–17, Paul discusses how when Moses was exposed to God's glory on Mt. Sinai he subsequently had to veil his face because it shone so brightly. Those who do not know Christ, Paul says, in some analogous way have a veil over their eyes. Importantly for our discussion, Paul says in verse 16, "But whenever anyone turns to the Lord, the veil is taken away." That is, Paul is emphasizing in this passage the *lack* of a need for a veil for those who are in Christ! But here is what verse 18 says: "And we all, who with *unveiled* faces contemplate *the Lord's glory*, are being transformed *into his image* with *ever-increasing glory*, which comes from the Lord, who is the Spirit." First, notice once again the connection between "glory" and "image." But second—and most importantly—notice that our encounter with the glory of Christ is supposed to result in the *removal* of a veil, not the donning of one. In Christ, veils are not necessary. It is difficult not to see a connection between Paul's teaching here and what we have observed in our interpretation of 1 Corinthians 11:2–16 in chapter 7 above (especially in Explanation B).

Conclusion

If we observe carefully what Paul taught about the relationship between God and Christ elsewhere in his writings, we find that he exalted Christ to the level of God, worshipping Father and Son as, equally, one God. Thus, Paul's analogy in 1 Corinthians 11:3 regarding that divine relationship and the male-female relationship *must* be taken to exalt women in Christ to an equal status with men, not to subordinate them. Furthermore, when we observe how Paul uses "glory" and "image" in connection with each other elsewhere in his writings, we find that 1 Corinthians 11:7 cannot be used as a basis for subordinating women under men either. If Christ is the glory of God, and yet is equal to God, it follows that the woman's being the glory of man makes her his equal in a similar way. It turns out that, even in 1 Corinthians 11, Paul's view of men and women is thoroughly consistent with the view of male and female we observed in Genesis 1 and 2. Paul's vision for a restored creation in Christ begins with the restoration of mutuality in the most basic of all human relationships. In Christ, men and women rediscover who they really are to each other—equal, mutually dependent partners, co-heirs and stewards of God's creation.

9

More Questions

THERE ARE SOME QUESTIONS that, in my experience, often appear in discussions about women speaking in the church. I don't know of a better way of addressing them than to do so one by one.

Question 1: Doesn't Adam's Naming of Eve Imply His Authority over Her?

Adam names his wife Eve in Genesis 3:20, and this fact has caused some to wonder if his doing so signifies his God-given authority. We might point out right away that Adam does this after the fall and, thus, his action should not be understood as evidence of a created hierarchy between the sexes. But, there is more that we can observe.

In the Bible, naming someone *can* be done by a person trying to assert authority over another. When Daniel and his three companions Hananiah, Mishael, and Azariah were taken into exile in Babylon, they were famously given Babylonian names by their captors (Dan 1:7). Joseph, who was also taken as a captive to Egypt, was likewise given an Egyptian name (Gen 41:45). This practice of renaming captives was clearly intended as a display of power, for it showed the desire of one party to shape and determine the identity of another. But, it seems clear that Adam's relationship to Eve is in no way analogous to that of an imperial power to its vanquished victims. That is not even close to how Genesis portrays man and woman's relationship in God's design.

We also know of momentous cases in the biblical story in which God gives people new names. God changed Abram's name to Abraham, Sarai's to Sarah, and Jacob's to Israel (Gen 32:28; 35:10). We might stop there and conclude that, since God is everyone's authority, and since God names some people in the Bible, naming must be a function of authority.

But naming in the Bible is much more flexible than that. Most of the time, mothers are the ones who name their children. Fathers do it too, but most of the time it's the mothers. I don't think we should draw any conclusions regarding authority from that custom, but it's worth pointing out just to show that the act of naming someone, which of course usually happens shortly after babies are born, is done by both women and men in the Bible.

More importantly for our present topic, however, some people give God special names in Scripture. The first to do so was Hagar. She called God "*ēl-ro'î*," which means, "The God who sees me" (Gen 16:13). While Hagar is unique in that she named God directly, in the second person, saying, "*You are ēl-ro'î*," others in the Hebrew Bible also give God new names.[1] The fact that we have examples in the Hebrew Scriptures of people naming God shows that the act of naming someone is not necessarily reserved for a person with a higher rank or status.

Besides, the name Eve should be understood as a descriptive title, not merely an arbitrary name. "Eve" means "life," and Adam names her that because she would become the mother of all the living (see 3:20). Adam does not seem to be asserting his own authority over Eve by naming her this. It makes more sense to see this as something like the endowment of an honorary title.

Question 2: Didn't Paul Intend to Appoint Men as Elders?[2]

Perhaps some of my readers have been posed this little riddle:

> A father and son are involved in a terrible auto accident. The father is killed and the son is seriously injured. An ambulance rushes the unconscious boy to the hospital and immediately admits him to

---

1. Abraham (Gen 21:33; 22:14), Jacob (Gen 48:15), Moses (Exod 17:15–16), and Gideon (Judg 6:23–24), for example.

2. For a summary of this explanation of 1 Tim 3:2–7 (and also indirectly Titus 1:6–10), see Table 9.1 in the appendix.

the operating room for emergency surgery. But upon entering the operating room the surgeon stops and says, "I cannot operate on this boy because he is my son." How is this possible?

When my college roommate, Kyle, told me this riddle, I was stumped. "How could the surgeon be the boy's father if he died in the accident?" I wondered. "It's a trick," I thought. "I've got to think outside the box. Hmmm . . . Did the boy's father really die? Is he a ghost? Was he really the boy's stepfather?" I've posed this riddle to a few other people, including my students. Most get it right away, but I've found I'm not the only one who *assumes* that the surgeon in the story is a man and who, as a result, cannot see that the story barely qualifies as a riddle. Of course, the solution to the riddle is that the surgeon was the boy's *mother*!

Even though I have never had anything against women's being doctors, and even though I personally know several women who are doctors, my stereotype of a doctor—and probably particularly of a surgeon—is male. I think my readers will agree that we do this a lot. We assume nurses would be women, and probably elementary school teachers, librarians, cashiers, switchboard operators, and secretaries too. We assume police officers, auto mechanics, engineers, taxicab drivers, and probably coaches and film directors would be men. We do this in many cases without consciously opposing the other gender's being in those roles. Stereotyping various roles in society usually involves assigning gender to them.

The formation of stereotypes is normal and probably unavoidable. However, when stereotypes become engrained over time, they tend to evolve into rules. Take the example we mentioned earlier about medical doctors being male. Today it is difficult to find anyone who thinks that women should not practice medicine. Even families whose cultural values are traditional with regard to male authority often encourage—or even oblige—their daughters to pursue careers in medicine. According to data published on the website of the Association of American Medical Colleges, there are now more women studying in medical schools in the United States than men.[3] If that trend continues, a profession previously reserved only for men will soon be more female than male.

Florence Nightingale is one of modern history's most celebrated stereotype-changers. In Nightingale's time, the stereotype of a hospital nurse was a woman of loose morals with a criminal history. Women who worked in hospitals were only the most desperate—the ones who had

---

3. Heiser, "Majority of U.S."

been rejected everywhere else. As a woman from a wealthy, high-class family, Nightingale openly defied society's expectation that she marry and lead a respectable life, and instead became a nurse and went off to care for soldiers wounded in the battles of the Crimean War. Through her efforts in the face of enormous opposition, Nightingale successfully transformed the stereotype of nursing. Largely due to her determination and sacrifice, nursing has become an honorable profession all over the world. So far-reaching was this transformation that, eventually, some men even began choosing to enter the nursing profession.

But despite Nightingale's incredible influence in changing society's outlook on the nursing profession, for most of her life she was against women's becoming doctors. This was due in large part to her negative experiences with doctors generally. But it also had to do with her stereotype of doctors as male. When women began graduating from medical schools, beginning with Nightingale's friend Elizabeth Blackwell, who became the first woman medical doctor, Nightingale thought they were wasting their time. Nightingale wanted to transform the nursing profession for women, but she was not interested in advocating for opening the doors of medical schools to them. Nightingale's argument, of course, was far from simplistic, and it would be beyond unfair to accuse her of ignorant, careless prejudice. Nevertheless, most would agree now that, hero that she was, she made a mistake in this regard. She should have supported women who wanted to become medical doctors. These things are always more complicated in the moment than in hindsight, and my readers will surely agree that Nightingale remains worthy of the honor she receives for her work, while simultaneously humbly agreeing that she probably let her stereotype of doctors as male persons limit her imagination of how women could be useful and excel in society.

Paul, no doubt, stereotyped the roles of his society, and those stereotypes surely included gender, just like ours do. When I was growing up, I always heard the word "elder" in the context of speaking about the leaders of a Christian church. But, of course, Paul's context was different. The church had barely started when he began working in it! When Paul thought of "elder" he thought of the officers of Jewish synagogues, and these were *all men without exception*. While I did not have a legitimate reason for stereotyping the role of a surgeon in the aforementioned riddle as a male person, Paul had every excuse for doing this with the role of elder. Paul had never met a woman elder, because no woman had ever been one! With that in mind, I can concede that Paul probably *did* assume that the people chosen to be elders in the churches he'd planted would be men.

For some, the admission that Paul assumed pastors would be men is tantamount to denying most of what I've argued for in this book up to this point. If Paul assumed elders would be men, shouldn't we assume the same?

I don't think so. We are not bound by Paul's stereotypes, especially if we can find evidence that he himself did not see them as binding rules. The doctrine of biblical inspiration requires Christians to attend carefully to what the Scriptures teach and command. But, it does not require that we pattern all of our assumptions after those of Paul, Peter, Moses, David, or any other biblical author. Paul himself would have agreed with this. He taught that the Christian should seek to have the mind of Christ, not the mind of one of Christ's apostles.

My conceding that Paul *does* seem to be assuming that Titus and Timothy would appoint male leaders in the churches over which they had charge is not the same as admitting that Paul was commanding Titus and Timothy to *only* appoint men to those positions. Let's consider the context. The context of the phrase "husband of one wife"[4] is clearly emphasizing the character of the person to be selected for the office of elder. If we read the list of qualifications—or character traits—ideal for an elder, we see readily that Paul's concern is with the moral and spiritual uprightness and maturity of the person to be chosen. For that reason, I think we have a strong basis for doubting that Paul intended through the phrase, "husband of one wife," to say to Titus and Timothy, "Hey, be sure whoever you get is a man, not a woman."

If that is not enough to persuade my careful readers, consider a second assumption Paul is making. Paul is not only assuming the gender of the appointees will be male; he is also assuming they will be married. Further, he assumes they will have children. These assumptions are no less apparent than the one about the gender of the appointees. Thus, to categorize these, we can say Paul made assumptions not only about an elder's gender, but also about his marital and parental statuses. Here is the problem: Paul was single. Granted, Paul's role was that of an apostle, which is slightly different from that of a local church elder. But, Paul *encourages* singleness as a vocation in 1 Corinthians 7, and even seems to think singleness is preferable to being married because it frees a person

4. 1 Tim 3:2; Titus 1:6.

to devote him or herself entirely to "the things of the Lord" (1 Cor 7:32; see also 39–40). On top of all this, we should point out the elephant in the room—namely, Jesus was a single, childless man! It would be unbearably inconsistent for Paul to *require* shepherds of the local church to be married fathers of children when the Good Shepherd himself was a single man.

The conclusion to be drawn from all this is that, while Paul assumed that the elders Titus and Timothy would appoint would be married men with children, these assumptions *do not* constitute restrictions. Rather, the point Paul is making is that these should be faithful persons—persons who are responsible and committed to their marriages, and who tend conscientiously to the well-being, both spiritual and physical, of their families. I think it is safe to say that, should Titus and Timothy have chosen to ordain a single man as an elder, Paul would not have objected in the least, so long as that man had demonstrated the required gifting, calling, and integrity necessary for a person in that position. For the very same reason, we can safely assume that Paul would not have objected to a woman's ordination either. Paul does not mention "husband of one wife" in order to mark maleness as a qualification for elders. The point is not "husband" but "one" wife.

It is important for us to note not only what Paul assumed, but also what he did not assume. The phrase, "husband of one wife" could be literally translated, "one-woman man."[5] While Paul assumed that the elders appointed in the churches under Timothy's care would be men, he could not assume that they would be sexually exclusive in their marriages. Both Greek and Roman culture, as well as Roman law, forbade men from having more than one wife at a time. However, it was common, at least among those who could afford it, for men to have concubines. Also, Roman men had the legal right to use their slaves sexually, as well as prostitutes. In such an environment, Paul's concern is not with the maleness of the person who would be leading a church, but with his moral character. Today, virtually all Christian denominations require elders and pastors to be monogamous. We take it for granted. But Paul, in his time, couldn't. Neither the Greek and Roman cultures in which he moved nor biblical precedent could support such a stipulation. After all, biblical heroes like Abraham, Moses, David, and others were all polygamous. Yet, Paul had the insight to require of elders *the same standard of sexual exclusivity in marriage that both the culture and biblical precedent required of all women*

---

5. In biblical Greek the word for "woman" and "wife" is the same.

generally. The effect of such a requirement would be equalizing to the sexes. Paul is not trying to *exclude* women from being elders. Instead, he is trying to set high moral standards for the office so that only a person of integrity—whom he assumes will be a man—will be able to fill it. In doing so, Paul ends up requiring of male elders the same standard for sexual exclusivity that was *already required* of women in that culture.

These are broad arguments based on general principles of coherent Bible interpretation. But there is one other small clue that lends credence to the conclusion I have drawn above. In 1 Timothy 3, immediately after providing the qualifications for the office of an elder, Paul provides the same for that of a deacon. The qualifications sound basically the same. Specifically, Paul says deacons also must be "the husband of one wife." The reason this is important to note is that Paul calls a woman named Phoebe "a servant of the church at Cenchreae" in Romans 16:1. The word translated "servant" in that verse is the same word that is translated "deacon" in 1 Timothy 3. This word—*diakonos*—can mean, generically, "servant," and can therefore refer to all sincere followers of Jesus. But, Phoebe is said to be a deacon of a specific church. Further, her official status is made clear in verse 2, where Paul instructs the Roman Christians formally to support her ministry. If the interpreter refrains from assuming beforehand that Phoebe cannot have been a deacon in the official sense of the word because of her gender, there is no reason to think she was not, in fact, an officially ordained deacon of the church, having responsibilities similar to those of the deacons in Acts 6:1–6. Therefore, while Paul *does* assume that Titus and Timothy will be appointing men as deacons, he does *not* thereby exclude women from consideration for those positions, as evidenced by Phoebe's being a deacon in the church at Cenchreae. Here is my point: If Paul did not intend the phrase, "husband of one wife" as an absolute gender restriction for deacons, there is no reason to think that he intended it as such for elders either. The phrase, "husband of one wife," therefore, should not exclude women from consideration for ordination to pastoral or other leadership positions in the church.

Question 3: Don't Male Priests Point to Male Pastors?

The tabernacle and temple priesthood ministry was reserved only for men. Some wonder, "Doesn't this set a precedent for pastoral ministry's being restricted to men?" That priests in the temple and tabernacle were all men is true, of course. Before this fact is used as an argument for a gender restriction in church ministry today, however, it is important to realize the ramifications of doing so. Not only were Levitical priests only men, they were also only Israelites and, further, were exclusively Levites (Num 3:11–13). If the church today is supposed to follow the gender restrictions of the Levitical priesthood, wouldn't this imply that national and tribal restrictions should also be taken into consideration? Further, no one who had a physical defect could serve as a priest, and the service of qualified priests was carefully guarded such that, if a priest was for any reason unclean, he could not serve until he had performed the requisite purification rites.

With regard to the gender restriction, there is one factor that is often overlooked. One of the reasons women could not serve as priests was because their monthly period made them unclean. Women could not enter the temple or tabernacle or be in physical contact with anyone at all while they were menstruating (see Lev 15). It would have been utterly impractical for women to serve as priests for that reason.

Hopefully, most of my readers think of menstruation as presenting no barrier in a person's ability to approach and worship God. Hopefully, words like "unclean" do not readily come to mind when the topic is broached. Unfortunately, I have to say hopefully instead of definitely because this isn't the case in some arenas. A young Coptic Orthodox girl in a youth group I used to lead once told me that her priest had instructed her to refrain from taking communion when she was having her period. This young woman, who had strong feminist leanings, was offended by this, as was I on her behalf. But, according to Coptic Orthodox reasoning, this is a biblical restriction. They draw it directly from Levitical law—the same law that requires priests to be men.

I assume most of my readers will probably be offended for this young woman along with me. "That was a requirement of the *old* covenant," most of us will immediately think. "*Jesus* makes us all clean now, and we can approach God with boldness." Amen and amen. But, what is the logical fallout of such a claim? If God through Christ has removed the cleanliness requirements of the old covenant, on what basis do many churches continue to exclude women from certain ministries because of old-covenant gender restrictions? If one is going to cite *one* priestly requirement as precedent for whom the church does and does not allow to be pastors, *all the priestly requirements* need to be put back on the table, at least for consideration. Actually, this is what the Coptic

Orthodox Church has done, and they've concluded not only that women shouldn't be priests, but also that they shouldn't take communion during their monthly period either. While I disagree with my Coptic Orthodox brothers and sisters about this, I have to admit that they are being more consistent in their application of the Bible than some of my fellow Protestants sometimes are.

Priestly qualifications not only reserved the priesthood for Israelite males descended from Aaron, but also to only "unblemished" men. Leviticus 21:16–23 provides the details:

> The Lord said to Moses, "Say to Aaron: 'For the generations to come none of your descendants who has a defect may come near to offer the food of his God. No man who has any defect may come near: no man who is blind or lame, disfigured or deformed; no man with a crippled foot or hand, or who is a hunchback or a dwarf, or who has any eye defect, or who has festering or running sores or damaged testicles. No descendant of Aaron the priest who has any defect is to come near to present the food offerings to the Lord. He has a defect; he must not come near to offer the food of his God. He may eat the most holy food of his God, as well as the holy food; yet because of his defect, he must not go near the curtain or approach the altar, and so desecrate my sanctuary. I am the Lord, who makes them holy.'"

If we were to use these as guidelines for choosing pastors today, we would have to exclude all persons with disabilities. Not to be crude, but just to establish the point, imagine what would happen if a seminary, as part of its application process, were to require a prostate examination! If a seminary wanted to apply Levitical restrictions for the priesthood to those it prepares to be pastors, a full medical checkup would be necessary.

My point is simple: singling the gender restriction out from amidst all the many restrictions surrounding the priestly office in Levitical law is cherry-picking and special pleading. It is not a consistent way to interpret and apply the Bible to Christian practice.

In fact, the impossibility of extending Levitical restrictions to the church's practice becomes abundantly clear when one considers Jesus. Jesus was not a Levite and, therefore, was not qualified according to Levitical requirements to be a priest. Apparently, this was a stumbling block for some of the earliest Hebrew Christians. The writer of the Epistle to the Hebrews in the New Testament had to go to great lengths to explain how

Jesus, a member of the tribe of Judah, not Levi, could be our high priest to represent humanity before God.[6]

Whereas Paul's requirements of an elder as outlined in Titus and 1 Timothy have to do with moral character and spiritual life, the qualifications of a priest had to do with biological heredity, bodily characteristics, and ritual purity. This is perhaps the sharpest contrast between the two sets of qualifications. One thing that stands out right away is that while Paul says a church elder should be the "husband of one wife," the marital and sexual history of a priest in Levitical law was not brought into question at all. Surprisingly, at least from our perspective, the marital history of *the priest's wife* (or wives) is what was important for whether or not a priest could be qualified to serve in the tabernacle or temple! Priests could only marry virgins. Even widows were off limits. But the priests themselves could be divorced. They could also have multiple wives, even though their wives could not be bigamous. Leviticus 21:13–15 says,

> The woman he marries must be a virgin. He must not marry a widow, a divorced woman, or a woman defiled by prostitution, but only a virgin from his own people, so that he will not defile his offspring among his people. I am the Lord, who makes him holy.

Paul's priorities for an elder and the Levitical law's priorities for a priest are fundamentally different from each other. While there may be some rough parallels between the role of a Christian pastor and that of a temple priest, the qualifications for the two offices have almost no overlap.

Still, my best argument is one I learned as a child growing up in my little Plymouth Brethren church, and it's a truth every Christian should know. Namely, in Christ, *every* person is a priest to God. Because we believe that Jesus is the incarnation of God, we draw the conclusion that God's presence is with us. At Jesus' death the veil to the holiest part of the temple was torn. In a sermon, pastor and scholar Craig Barnes says,

> [Matthew, Mark, and Luke] tell us that at the time of Jesus' crucifixion, the veil that separated the Holy of Holies from the rest of the temple was ripped from top to bottom, as if it was done by heaven. I used to think that the purpose of that was so that anybody could go into the Holy of Holies—priesthood of all believers; we can all go in now. But I've since come to think that, maybe, it's so the holiness could rush out.[7]

6. See especially Heb 4:14—5:10; 7–8.

7. Princeton Theological Seminary, "President Barnes Preaches on Exodus

By the Spirit of God, all who are in Christ are, in fact, not only priests to God, *but also the temple of God itself* (1 Cor 3:16; 6:19)! Because of Jesus we have come to know that access to God's presence is not restricted. There is explicit New Testament evidence of this truth (Rev 1:6; 5:10) as well as foreshadowing of it in the Hebrew Scriptures (Exod 19:6). Thus, *all* believers are priests under the new covenant in Christ, and there is no distinction based on the Levitical system. The New Testament is not ambiguous about who is and who is not qualified to be a priest in Christ. If a person is in Christ, he—*or she*—is a priest to God.

Question 4: Doesn't Male Biblical Authorship Point to Male Pastors?

As far as we know, the Bible was written only by male authors. Doesn't this imply that God prefers male messengers? The first thing that should be said is that we do not know whose actual, physical hand penned any of the books in the Bible. In some if not most cases the biblical authors probably used scribes to help them. Of course, when I say, for example, that Paul wrote the Epistle to the Romans, no one stops me and says, "No, he probably used a scribe." Why? Because it doesn't matter whose hand penned the original text; what matters is whose mind was the source of its content. Who composed the text is what matters. Who provided the theological material is what matters.

If we think in terms of who provided its content, the Bible's authorship becomes a little less male. Certainly, the vast majority of voices heard in the Bible are men's. But, women's voices are heard in the text often enough to refute the claim that women did not participate in the Bible's composition. Hagar, an Egyptian slave woman, is the first person in the Bible to give God a name, and the promise that she receives from God for her son Ishmael and his descendants is similar to the one Abraham received about Isaac. Hagar could be classified among the prophetesses of the Hebrew Bible, in fact, for she certainly received a prophecy from God. Miriam, Moses' older sister, composed the Israelites' victory song after the Red Sea crossing. Both these women thus "wrote" parts of the Bible. Miriam, along with Huldah and Deborah, is called a prophetess in the Bible as well. Hannah, the mother of Samuel, wrote a song after Samuel's birth that is echoed, with tremendous theological import, in the song of

20:7–11," 10:33—11:00.

Mary in the Gospel of Luke. Put these two women down on the list with Deborah and Miriam as women who wrote parts of the Bible.

If my readers are like me, this short list will be slightly underwhelming. Compared to the amount of male influence in the Bible's composition, female influence is, admittedly, pretty small. No one can truthfully claim that women and men are equally represented in the Bible. But, at the same time, no one can truthfully claim that *only men* wrote the Bible.

I'll make one last observation that may interest some of my more inquisitive readers. Christians believe that all of Scripture is inspired by the Holy Spirit. It just so happens that the word for spirit is neuter in Greek. In English, a spirit could be he, she, or it. But in Aramaic, the language spoken by some of the earliest followers of Jesus, spirit is feminine. Some of the most important early Christian translations of the Bible are in Syriac, a dialect of Aramaic. In the Syriac Bible, the Holy Spirit is referred to as she and her. For many of the earliest followers of Jesus, the Bible was inspired by *her,* the Holy Spirit!

This doesn't prove anything, really, because the Spirit is immaterial and eternal and, therefore, has no gender. This is just my roundabout way of pointing out that, ultimately, what gives the Bible authority is not the Bible's human authors but the Spirit who inspires what they wrote. The fact that God inspired the writings of men is merely evidence of God's gracious wisdom in condescending to our human social and cultural mores. God did not drop a perfect book out of the sky; God worked in and through people—particularly the Hebrew and, later, Israelite and Jewish people—to bring God's word into the world, a word that ultimately points to Jesus, the Word made flesh. Given the utterly male-dominated societies into which God spoke, one would expect women to be considerably less prominent than they are in the Bible.[8]

At the end of the day, Christians are not supposed to model their lives or their church communities after the Bible's literary characteristics or compositional provenance. Rather, they are supposed to be *Christ-ones* (Christians)—followers of Jesus. In God's providence, the first people who bore witness to the resurrected Christ—which is what preaching the gospel is at its core—were women. The prophet Joel famously predicted that the preeminence of a single gender in prophecy would balance out in a future time when God would "pour out" the Spirit on everyone. Specifically, he wrote, "your sons *and daughters* shall prophesy" (Joel 2:28). In

8. See Frymer-Kensky, *In the Wake of the Goddesses,* for a thorough, illuminating study of the Bible's uniqueness among ancient literature in its inclusion of women.

Acts, a woman named Priscilla is portrayed as an effective teacher (Acts 18:26). Also in Acts, Philip's four daughters are said to have the gift of prophecy (Acts 21:8–9). In Romans 16, Paul mentions a woman named Junia along with a man named Andronicus whom he seems to number among the apostles (v. 7). He also mentions Tryphaena and Persis, noting that they are women who labored along with him "in the Lord" (Rom 16:12). It is conceivable, of course, that these women merely supported the gospel by doing something like what some today would consider traditional womanly things in the church—cooking, cleaning, teaching Sunday school, leading women's groups (all of which are extremely important and valuable). But I think this is highly unlikely. I think, rather, that Paul is naming people who have become well-known in the early church as ministers of the gospel—people who were engaged in work very similar to his own. Why else would Paul be mentioning these people specifically in a public letter like this? Paul seems to be commending the *vocal* ministries of these people to the Christians at Rome.

All this to say, women have more influence in the Bible—including in its composition—than they are often given credit for. This in and of itself doesn't prove that women should be allowed to speak in the church. But, it does show that women's voices cannot be theologically irrelevant. Anyone who reads the Bible attentively will end up learning from women. It can't be avoided. Why, then, should men try to avoid learning from women in the ongoing work of the Spirit through the voices of Christian women today?

Question 5: Don't Male Disciples Point to Male Pastors?

Jesus' twelve disciples were men. Doesn't this set a precedent for male leadership in the church? This is one of the tougher questions for a person who holds my position. Couldn't Jesus have done more to include women than he did? Couldn't he have had six men and six women as his disciples, just to make things clear? The truth is, I don't have an answer to this question (yet) that completely satisfies me, so I must warn my gracious readers that what follows may have the same effect on them. Nevertheless, here is what I have to offer.

First, it is important to understand why Jesus chose *twelve* disciples. Leaving aside their maleness, consider their number. Why twelve? The reason is that they represented the twelve tribes of Israel. Jesus came to proclaim the reign of God in the world, and this was something for which Israel had been waiting centuries before his arrival. Jesus' choice of twelve primary disciples was a not-so-subtle allusion to the nation of Israel itself and, thus, to Jesus' role as Israel's king. When one bears in mind the male-dominated environment into which Jesus was preaching his message, his choice of twelve men becomes understandable. It probably would not have been possible for this message to reach those who were observing Jesus' activities if some of those twelve disciples had been women. After all, the twelve tribes of Israel were named after the twelve patriarchs—the sons of Jacob, whom God had called "Israel."

Second, Jesus *did* have female disciples. According to what the scholars tell us, it was extremely rare—or even completely unheard of—in Jesus' day for a Jewish rabbi to choose women as his disciples. Yet, Jesus did so. Here are two passages from the Gospels that mention Jesus' female disciples:

> In Galilee these women had followed him and cared for his needs. Many other women who had come up with him to Jerusalem were also there. (Mark 15:41)

> After this, Jesus traveled about from one town and village to another, proclaiming the good news of the kingdom of God. The Twelve were with him, and also some women who had been cured of evil spirits and diseases: Mary (called Magdalene) from whom seven demons had come out; Joanna the wife of Chuza, the manager of Herod's household; Susanna; and many others. These women were helping to support them out of their own means. (Luke 8:1–3)

Perhaps the most striking example of a female disciple is Mary, Martha and Lazarus's sister. Most Christians will have heard the story of Mary and Martha. In sermons I have heard about this story, Martha is usually portrayed as the busy, dutiful woman who failed to see the importance of slowing down to spend time with Jesus. Mary, on the other hand, knows how important it is to have her quiet time with Jesus. But this story also has a more socially revolutionary message, for it portrays a Messiah who is willing to resist traditional gender expectations.

In Acts 22:3, Paul says that he "sat at the feet" of the famous rabbi Gamaliel. This means that Paul was Gamaliel's disciple. "I sat at so-and-so's feet" was an idiomatic way of saying, "I was so-and-so's disciple." This was something that could only be said of a man because all rabbis were men. Luke is the author of Acts, so there is good reason to expect that the same idiom means the same thing elsewhere in his writings. Thus, in Luke 8 when Jesus casts out a multitude of demons from a man and the text says that the man was found "sitting at the feet" of Jesus, we can conclude that the man was sitting there learning from Jesus' teaching, like a disciple would. The point is not that the man was sitting physically near Jesus' feet; it is about his new relationship with Jesus as his follower. Thus, when Luke 10:39 says that Mary "sat at the Lord's feet and listened to his teaching," it means that Jesus was welcoming Mary into a circle that was normally reserved exclusively for men. Mary was being treated by the great rabbi Jesus as his disciple—a student in Jesus' school. Martha's indignation about the situation came from far more than her frustration at having to clean all the dirty dishes by herself. Martha was angry with Mary because she was doing something very improper—something no woman should have been doing (that is, according to people other than Jesus).

In twenty-first-century, Westernized parts of the world, we have become accustomed to a great deal of overlap between the roles of men and women both in the home and in many other areas of society. Few of us would be surprised to go to our friends' house for dinner to find a man preparing the meal. But in the time and place of Jesus—and in traditional Mediterranean cultures today as well—it would have been extremely awkward for a woman to choose to sit and chat with the men while someone else prepared the food, especially if she is the *younger* sister in the household.

Note that Luke makes a distinction between Jesus' relationship with Martha *vis-à-vis* Mary. Martha is the hostess (v. 38), while Mary is the disciple. Certainly, Martha was Jesus' friend; but Mary positioned herself as Jesus' *disciple* (v. 39). What is so remarkable about this story is that Mary felt the confidence to do such a thing. Again, probably neither I nor most of my gracious readers will be able to feel the full significance of Mary's action from our cultural perspective. Most of us probably wonder why Martha wasn't upset with Lazarus too for not helping her in the kitchen. Shouldn't Lazarus have helped with the preparations for the meal just as much as Mary? Well, no—not in a traditional Mediterranean culture, especially in the first century. Lazarus was a man. If a famous teacher graced his house, the proper thing for a man to do would be to sit and chat with the visitor. The women's responsibility was to serve the guest and the men of the house while they visited, and to do so quietly and meekly.

Jesus and Mary's behavior in this story says far more to us as readers about Jesus' sociocultural agenda than it does about taking a daily quiet time. Certainly, taking time out of our busy lives to spend in quietness before God is *part* of what this little story can teach us. But it is more important for our current discussion to see *the other part* of what is at stake in this little episode. It is important to note that the ultimate goal of being a rabbi's disciple was to eventually become a teacher of that rabbi's lessons oneself (2 Tim 2:2). It is safe to assume this is what Jesus had in mind for Mary.

I haven't mentioned all the examples available. But this is enough to make the point that Jesus actually *did* have female disciples. True, none of the twelve disciples were women. But on the other hand, none of them were gentiles either. Jesus largely followed the conventions of his day. People called him rabbi because they recognized him as filling the role of a Jewish itinerant teacher of the Torah, and this role involved having a core of young male students. Jesus did enough to push the boundaries of accepted norms, however, to show us that he was far from satisfied with the status quo. We have mentioned briefly in our previous discussions his unconventional and—by his contemporaries' standards—inappropriate affirmation of women in Luke 7 and John 4. Jesus seems to purposely hold women up as models of true discipleship in those passages. He planted the seeds for a transformed view of women among his fledgling church. The question was (and is), would (and will) his followers water those seeds?

As I noted, this doesn't quite satisfy me completely. I can't help but wish that Jesus had been more explicit about this. That lingering question, "Couldn't Jesus have been just a bit more radical?" still nags at me. I have similar questions about how the Bible addresses slavery. "Why," I often wonder, "doesn't the Bible just condemn slavery outright?" That's a discussion for another time, but it's relevant enough to at least mention here. It's impossible for me to claim that the Bible treats men and women equally. In fact, I would probably have to admit that even Jesus did not treat women as if they had equal *social* standing to men.

However, I *can* claim that the Bible gives more than a sufficient number of hints to goad the Spirit-led church of Jesus' disciples in the future toward realization of what Jesus was ultimately expecting of the community that he started. It took centuries for significant parts of the church in my home country to finally formally repent of slavery and racism. The church's responsibility for perpetuating those evils has still not been fully acknowledged, or even realized, by many in the church in my home country. The price for our lethargy will no doubt continue to be paid for some time to come. Still, I maintain that those who have used the Bible to support slavery and white supremacy have been wrong all along—that the fundamental message of Scripture has always been diametrically opposed to them. It is undeniable that the Bible was *used* to support slavery and racism; I'm just claiming that such a use perverts its true message.

Likewise, I think the majority of the church has missed the Bible's push toward a new way of thinking about male and female because they are waiting for someone to find a verse in the Bible that says outright, "Hey, women and men are equal. Let the women speak in church too." No such verse exists! But, no such verse exists to condemn the institution of slavery outright either. The Bible, generally speaking, doesn't work that way. The Bible doesn't have to overtly say a thing in order for us to affirm that its message points in a particular direction. Stackhouse explains, "God works along the general social contours of patriarchal society, taking us as we are, even as the creative and liberating pressure of the Holy Spirit on that society first ameliorates some of the most oppressive aspects of patriarchy and then ultimately opens it up to the full equality of women."[9] Just as the Bible was against slavery all along *without saying so outright,* so the Bible is against limiting the speaking ministry of women, and also subordinating them under men because of their gender. We ought to realize this now and humbly make a change. In my opinion, the quicker we can do that the better things will be for the church's future.

Question 6: Isn't It Dangerous to Allow Women to Lead?

Men who listen to their wives' advice in the Bible sometimes go wrong. Doesn't this point to the need for women to follow, and for men to lead?

The most commonly cited example of a man going wrong by following his wife's lead is in the story of Adam and Eve. Genesis says that Eve gave the fruit to Adam. It appears that Eve is taking the lead, at least in that episode. Sometimes hierarchicalists argue that Adam should have taken the lead. "If he hadn't been predisposed to following his wife's leadership—if he had been the authoritative party in the relationship—maybe the story would have ended differently," it is thought.

---

9. Stackhouse, *Partners in Christ*, 108.

There are other examples in the Bible of men doing the wrong thing after following their wives' or some other woman's counsel. Ahab took the role of a follower in the story of Naboth's vineyard (1 Kgs 21). In this tragic story, Ahab, king of the northern kingdom of Israel at the time, stands by while his wife Jezebel employs scoundrels and a kangaroo court to brutally execute an innocent man in order to steal his vineyard. I remember chatting after a church service about this story with a man once. Chuckling, he said, "One thing we learn from that story is, never listen to your wife!" Is that what the story is supposed to teach us?

Abraham provides another example of a man who followed his wife's poor advice. When Sarah could not bear children, she suggested he try to have a child by her maidservant Hagar. Abraham complied and this led to family problems that ultimately proved unresolvable. Job's wife tells him to "curse God and die" (Job 2:9). That doesn't sound like very good advice! And then there is the oft-told story of Samson and Delilah. Samson finally gives in to his mistress Delilah's nagging and tells her the secret of his great strength. She then famously betrays him to his Philistine enemies, thereby producing yet another biblical example of how a man's trusting a woman's lead can send him on a path to his undoing (Judg 13–16). And as we mentioned in the introduction, Herod Antipas ordered the beheading of John the Baptist at the request of his wife Herodias.

Maybe there are some other examples I'm missing. If one were to *only* list the episodes in the Bible in which men do wrong by following their wives, one might be persuaded that there is something compelling about the assertion that following the lead of one's wife is a bad idea. But to be fair, and to draw an objective conclusion, it is of course necessary to include the places where women make serious mistakes by following their husbands too. Examples of this are just as easy to find.

Before the episode where Abraham follows Sarah's poor advice and impregnates Hagar, we find Abraham *twice* telling Sarah to hide her relationship to him in order to save his own skin (Gen 12:10–20; 20:1–18). Though the text does not say so openly (probably as a way of respecting Sarah), it seems that on the first of these occasions Sarah found herself in the harem of the king of Egypt (Gen 12:15). That is, by following her husband's advice she became, at best, a king's concubine. To put it in a less generous way, she became a sex slave. (This is the story that makes me uncomfortable with the way Peter refers to Sarah as a model wife in 1 Pet 3:6.) It is abundantly obvious that Sarah should *not* have followed

Abraham's lead in these situations—for her own good if for no other reason. Who knows the emotional trauma she had to deal with after that event? Who knows how much strain this put on her relationship with Abraham? Could this event help explain Sarah's oppressive treatment of Hagar later in the story? Isaac later commits the same cowardly act in Genesis 26, placing his wife Rebecca in the same perilous situation.

The fact is, men give bad advice to their wives sometimes too, both in the Bible and in human experience generally. I myself have made mistakes when I've taken the lead in my marriage. Thankfully I've not made any errors as calamitous as Abraham did, but he and I—and all husbands— miss the mark at some point. When that happens, and a wife is insightful enough to see it, blessed is the man who is ready to listen to her!

But let's take this exploration a step further. Are there any examples in the Bible of women leading their husbands, or other men, in the *right* direction? Almost everyone who goes to church has heard the story of Esther. What would have become of the Jewish people in Persia had Esther's husband, the Persian emperor Ahasuerus (Artaxerxes), not listened to his wife's advice? Wicked and ruthless man that he was, he at least had the wisdom to let his wife expose and correct his own blunders in that particular story.

In 1 Samuel 25, we find the story of Abigail. In this story, Abigail's husband Nabal is portrayed as a foolhardy, lazy man who seems to care more about partying than managing and protecting his household. The reader gets the definite impression that Abigail is the brains in the home. When Nabal insults David, David decides to rally his band of outlaws and raid Nabal's house. David fully intends to kill Nabal and to slaughter every other man in his household (something David was absolutely capable of doing [1 Sam 27:8–12]). Indeed, this particular story doesn't reflect too well on David's character either. The men are not looking very good in this story. But when she hears of David's plans, Abigail flies into action without her husband's permission (he is partying at the time). She gathers a peace offering and goes out to meet David and his band of angry men before they arrive to massacre her family. Abigail's smart, swift response is exemplary leadership. This is the kind of woman anyone would want to be president or prime minister during a national emergency. Abigail saves not only her husband's life, but also those of all the male servants in their large household. Nabal dies of heart failure shortly thereafter—but thanks to Abigail his heart doesn't fail because David had stuck a sword through it.

In the New Testament Joseph listened to his betrothed's outlandish claim that she was both pregnant and still a virgin. What kind of man believes such an absurd claim from a teenage peasant girl? Well, a wise and good man like Joseph, apparently. (Unfortunately, there are still plenty of people around who still don't believe her.) This isn't a case in which a woman gives a man advice, but it *is* a case in which a man does well to listen to a woman. We might say that Mary is Eve's redeemer—not in every sense of course, but in terms of how we should view women. Why should Eve be the woman who first comes to our minds when we think about how a stereotypical woman behaves? Why not Mary instead—the one whom God chose to be God incarnate's first dwelling place? The one who trusted God and submitted to God's will?

Zipporah, Moses' first wife, is another example of a woman whose husband depended on her leadership in a desperate situation. The incident is so strange and is given such short attention in Exodus that many Bible readers skip over it without appreciating how important it is. Here's what it says:

> At a lodging place on the way the LORD met him and sought to put him to death. Then Zipporah took a flint and cut off her son's foreskin and touched Moses' feet with it and said, "Surely you are a bridegroom of blood to me!" So he let him alone. It was then that she said, "A bridegroom of blood," because of the circumcision. (Exod 4:24–26 ESV)

There is a lot upon which to comment in these three short verses. Suffice it to say for our purposes that Zipporah is portrayed in this story as a wise, resourceful wife whose husband depended on her. She clearly takes the role of the leader in this little story, making all the decisions and taking all the important actions.

Still, there is one example in the Bible of a wife who offered her husband good leadership advice that trumps all others, and should settle the matter of whether or not men should listen to their wives' counsel once and for all. Sadly, we're not told this brave woman's name. She is simply mentioned, almost offhand, as Pontius Pilate's wife. When no one else, not even Peter, stood up for Jesus, this woman confronted her husband and warned him that executing Jesus would be a horrible error (Matt 27:19). Foolishly, Pilate chose to ignore her. As a result, he has passed into history as a byword for cowardice. Had Pilate been willing to heed his wife's warning, *he could have avoided committing the crime of crucifying the incarnation of God!* In my estimation, this story alone is enough to refute the notion that men go wrong when they follow their wives' lead. No, a wise man often listens to his wife's advice.

The bottom line is this: both men and women can be wrong. Both are human, and therefore finite *and* broken by sin. Husbands and wives, ideally, should be able to listen to each other and follow one another's lead. Sometimes the husband will have the requisite knowledge and insight to be the leader. At other times the wife will. A husband can lead his wife straight into a living hell; and a wife can lead her husband to heaven. If they want to head in the right direction, both should be following Jesus, together. "Who's in charge?" is not a very helpful question in a healthy Christian marriage.

Question 7: If Husbands Are Not Their Wives' Authorities, How Can Parents Be Their Children's Authorities?

Of all the questions we've addressed in this chapter, I hear this one the most. The reasoning goes like this: "If we decide that Christian husbands shouldn't think of themselves as their wives' authorities based on the biblical command that wives submit to their husbands, doesn't it follow that parents shouldn't consider themselves their children's authorities based on the biblical command that children obey their parents?"

I don't think this reasoning holds water. Women are not children. Children are immature by definition. They need parents who will guide them to maturity. Children need to obey their parents *not* because of a particular role that needs to be filled, but because this is the only way that they can successfully be prepared for the responsibilities, challenges, and hazards of adulthood. Wives, on the other hand, are adults just like their husbands. It is not a husband's responsibility to raise his wife. Her parents should have done that when she was a child. A husband's responsibility, rather, is to nurture, care for, and serve his wife. She should do the same for him.

As we noted previously, in the context of the same passages in Colossians and Ephesians in which Paul tells children to obey their parents and wives to submit to their husbands, he also tells slaves to obey and submit to their masters. Though Paul could not have anticipated it in his day, his words were later to be torn from their contexts and used to justify one of the most horrific sins in modern human history. As an American, it is impossible for me to hear the word "slave" without calling to mind the enslavement of African and Native American people by European colonists and, later, white Americans over the past five centuries. Everyone knows that slavery existed for a long time before white Europeans began enslaving the peoples of other lands as part of their colonizing projects. The institution of slavery *per se* was not invented by European colonialists. But, the means of justifying slavery was new. By the time Christopher Columbus set out to find the "New World," Europe had been influenced by the Bible for well over a millennium. Once the economic benefits of enslaving people from other parts of the world became clear, European Christians had to find some way to justify their doing so in a way that would, ostensibly (but, in fact, perversely), fit with their Christian worldview. Their cultural forbearers, the Greeks and Romans, had not needed to do this. In the Greco-Roman mind a racist ideology was not necessary to justify slavery. If one group of people was stronger than another militarily, no further justification for enslaving them was required. One town might suit up, go to battle, and take a bunch of slaves from the town a few kilometers away—even though the people in both towns were virtually identical ethnically. Of course, a person's citizenship status mattered in the Roman Empire. But, Roman citizenship was not determined by ethnicity or race. The heirs of Roman power—European Christians—by contrast, knew because of their exposure to Christian teaching that might does not make right. Nevertheless, they still wanted to exploit slaves. So, they developed a way of categorizing people based on physical attributes, thereby giving birth to what shortly developed into full-blown white supremacist ideology, with all its accompanying horrors. In this way, they could justify slavery not by an appeal to brute power and glory (as the Greeks and Romans had done), but by an appeal to God's design. God, they decided, had created darker-skinned people to serve, and lighter-skinned people to rule. This was simply the place of darker-skinned and white people respectively, and all parties would do better to accept that.

The Bible, in the hands of white Christian slaveowners, was thus perverted from its purpose as the vehicle of a gospel message of liberation and made into a tool of violence and exploitation. And, it would not be an exaggeration to say that the "submit" passages of Ephesians, Colossians, and 1 Peter have been used more than any other texts in all the Bible as such. Sometimes, one wonders if these texts are redeemable at all, for in the minds and hearts of many people their warped interpretation has become so thoroughly linked to the texts themselves as to make the two impossible to separate. In his classic work, *Jesus and the Disinherited*, the great American theologian and pastor Howard Thurman writes about a conversation he had with his grandmother. Thurman's grandmother had grown up enslaved, and thus had been deprived of the opportunity to learn to read. As a child, one of Thurman's chores was to read the Bible to her. She would choose passages from various parts of the Bible, but she almost never asked Thurman to read from Paul's letters. Later, as a young man, he asked her why this was. She replied,

> "During the days of slavery . . . the master's minister would occasionally hold services for slaves. Old man McGee was so mean that he would not let a Negro minister preach to his slaves. Always the white minister used as his text something from Paul. At least three or four times a year he used as a text: 'Slaves, be obedient to them that are your masters . . . , as unto Christ.' Then he would go on to show how it was God's will that we were slaves and how, if we were good and happy slaves, God would bless us. I promised my Maker that if I ever learned to read and if freedom ever came, I would not read that part of the Bible."[10]

This is just one example of how the Bible has been used to steal, kill, and destroy. Just as a murdered person can never be restored, even when the murderer repents, I admit that I sometimes wonder whether certain passages of the Bible have been murdered by those who have used them to sap the life out of other people. I'm aware, given the history of how certain passages have been weaponized over the past two millennia, of how feeble efforts to restore them to their rightful place as part of the Bible's freeing gospel may prove to be. And, in light of how the "submit" passages *in particular* have been used by some to assert power over others, they should be approached with *extreme and exceptional* caution. If the "submit" passages were used so effectively to support and perpetuate a sin as monstrous as American slavery, it seems likely that they could easily be used to support abusive male domination of women (and, indeed, they have been).

I note this in order to put the question at hand in perspective. Some worry about whether or not children will need to obey their parents if husbands are not construed as their wives' authorities according to Ephesians 5. But, given the very recent history of how the "submit" passages

---

10. Thurman, *Jesus and the Disinherited*, 20.

have been used, shouldn't the overwhelmingly more urgent concern be, "If we say that husbands are their wives' God-given authorities based on the 'submit' passages, what exploitation and abuse might we be in danger of perpetuating?"

I've given an all-too-truncated version of the story of how the Bible came to factor into the racialized justifications of slavery, and how it and its legacy have plagued the world for centuries. But if for no other reason than to be fair to Paul, the point to be made for our present discussion is that Paul lived and wrote before the racist theology that propped up Euro-American chattel slavery developed. Paul was not speaking into a Christianized culture that justified slavery based on God's will. Instead, he was speaking into a culture in which raw power, honor, and glory alone were enough to justify slavery, along with a host of other forms of oppression—that is, the world of the Roman Empire. Paul was emphatically *not* trying to support a perverse Christian theology of slavery. Rather, Paul was attempting to shepherd Christian slaves as they tried to follow Jesus in the midst of an unjust worldly system of abusive power.

Paul was certainly aware that slave revolts were a possible option on the table in the Roman Empire. Most famously, a revolt led by a slave named Spartacus had been crushed a little over a hundred years before Paul's day. In the end, 6,000 of the slaves who survived the uprising and subsequent war were crucified in a line stretching for miles along the Appian Way leading to Rome. Everyone in the Roman Empire knew about that event. Perhaps Paul *could* have incited such a revolt. But as counterintuitive as it might be, Paul was telling Christian slaves that Jesus' life and work had opened up an entirely different and new way of confronting the evil powers that are at work within unjust systems, like slavery. When Paul tells slaves to submit, he is not telling them to do so because of a God-given role they occupy. Rather, he is showing them how to live like Jesus within their present, unjust circumstances. Paul's hope was not to make all slaves like their masters, *but to make all masters like their slaves.* He envisioned a community in which, like Jesus, all its members saw themselves as servants of one another. A faith that constantly tells its adherents to serve, serve, serve, and *never once* tells them to rule over others undermines the very idea of a static slave-master relationship.

On the other hand, Paul would have had no interest in dissolving the parent-child relationship. Parents provide guidance for those who are less mature than they, and prepare those little persons to someday become the guides of others. The goal of parenting is to bring children ultimately to maturity as adults. Slavery, however, only seeks the maturity of a slave insofar as that maturity will benefit the slave's master. In the case of American slavery, slaveowner practices and laws actively sought to *stunt* the maturity of slaves. For example, after the year 1830, most slave states forbade slaves by law from learning to read, imposing fines on anyone who tried to teach them. Even without such laws, only about 10 percent of slaves had learned to read.[11] The situation was, of course, different in Greco-Roman times when many slaves were encouraged to be educated because they served as tutors or stewards for wealthy masters and their families. The point is, when it comes to the master-slave relationship, the education of, *or* the withholding of education from, slaves depends on the needs and desires of their masters, not those of the slaves themselves. Good parents, by stark contrast, seek to provide their children with as many enriching, character-building, and educational opportunities as possible not for their *own* good as parents, but for the good of the children themselves. In their essences and goals, parenting and slavery could not be more different! Slavery is the utilization of the weak and poor to benefit the strong and wealthy, while parenting is the utilization of strength, wisdom, and resources to bring the young and immature to wisdom, effectiveness, and enrichment. Parenting, at its best, benefits the parented; slavery, at its "best," benefits the enslaver. The fact that both the parent-child relationship and the master-slave relationship are mentioned in Ephesians 5 does not erase this fundamental difference between them.

I think an attentive reading of Pauline theology leads ultimately to the abolition of slavery as an institution, even though Paul tells slaves to obey and submit to their masters. By contrast, I think Paul did *not* envision the abolition of parenting. If this is correct, it is clear that Paul's admonishments regarding Christian submission and obedience to this or that human being or institution is not always for the same reason. *But notice that neither a Christian slave's submission to his master nor a Christian child's submission to his parents has anything to do with God-given roles.* Paul tells slaves to submit because serving others models Christ as the Servant-King. He tells children to obey because this is good for them. When Christian parents tell their children to obey them, they do not explain why by stating, "Because this is your role to play." Instead, they say,

---

11. Coleman, "How Literacy Became a Powerful Weapon."

"Because you need my guidance, and God has given me that responsibility as your parent. Your obedience to me is for your own good."

To corroborate my point in a roundabout way, I'll borrow a quote from an expert on the status of women in the New Testament world. In her fascinating commentary on Ephesians, New Testament scholar Lynn Cohick notes, "[A] patron or master could be female, and her client or slave a male, which means that subordination in the ancient world was not limited to male/female."[12] That is to say, Paul was probably telling at least some men—slaves—to obey some women—their mistresses—in Ephesians 6:5. Of course, husbands are always men and wives always women. But, if Paul's telling women to submit is due to a gender-role ideology, why doesn't he say anything about the gender of slaves and masters—a social relationship in which he just as often encourages submission?

It seems that a static roles ideology fits neither Paul's teaching that children obey their parents nor his command that slaves submit to their masters. I suggest that Paul's telling women to submit to their husbands wasn't about an ideology—much less a theology—of roles either. Unlike slavery, Paul provides ample theological backing in support of marriage as an institution. He didn't want to abolish marriage. But still, Roman law gave husbands tremendous power over their wives and children. When Paul tells wives to submit to their husbands, he is doing something *very* similar to what he is doing when he tells slaves to submit to their masters. It is somewhat ironic that Paul's command that children obey their parents is so often brought up in conversations between Christians about women and submission in the church and home today. The truth is, the status of a wife in Paul's world paralleled that of a slave much more closely than it did that of a child. In terms of their ability to choose freely how and where they wished to spend their lives, most women were not much better off than slaves. Unlike children, women cannot grow up and achieve the new status of adulthood. Women are adults already. Once they've reached adulthood, their maturity level cannot be used to justify their subordination to another person, whether a master or a husband. But a child's maturity level, of course, can!

All this is to say that the relationship between two married adults *should be* thought about very differently from a parent-child relationship. The trouble is, again, we modern folk often come to the Bible hoping that it will give us a blueprint, from scratch, for how a Christian household

12. Cohick, *Ephesians*, loc. 2845 of 4036.

should be arranged. That is simply not what the New Testament does. The New Testament, not unlike Jesus, is incarnated into real-world times and places. The original readers of Paul's letters were *not* asking, "What does an ideal Christian household look like, apart from any real-world context?" Rather, they were asking, "How, given the sociocultural norms, expectations, and predetermined relationships of my present, everyday situation, can my life be a testimony to the reign of God that is coming into the world through Jesus?"

As Genesis 3:16 predicts, marriage quickly devolves into something that resembles a slave-and-master relationship when a society allows sinful passions to prevail. Fallen humanity easily defaults to an arrangement in which the strong rule the weak. (Men, generally speaking, have shown this to be true repeatedly throughout human history.) Human community can thrive without the institution of slavery; it cannot, in Paul's view, survive and thrive without marriage. When it comes to slavery, the gospel's ultimate word is *abolition*. But when it comes to marriage, the word is *redemption*. As we have argued throughout this book, partners in a marriage who find themselves redeemed by Christ will become servants of each other. In an authentically Christian marriage, there are no masters. There are only servants.

Closing Remarks

I WANT TO THANK my readers for giving me a hearing. I am grateful when any person cares enough about this issue to read a book about it. I hope that I have been as fair as possible to those who disagree with my position. On the one hand, claiming that "I am right, you are wrong" is inevitably going to ruffle feathers. But on the other hand, I have known so many wonderful Christians who disagree with me on the question of male-female equality that, despite my passion to change their minds, I cannot deny that I have experienced the Spirit of Christ through them. I hope that my stronger comments in the foregoing pages have not been understood as attacks on every individual who disagrees with me. Indeed, I hope that I have not attacked persons at all, but only an idea.

I hope that my readers will have noticed that none of my arguments were based ultimately on a concern for the rights of women. I am not against the concept of human rights generally, or of women's rights in particular, and I celebrate the improvements that the concept of rights has spearheaded for the lives of both men and women in many societies around the world. I would even be honored to be called a feminist, and I applaud the bravery of those who advocate for women's rights. Still, I find the biblical doctrines of the image of God and the body of Christ to be more philosophically complete and, therefore, more true to reality as we experience it, than the concept of human rights. I have not argued that women should speak in church because they have a right to do so; I have argued instead that we—the church as a whole with both genders included—*need* the voices of Christian women in order to fulfill our symbolic function as God's redeemed, restored humanity in the world. If the church needs pastors and teachers at all, it needs at least *some* women to fill those roles. The situation now is lopsided. I, frankly, have a lot of questions about why God created humanity as two sexes. But nevertheless, here we are. Humanity *is* male and female, and the church as the living testimony of a redeemed humanity must recognize this in its practical life. When we fail to affirm fully and equally the voices of one half of humanity in the church—even a little bit—we fail ultimately to affirm the image of God in the whole. If the church is the earthly witness to God's redemption of humanity in Christ, and if humanity is made in the image of God, the voices that speak for, and to, the church must represent the wholeness of that image. Our sisters' voices should be heard. This is not only for their own sake, but for the good of the church and, by extension, of humanity and all of creation. The issue is really that far-reaching.

Genesis teaches that the tendency of fallen humanity will be for men to dominate (see 3:16). Unfortunately, recent history has shown that, quite often, when one branch of the church makes moves to raise the status of women, another branch reacts by taking steps in the opposite direction. I wish I could say this is the kind of issue that could be decided once and for all, in this generation. But I don't think it is. It is likely that the legitimacy of women's voices in the church will continue to be questioned in some way in every generation for as long as humanity continues in its broken state. Progress toward a Christ-like ideal has never been inevitable. Nevertheless, we have an opportunity, in our generation, to tell our sisters that we want to hear their voices—indeed, that we *need* to hear their voices.

Too many churches bind the voices of women rather than untie the cords of silence. The fact is, Christian women always have been, and always will be, teachers, preachers, and pastors in the midst of God's flock. But only occasionally has this fact been formally recognized and, consequently, the church has not as actively or consciously sought to equip women for these tasks as they have sought to do so for men. I am utterly persuaded that it is time for the whole church to embrace the whole of humanity in every aspect of its ministry and, where it can, to encourage the same in wider society. I envision a church environment in which women who are called to serve Christ's body with their voices will be encouraged to do so even as I was encouraged by so many as a young man. As a young man interested in and called to preaching and Bible teaching, I was encouraged and affirmed by multitudes of people around me to pursue preparation and to cultivate those gifts and passions. In many churches today, the faintest spark of interest in these things will be enthusiastically fanned into flame so long as that spark is found in the soul of a young man. But tragically, a young woman growing up in those same churches and with the same spark will not be encouraged to develop her gifts or to pursue vocations in vocal Christian ministry, at least to the same degree. The bellows that fan the spark in the young man will be turned about and used to tamp out the same spark in the young woman.

In too many Christian circles, a woman called to use her voice faces an uphill battle. What should be a normal process of discernment quickly turns into a skirmish of Bible verses and a clash of ideologies. Women find themselves caught in the crossfire of culture wars—wars not without their collateral damage. Few people have the energy or stamina to stand up in that crossfire, especially if they haven't had the chance to get the necessary training to do so. Many Christian women will grow up in church environments in which they will not even be encouraged to be open to the Spirit's leading them toward a speaking ministry. How likely is it that a little girl—or even a young woman—who grows up literally never seeing a woman behind a pulpit, and is occasionally taught that it is wrong for women to preach, will ever even consider pursuing the vocation of a pastor?

Our failure to recognize and encourage the voices of women has stunted our growth. We are *all—men and women alike*—the worse off for it. This is not a "women's issue," as it is sometimes framed; it is an issue for all of God's people. We are the body of Christ. If the cords of silence bind our sisters, they bind us all. The good news is that God has not abandoned us, and the door of repentance stands wide open. God is patient, and the Spirit remains willing. Yes, the church as a whole—and every local church too—*can* change.

I had originally entitled this book, *Let Our Sisters Speak*. But that title would have implied too much deference to the control that men have over women in the church. As Dr. Barr says, "Women, despite patriarchy's ever-moving goalposts, have always found a way to preach and teach the Word of God."[1] Women of God are already speaking, and have been doing so throughout the history of God's self-revelation. But, can we hear them? Or rather, can we hear what God is saying through them? It is time for us to open our eyes and see that, from God's perspective, the cords of silence are already untied, and lie on the ground under our feet.

---

1. Barr, *Making of Biblical Womanhood*, 169.

Afterword

by Marisa Lapish

DECIDING TO GO BACK for a graduate degree in theology and culture as a sixty-year-old woman was daunting, to say the least, but the added dimension of pandemic learning in an online classroom with younger faces staring at me was disorienting. I believe it was the first day of my Interpretation of Sacred Texts class when my professor asked the question to be discussed in the breakout room: "What were your earliest experiences with the Bible?" As the younger generations shared their stories mostly set in evangelical church culture, I realized my journey with the sacred biblical text was a divergent one, since I grew up in a liturgical church setting.

Every Sunday for my first twenty-three years of life, I heard a story about Jesus read aloud from the Gospels, as I simply listened. As a young child, that also meant finding the story expressed on stained glass windows, painted murals on cupolas, and the crucifix sculpture directly before my eyes on center stage. My faith came through hearing the word of God (Rom 10:17). There was a sense of Jesus himself telling me his stories while I sat in a church space that held me in a listening posture. In my earliest listening experiences of the sacred text, Jesus was never absent, week in and week out. My earliest experiences of Scripture never came from my reading the pages of the Bible, but were experienced as the words of Jesus spoken aloud through human voice.

It was natural, in my family culture at home, to ask my father questions, including spiritual ones, as we drove through town or sat around the house. The answers were debatable; faithful questioning was encouraged. "It's a mystery," was an acceptable answer. I remember asking God questions silently in church as the gospel stories were read and time was suspended in that sacred space. I later recognized that my questions about the faith were my seeking prayers.

In my teen years, a revival that later came to be known as "The Jesus Movement" swept through the liturgical churches of Northeast Ohio, and I encountered God experientially, liberating me from destructive sins, mindsets, and addictions. Moreover, I experienced an insatiable hunger to read the Bible. I was encouraged to start with the Gospel of John and to follow Jesus through the rest of the Gospel accounts, which were so familiar to me. I read, meditated, memorized, and studied the life-giving words which were such very good news. I fell in love with Jesus as the Word of God (John 1:1), as Jesus' words remained in me (John 15:17) through reading the pages of this sacred text, the Bible.

Not long after this time in my life, my orientation toward the Bible began to shift from listening to and meditating on the words of Scripture, to reading and studying the Scriptures for knowledge and belief. Loving women and men, mothers and fathers in the faith, discipled me and graciously modeled a self-giving, hospitable lifestyle of love. Because of their embodiment of the Christian ethic to love God and love neighbor as the greatest of all commandments, I was motivated to grow in my relationship with God. I soaked up what was taught me and set out to walk in the Spirit accordingly. It was a relief and inwardly gratifying to have some certainty to replace so many of the unsettled mysteries about spiritual things I wondered about. The answers, I was told, were clearly and literally spelled out in the Bible, so I immersed myself in the words of the book.

As I look back at my journey with Scripture, I see that my thoughts about God emerged over time as I was discipled and grew spiritually, depending on the questions I asked, the teachers I learned from, and how I approached Scripture. Some things that were crystal clear in previous seasons of my spiritual journey gave rise to more questions which changed with each new season of my life. Working with pastors and others in ministry has convinced me that students of the word change their ideas about Scripture over time as they seek to know God and as they search the Scriptures and study more deeply. This is good and healthy and to be expected of any disciple of Christ who has a longing to know Jesus more intimately as revealed through Scripture. Faithful questioning is our biblical heritage, demonstrated not only by Jesus, who welcomed the questions and ideas of curious people as recorded in the Gospel stories, but also by the God who inspired the questions of Job, the psalmists, and a host of prophets. For a time, our questions seem settled by acceptable answers until more questions surface as we navigate days of suffering and trials of our faith, or encounter new experiences and seasons of life.

I remember taking a spiritual gift assessment at the evangelical church I attended after I was married. The results showed that teaching, prophecy (interpreted as preaching), and administration were my gifts. The results were not especially surprising to me since I was an avid and passionate learner and leader with a dream of being a college professor. But what was surprising to learn, as a new disciple of Jesus, was that my gender determined how I could use those gifts in marriage and in the church. I was taught that I could teach, preach, and lead women and children, but never men. I could not stop thinking about how that idea did not align with the stories I had learned so well about Jesus and the women who followed him. Wasn't the central gospel message, "He is risen!" proclaimed in Scripture through the female voice of Mary Magdalene, as she obeyed Jesus, the one who had told her to go and preach this good news to the male disciples (John 20:17)? Nonetheless, since women were to be silent in the church, I decided to obey what seemed to be the clear teaching of Scripture to teach and preach and administer as a woman only to other women and children. This self-regulation of speech and behavior, and the inner chatter that went on in my head, was exhausting for a new learner like me who desired to obey the biblical texts literally.

My child-bearing years were fulfilling and deeply enriching to me. As a stay-at-home mom with ten beautiful children, I was blessed to pour myself into teaching and preaching and administering as I homeschooled, taught toddler Sunday School at church, and held neighborhood Bible clubs and women's Bible studies in my home almost every week. The content of my Bible teaching was largely about what consumed my days: homemaking, child rearing, and marriage. Meanwhile, my wonderful husband worked hard, serving at the Christian camp where we lived. The focus of Bible teaching and preaching that interested us most was about our roles in marriage and the church. The teaching we came to believe was clearly hierarchical. This is what our church believed as doctrine and preached as truth to obey; this also is what I taught other women as clear biblical teaching.

For my husband, that meant as a leader of the home it was expected that he would be responsible for leading family devotions. The only problem was that my husband also had taken that spiritual gift assessment, which accurately divulged that his primary spiritual gifts were serving and giving—two gifts more typically identified with females, it would seem. Why had God divinely reversed our spiritual gifts in dissonance with our gender roles? Didn't God know my husband's struggle to teach and my struggle to serve? These biblical role expectations felt contrived, inauthentic, and deprived of power, and they created friction within our hearts toward each other. Surely, our growing resentment was not helpful in bringing the loving oneness God intended for marriage as instructed in the Bible. I am not totally cognizant as to how, when, or why it happened, but at least behind closed doors, I dropped the expectations for my husband to be a Bible teacher, and I freely and fully taught from my home "pulpit." My husband, in turn, was set free to serve and selflessly give in his vocation at the Christian camp he has worked at with joy for thirty-seven years. Our marriage considerably improved as we united our gifts in love as they were given, supporting one another. Were we disobeying Scripture when we reversed our roles in this way in order to live more harmoniously and with deeper joy in using our gifts to serve each other and our family?

I was not alone in my experience of dissonance. My friends shared the same frustrations as they sought to live out biblical marriages with obedience to this interpretation of Scripture. We tried to encourage each other in these biblical principles to submit, to deny ourselves, and to exercise silence. Instead of speaking, we engaged in prayer for our husbands and church leaders. Some of the complementarian pastors we knew confided in us that they did not personally believe what they were teaching, but were silent about changing their doctrinal stance because, on the surface, it seemed to be the only biblical way to explain many of the Scripture passages that Michael interpreted alternatively in the previous pages of this book. I remember clearly one missionary pastor expressing himself this way: "I'm a complementarian with an egalitarian heart." Perhaps most complementarians in everyday relational practice *are* egalitarians. Christian ethics of love in today's culture seem to facilitate the egalitarian response in marriage. Yet, perhaps, as Michael suggests, some Christians—including leaders—have never been presented with an alternative biblical explanation that seems reasonable and supports the Christian ethic to love our neighbors as ourselves without necessitating relational hierarchy. Could complementarians with egalitarian hearts instead simply embrace biblical egalitarianism with its more relatable and relational love ethic trajectory?

Actually, I was perfectly content to teach women and children in my home and at church, at homeschool events and missions conferences, until one day something unexpected happened in my home during my neighborhood ladies' Bible study. A young man burst through my front door, sat down on the couch, and opened his Bible to join the study. "What passage are we studying today?" Jay asked. Jay was a young man with whom our neighbor had shared the good news of Christ in their workplace. We had come to know and love and pray for him over the previous few months. The result of his new life in Christ was a deep hunger to know God through Scripture. Undeniably, his spiritual gifts were in teaching and preaching. I remember feeling a little unnerved when he joined us. I wondered to myself, *"Is this okay for him, a man, to be learning Scripture from me, a woman? Should I stop teaching now that he is here?"* Of course, I had taught my sons Scripture as I homeschooled them, but what about men that were not my children? My experience as I taught at homeschool conferences showed me that when *my* teaching sessions began, the men in the group left the room. I had also seen this occur in a church when a female pastor preached from the pulpit: some men left the sanctuary. Again, some words sown inside of me remained, reminding me of the Jesus revealed through Scripture, who talked with a woman at a neighborhood well about relationships and the theology of worship. The woman left her water jar empty, and with heart overflowing with the living water of love, ran off to tell her male and female neighbors alike about Jesus as the Savior of the world (John 4:1–42). Of course I would teach Jay these words of life from the Bible as he sat on my living room couch surrounded by a group of fellow teachers and learners. Why wouldn't a young man have much to learn from this group of lovers of Scripture? Why should women have the benefit and blessing of learning from *both* men *and* women, while men have the benefit and blessing of learning from *only* men? What insights might be lost when our brothers are not given the opportunity to learn Scripture through female lenses? I recently recognized that the people who were fanning the flame of my ministry gifts, besides my family, included young men who called me their mentor. Michael was the first one who voiced that word about me aloud and in a public setting. This verbal validation was powerful, liberating me to use my speaking gifts with greater freedom. The encouragement of younger men as open learners served to untie the cords of silence so I could open my mouth and speak with deeper humility than I had previously experienced.

Interestingly, this teaching ministry organically spread from my home to my neighborhood to my community and outward through a small Bible school called INSIGHT, hosted on our camp premises. At the same time, I also served as the director of a small faith-based nonprofit organization, Following Christ International, a ministry of love to our immigrant and refugee neighbors in the Cleveland area. Community work was a sweet spot for ministry that provided much freedom for men and women to serve together and to bring the love of Jesus to people in both practical and spiritual ways. I decided to become a licensed, ordained chaplain in order to gain entry into places like hospitals and prisons to be a voice for restorative justice in my community. Still there was a disconnect between the freedom I experienced to teach about and proclaim the gospel of Jesus' love outside in the community, in contrast with the restrictions based on my gender to do the same kind of ministry within the walls of the church. It made no sense to me why my gender, and the gender of others, determined the location of where and how spiritual ministry could be done.

I often wondered if that was why so many gifted women write or teach in Christian schools and universities in order to be faithful to their calling to use their spiritual gifts of preaching and teaching. Where else can women teach, preach, and minister to adult men and women alike? Perhaps this is also why historically we see pioneering missionary efforts by women called to preach and teach in apostolic ministry. I remembered reading missionary biographies and Christian biographies relating stories of women who worked in small ways for God's kingdom, teaching only a few gifted men who sought them out. Their faithfulness in sharing their ministry gifts of teaching and preaching with men bore fruit in the form of underground churches in China and the Middle East. Such movements seem to grow most freely and rapidly in the margins of the institutional church, free of gender-based doctrinal barriers, with the deep beauty of diversity in race and ethnicity for sharing the gospel story of Jesus. Personally, I have witnessed and experienced the fertility and fruitfulness of that organic soil on the outskirts of traditional church experience, in homes and playgrounds, in coffee shops and restaurants, at the public workspace and neighbors' backyards. The legacy of Christian women ministering where they live and move and have their being rings true and echoes through the scriptural examples of Lydia's church on the river (Acts 16:13–15); Nympha's house church (Col 4:15); the courageous apostle Junia in prison with Paul (Rom 16:7); Priscilla's local business as Paul's co-worker and teacher of men (Rom 16:3); Paul's gospel co-workers, Mary, Tryphaena, and Tryphosa (Rom 16:6, 12); and his choice of Phoebe as a deacon, messenger, and reader of his letter to the church in Rome (Rom 16:1–2). Some see these women as exceptional cases. Yet, I suspect the organic movement of church along the margins even today is surprisingly more populated and more mobile to advance good news than one might expect, particularly as it offers greater access and freedom for both genders of teachers and preachers to communicate the gospel to people outside conventional churches. Sometimes the doors that seem more open to voices of women freely proclaiming the gospel swing outward into the community rather than inward into the sanctuaries of churches.

I do have increasing hope that those active in the institutional evangelical church can embrace each other as brothers and sisters within the family of God, and can truly become the beloved new humanity reflecting the kingdom of God on earth as it is in heaven that Jesus envisioned. In my own community, I have witnessed pastors and leaders wrestling with these doctrinal and ethical questions in order to lead their churches more gracefully. One such local pastor, Aaron, invited Michael and me to share with their leadership team the biblical foundation for women in leadership in their young church plant. He said that in their church culture, women already were functioning as leaders in their church, but they wanted to formalize their doctrinal stance to reflect their ministry practice. The heart of their church was for women to be affirmed in their calling and in their giftedness, and therefore they wanted to wrestle with the Scripture passages in question. Michael shared the corpus of texts interpreted in this book as the leadership team asked questions and fleshed out what an official doctrinal change would encompass and how it would be communicated to their congregation in order for women and men to minister without hierarchical encumbrance in church ministry together. The church transformed into one whose egalitarian heart for men and women in ministry together was established now with an egalitarian biblical foundation.

As I review my experiential journey with the Bible in retrospect, I am humbled and moved by the beautiful ways Jesus has been revealed to me—and is continuing to be revealed to me—through the words of sacred Scripture. In my current season of life as a graduate student, spiritual director, and Bible teacher, those sacred texts inspire me to deeper meditation as I hold the open, listening posture of a disciple of Jesus, like Mary of Bethany (Luke 10:38–39). I am smitten once again by the way Jesus interacts with people as I read stories in Matthew, Mark, Luke, and John. It does my soul good to regularly follow Christ in the Gospels, putting myself in those stories as each of the characters—men, women, Pharisees, disciples, onlookers—to imagine the effects that his words and his silence, his actions and restraints, had on each character. As one might expect, new questions also arise as I continue to grow in my love for God and neighbor as a lifelong learner who desires to walk in humility with other believers.

I find myself asking theological questions which seem important today in light of our current cultural milieu, and wondering how these questions might affect the church of the future for my children and grandchildren. From my experience in both worlds, I can now appreciate that the egalitarian view has a biblical foundation supporting its perspectives while also recognizing difficult, problematic texts where there are no easy answers. I long for a theology which practically encourages deeper oneness in marriage and greater unity in the church at large. Moving forward together in this discussion will require a spirit of humility when considering theology which affects the lives of human beings and their relationships in marriage and with others in the church and in the community.

I am convinced that the ethical considerations that Jesus teaches in the Sermon on the Mount (Matt 5–7) demonstrate the priority of relational love and honor toward those most easily silenced by the more powerful voices. Jesus illuminates that there *is* a first-and-foremost commandment that bears greater weight than all others: "Love the Lord your God with all your heart and with all your soul and with all your mind. This is the first and greatest commandment. And the second is like it: 'Love your neighbor as yourself'" (Matt 22:37–39). St. Paul reflects his understanding of Jesus' priority of love in the specific context of spiritual gifts when he reminds the church that the greatest and most enduring of all God-given gifts is love (1 Cor 13:13). We are also wise to consider the advice of St. Augustine: "Whoever, then, thinks that he understands the Holy Scriptures, or any part of them, but puts such an interpretation upon them as does not tend to build up this twofold love of God and our neighbor, does not yet understand them as he ought."[1] The love factor must enter into our embrace of specific doctrinal teachings around gender.

---

1. Augustine, *On Christian Doctrine*, 1.36.40.

My heart resonates with a question posed by Mimi Haddad: "As the world evaluates Christian faith and its treatment of women, can we really afford to overlook the biblical foundations for gift-based, rather than gender-based, ministry?"[2] Maybe the decisive key to resolving doctrinal issues about gender involves discerning which perspective more clearly witnesses to the love of Jesus in our suffering world today. Which view has less potential for facilitating a culture of domestic abuse in marriage or spiritual abuse in church? Which view is more likely to be aware of power differentials which silence dissenting voices or vulnerable victims? Which perspective enables people to become more loving and compassionate in a world searching for an expression of the reality of Christ's self-giving love, the good news for *all* people?

When both men and women faithfully question and wrestle with Scripture together, they can better understand the holistic love ethic that is modeled in the gospel. This shared understanding will create a more unified church that mirrors the cruciform love of Christ as the truest witness of the good news to the next generation and to our wider communities. Certainly, there is time, space, and grace for our biblical views and resulting ethical practices to change as we personally are transformed through seasons of spiritual formation, through scriptural meditation and prayer, over a lifetime. We are people capable of *metanoia,* repentance reflecting a change of direction and thinking; this is essential and constant for our personal maturity and growth as disciples of Jesus. Likewise, corporate practices and doctrinal changes are possible in the church whose leaders have the courage to faithfully question Scripture in order to reflect a more Christ-centered relational expression for men and women in the beloved community. May our future generations of men and women disciples, gathering together in both institutional and organic expressions of church, seek to follow the example of Jesus who *is* the Word of God, our final authority for faith and practice.

2. Haddad, "Women Leaders," para. 8.

Appendix

THE FOLLOWING ARE SHORT summaries of the various interpretations of Scripture passages offered in this book.

Table 3.1—A Summary Explanation of Genesis 1:26–31

Text	Explanation
26*Then God said, "Let us make mankind in our image, in our likeness, so that they may rule over the fish in the sea and the birds in the sky, over the livestock and all the wild animals, and over all the creatures that move along the ground."*	The word "mankind" translates the Hebrew word *adam*. Some translations simply translate this word "man." Both translations are correct because the word *adam* can refer either to a person or to humanity generally. In this context, the word clearly means "mankind" or "humanity" because the following verse specifies that both male and female are included. Humanity, consisting of both male and female, have the shared responsibility of ruling over and caring for creation. There is no evidence here of differentiation in authority level between man and woman.
27*So God created mankind in his own image, in the image of God he created them; male and female he created them.*	This verse states clearly that man and woman together are God's image-bearers in the world. The word *adam*, translated as "mankind," includes both man and woman.

Table 3.1—A Summary Explanation of Genesis 1:26–31

Text	Explanation
28*God blessed them and said to them, "Be fruitful and increase in number; fill the earth and subdue it. Rule over the fish in the sea and the birds in the sky and over every living creature that moves on the ground."*	The only authority structure mentioned is that of humanity over creation. The previous verse says specifically, as if to preclude any doubt, that both man and woman share the stewardship responsibilities relating to God's creation.
29*Then God said, "I give you every seed-bearing plant on the face of the whole earth and every tree that has fruit with seed in it. They will be yours for food.* 30*And to all the beasts of the earth and all the birds in the sky and all the creatures that move along the ground—everything that has the breath of life in it—I give every green plant for food." And it was so.* 31*God saw all that he had made, and it was very good. And there was evening, and there was morning—the sixth day.*	The blessings of creation are also given equally to man and woman as the two representatives of one humanity. God's declaration that the creation is "very good" indicates that it reflects God's intention. In God's restoration of creation in Christ, we should expect a move toward God's intention. Whereas God created humanity to have authority over the animals, God created man and woman to live in a nonhierarchical relationship with each other, sharing both in the stewardship responsibilities over creation and in the enjoyment of its blessings.

Table 3.2—A Summary Explanation of Genesis 2:7, 18–25

Text	Explanation
⁷*Then the LORD God formed a man from the dust of the ground and breathed in his nostrils the breath of life, and the man became a living being.*	The man is created out of the earth. We cannot infer from this that the earth is man's authority, for God has already declared humanity to be in authority over creation in the previous chapter. Consistency demands, therefore, that the woman's being taken from the man's side in verse 21 does *not* imply her subordination to him either. Being something or someone's origin does not entail a higher position of authority. It does, however, imply dependence. In the case of man and woman, woman was made from man, but all men are born of women. Thus, we should see this passage as emphasizing the mutual dependence of man and woman upon each other.
¹⁸*The LORD God said, "It is not good for the man to be alone. I will make a helper suitable for him."*	The words "helper suitable" do not refer to a subordinate, but to an equal and opposite partner.
¹⁹*Now the LORD God had formed out of the ground all the wild animals and all the birds in the sky.*	The fact that not only the man but also animals are created out of the earth is important. They are not the same kind of being as the man. The man is special, as can be seen from verse 7. When God later creates an equal and opposite partner for the man, God creates her from the man's flesh instead of from the ground. This emphasizes that the woman and the man, while different from each other, are nevertheless of the same substance.
He brought them to the man to see what he would name them; and whatever the man called each living creature, that was its name. ²⁰*So that man gave names to all the livestock, the birds in the sky and all the wild animals.*	As the steward of God's creation, the man has authority to name the animals. However, when the woman is created, he does not give her a name. Rather, he describes her as "woman," because she was taken out of man. She is the same kind of creature as he. The "breath of life" that he possesses also belongs to her. The man names the woman "Eve" later, but this is after the pair had sinned and been expelled from the garden.

Table 3.2—A Summary Explanation of Genesis 2:7, 18–25

Text	Explanation
But for Adam no suitable helper was found.	This is the second occurrence (though inverted here) of the term "helper suitable." This term does not refer to an assistant or underling, but to a strong deliverer upon whom one can—and must—depend. In fact, God is sometimes given the same title of "helper" elsewhere in the Hebrew Bible.
21*So the LORD God caused the man to fall into a deep sleep; and while he was sleeping, he took one of the man's ribs and then closed up the place with flesh.* 22*Then the LORD God made a woman from the rib he had taken out of the man, and he brought her to the man.*	The woman's formation out of the man's body emphasizes the equality of the two as human beings. The woman's being created after the man does not show her inferiority or subordinate status to him, for the animals were created before the woman and they are not her authorities, as the previous chapter makes clear. Paul's reference to "head" as a metaphor in the New Testament refers, at least in part, to the idea that woman's source is man.
23*The man said,* *"This is now bone of my bones* *and flesh of my flesh;* *she shall be called 'woman,'* *for she was taken out of man."*	The man recognizes the importance of the woman as another being who is of the same kind of flesh as his own. "Woman" is not a name, but a description of who she is in relation to the man. It is a relational term. The word *adam*, in fact, also means "ground," and the same word carries both meanings in verse 7. Thus, the title *adam* also refers to the man's origin—the thing from which he was formed. Of course, the fact that the man came from the ground does not subordinate him to it. Therefore, the fact that the woman was taken from the man does not subordinate her to him either.
24*That is why a man leaves his father and mother and is united to his wife, and they become one flesh.* 25*Adam and his wife were both naked, and they felt no shame.*	In male-dominated cultures, it is typical for a woman to leave her homeland and family to go and live with her husband. But here, the opposite is described. In Ephesians 5, Paul quotes this passage to illustrate God's design for husbands to love their wives self-sacrificially.

Table 4.1—A Summary of Explanation A of 1 Corinthians 14:34–38

Text	Explanation A
34_Women should remain silent in the churches._	The word translated "silent" here means to not make noise, indicating that the problem Paul was dealing with was not that these women were communicating ideas, but that they were making noise that was disrupting the church's worship.
They are not allowed to speak,	The word "speak" does not mean a specific kind of speaking like preaching, teaching, or prophesying. Rather, the problem had to do with talking as such. Because 1 Corinthians 11:5 implies that Paul allowed women to speak at times in the public worship of the church, we can logically conclude that Paul is not here forbidding women from _all_ speaking in church. And, given that in the whole context of this passage Paul is addressing issues of orderliness in worship, it is likely that Paul has some kind of disruptive or inappropriate speaking in mind—speaking that disrupts the worship service in some way.
but must be in submission, as the law says.	Submission is necessary for anyone who wishes to learn, not just women. "As the law says" is a mysterious phrase for two reasons. First, it is not normal for Paul to use the Mosaic Law as a final authority for Christian living. Second, there is nothing in the law that tells women to be silent, or even to submit, based on their gender. The best explanation is, again, to observe that the purpose of the law was to order a society, and Paul is advocating here for orderly worship.
35_If they want to inquire about something, they should ask their own husbands at home;_	At least part of the disruptive speech in which these women were engaging seems to have been asking questions at inappropriate times during the worship. Paul wants these women to learn. In a culture in which education outside the home was virtually unavailable to women, Paul wisely advised women to ask their husbands their questions at home. Whatever the reason, what is clear is that question-asking during the worship service was part of the problem that Paul wanted to address.

Table 4.1—A Summary of Explanation A of 1 Corinthians 14:34–38

Text	Explanation A
for it is disgraceful for a woman to speak in the church.	Again, Paul does not say that it is disgraceful for a woman only to "teach" or "preach" in the church, but to speak. He has in mind disruptive speech, for the reasons mentioned above. Paul uses the word "disgraceful"—a strong word that could be translated "shameful"—to emphasize the inappropriateness of what these women are doing. It is the disruptive nature of the speech, *not* its female provenance, that makes it inappropriate. A woman's speaking in church is disgraceful *for her,* and Paul wants her to be spared that disgrace.
³⁶*Or did the word of God originate with you? Or are you the only people it has reached?* ³⁷*If anyone thinks [he is] a prophet or otherwise gifted by the Spirit, let [him] acknowledge that what I am writing to you is the Lord's command.* ³⁸*But if anyone ignores this, [he] will [himself] be ignored.*	These verses present a problem for what we are offering here as "Explanation A." This explanation has a hard time explaining Paul's change of tone. Paul's use of "he" and "him" in verse 37 (this is the accurate way to translate from the Greek—the NIV inaccurately translates it "they" and "them") shows he does not primarily have a female audience in mind. He seems to be rebuking the men, whereas our "Explanation A" of verses 34 to 35 argues that it is the women who are causing the problem in the church. If women were causing a problem, why does Paul seem to be rebuking the men in verse 37? Thus, if we opt for the above interpretation of the passage, we would have to take these two verses as relating to all of chapter 14. Paul is saying something like, "If anyone thinks he has the authority to disregard what I have been teaching here, he should remember that the word of God did not originate with him. He needs to take heed to the need for orderly worship, so that God can speak in a way that will edify the body as a whole."

Table 4.2—A Summary of Explanation B of 1 Corinthians 14:34–38

Text	Explanation B
34*Women should remain silent in the churches. They are not allowed to speak but must be in submission, as the law says.* 35*If they want to inquire about something, they should ask their own husbands at home, for it is disgraceful for a woman to speak in the church.*	Paul is quoting the Corinthians in order to correct their thinking. Thus, these two verses should have quotation marks around them in an English translation. Paul apparently had written to the church at Corinth at least once before (see 5:9), had heard a report about them, and had received a letter from them as well (see 1:11; 7:1). Modern readers of 1 Corinthians must realize they are jumping into an ongoing conversation. All we have are clues regarding what has been discussed between Paul and the Christians at Corinth before this letter was written. Paul sometimes quotes the Corinthians, then responds to them. Because there are no quotation marks in New Testament Greek, modern translators must discern by looking at the context of a passage when this is happening. Some scholars have proposed that this is what is happening in these two verses. If this is so, these two verses do not reflect Paul's thinking at all. To the contrary, he opposes this way of thinking. In this interpretation, the phrase, "as the law says," is not Paul's argument, but that of the mistaken Christian men at Corinth who were trying to silence women in the church's worship services. Paul rejects this application of the law. The fact is, there is no law in the Hebrew Bible that forbids a woman's speaking or that commands her to submit. Paul was a devout Pharisee and an expert in the Mosaic Law, and he would have known this. Here again, Paul is reiterating an idea that was circulating among the Corinthian Christian men. If Paul is alluding to something that the Corinthians had written in their letter to him, this would have been clear to them. To the modern reader, however, it takes careful observation and reconstruction of the situation to discern what is happening.

Table 4.2—A Summary of Explanation B of 1 Corinthians 14:34–38

Text	Explanation B
36*Or did the word of God originate with you? Or are you the only people it has reached?* **37***If anyone thinks [he] is a prophet or otherwise gifted by the Spirit, let [him] acknowledge that what I am writing to you is the Lord's command.* **38***But if anyone ignores this, [he] will [himself] be ignored.*	Having quoted or summarized the Corinthian notion that women ought to be silenced, Paul here dismisses the idea. The implied answer to the rhetorical question, "Did the word of God originate with you?" is, "No, it did not." The phrase, "If anyone thinks *he* is a prophet," shows that Paul is addressing men, or at least that men were included among those he was addressing. If women were primarily the ones causing the problem, Paul would have said, "she" instead of "he" here. On this reading, Paul is saying something like, "You want to silence the women, but who gives you the authority to silence God's word? Did God's word originate with you (men)?"

Table 5.1—A Summary Explanation of 1 Timothy 2:11–12

Text	Explanation
11*A woman should learn in quietness and full submission.*	The word "quietness" does not mean complete silence. Instead, it refers to a quality that, elsewhere, Paul encourages all Christians to cultivate. A learner must be submissive in order to learn. This instruction is also good advice for men, even though Paul specifically addresses it to "a woman" here.

Table 5.1—A Summary Explanation of 1 Timothy 2:11-12

Text	Explanation
12*I do not permit a woman to teach*	Whereas Paul commands "a woman" to learn in the previous verse, verse 12 is not a command. Rather, Paul is describing, using the present tense, his own practice regarding the matter of "a woman" teaching. There is no indication in the text that Paul is talking about the church context here. The only place a woman would have a chance to learn in the time and culture of Paul and Timothy was with a tutor at home. Paul wants women to learn first, before teaching. It seems that some women in the Christian community at Ephesus had been ignoring this principle and had been engaging in unfruitful tale-telling (see 2 Tim 3:6; see also 1 Tim 5:13). Again, there is no indication in the text that this was happening during church gatherings. Rather, it seems it was happening in homes.
	Some interpreters find the wording "a woman" and "a man" as opposed to "women" and "men" significant. It could be that Paul has a particular couple in mind here. That would seem strange unless we remember that this is a personal letter to Timothy. It could be that Timothy and Paul were aware of an ongoing pastoral situation about which Timothy had asked Paul for advice.
or to assume authority over a man;	The word translated "assume authority over" has a negative connotation, especially when used in reference to one person's relationship to another. It should be translated "domineer," "dominate," or "be the master of." It refers to a person who has the power to execute another. While men in Roman and Jewish cultures *did* have legal authority over their wives just as they did over their slaves and children, Paul never encourages men to think of their wives as their subordinates. The fact that this negative word comes along with the word "teach" shows that Paul was trying to prevent "a woman" from doing something negative— something that men shouldn't do either. Paul is not against a woman's teaching a man, but a woman's teaching a man in a domineering way. There are sufficient examples of women teaching men in both the Hebrew Bible and the New Testament to eliminate the possibility that Paul was categorically against women's teaching men.

Table 5.1—A Summary Explanation of 1 Timothy 2:11–12

Text	Explanation
she must be quiet.	Again, the word "quiet" refers to a quality all Christians should cultivate, especially those who want to learn and grow. The fact that this word is juxtaposed with what comes before—"dominate" or "domineer"—is a clue that Paul intends something *negative* by that term.

Table 5.2—A Summary of Explanation A of 1 Timothy 2:13–14

Text	Explanation A
13 *For Adam was formed first, then Eve.*	Adam's being created first does not mean that he is Eve's authority. Given that Paul has just commanded "a woman" to learn, we can safely assume that this verse has something to do with teaching and learning. In Genesis, God gave Adam the command not to eat from the Tree of the Knowledge of Good and Evil before Eve was created. Perhaps Paul is referring here to the idea that Adam was responsible to "teach" Eve that information.
14 *And Adam was not the one deceived; it was the woman who was deceived and became a sinner.*	Adam ate the fruit just like Eve did. But, whereas Adam did it with his eyes wide open, Eve had been deceived. In Eve's conversation with the serpent in Genesis, it does seem that she had not learned well. She says God had told them not to "touch" the fruit, but God had not said that. Perhaps for this reason, Paul is able to draw a distinction between the nature of Eve's sin and the nature of Adam's sin. In 2 Corinthians 11:3, Paul uses Eve as an example of how any person can fall prey to deception. This shows that Paul does not see Eve as a stereotype of female gullibility, but of the universally human vulnerability to deception. The only way to prevent someone from being deceived is by helping him or her learn. Learning, however, could not have prevented Adam from sinning because Adam's sin was somewhat different. Adam was *not* deceived; he sinned with full knowledge of what he was doing. This is why Paul only speaks of Adam elsewhere in his writings as an example of a sinner, but never as an example specifically of a *male* sinner (see for example Rom 5:18 and 19).

Table 5.3—A Summary of Explanation B of 1 Timothy 2:13–14

Text	Explanation B
13*For Adam was formed first, then Eve.* 14*And Adam was not the one deceived; it was the woman who was deceived and became a sinner.*	Paul here draws an analogy between "a woman" in the church at Ephesus and Eve. Eve sat under the false teaching of the serpent, as it were, and then turned around and became a teacher of Adam. In doing this, she became Adam's false teacher. Paul is worried that a similar thing will happen in Ephesus. False teachers were actively targeting women, and some women had sat under their teaching. If those women (or, "a woman," as the text reads) were to then teach "a man," bad things could come of it. Paul's solution is to (provisionally) bar such a woman from teaching.

Table 5.4—A Summary of Explanation C of 1 Timothy 2:13-15

Text	Explanation C
13For Adam was formed first, then Eve. *14And Adam was not the one deceived; it was the woman who was deceived and became a sinner.*	Paul mentions the order of creation not to point out man's superiority to woman but to balance a misconception pervasive in Ephesian religion. The magnificent Temple of Artemis was the most prominent building in Ephesus, and her worship dominated Ephesian culture. Artemis was a virgin goddess whose priests were eunuchs and priestesses virgins. Further, she was the goddess of childbirth, having the power in her hands both to preserve and to kill pregnant women and their babies at will. Artemis was the twin sister of Apollo, whom she served as a midwife as their mother Leto gave birth to him, and this "creation"—or, more accurately, "origin"—event had supposedly happened very near the city of Ephesus. This provides the background for Paul's comments in these three verses in particular, but also for much of what Paul says in his letters to Timothy. The reason Paul emphasizes the fact that Adam was created first was because the Artemis cult, which exalted the female over the male in religious matters and which looked down on marriage, stressed so strongly the birth order of Artemis and her brother Apollo. Paul is saying, "No, actually, God created the man first. Artemis can't save you. Instead, honor God, honor your marriage, and trust in God to protect you during childbirth." Paul is not trying to merely *flip* Artemis religion entirely such that men would begin to see themselves as women's religious superiors. Rather, he is trying to bring balance to the situation. While it is true that women give birth to all men, and that men depend upon women in a special way as a result, it is also true that, in the beginning, the first woman came from the man. Paul hopes this teaching will correct an un-Christlike power dynamic that was affecting marriages in the church at Ephesus.
15But [she] will be saved through childbearing—if they continue in faith, love and holiness with propriety.	Because childbearing was done in the home in Paul and Timothy's culture, this verse shows that Paul is addressing the home context. The promise of deliverance during childbirth almost certainly has Artemis worship behind it. Paul is telling women to resist falling back into trusting in the goddess Artemis and instead to trust in the one, true God, even for childbirth. In this time, childbirth was extremely dangerous and was probably the thing that women worried about the most.

Table 6.1—A Summary Explanation of Ephesians 5:21–33

Text	Explanation
21Submit to one another out of reverence for Christ.	The word "submit" means to order oneself under another. Becoming another's servant requires submission. This command is the premise for what follows. While some have argued that "one another" actually means, "some to others" in this context, it is more consistent with Paul's theology and grammatical style to read it as simply, "one another." Paul is not interested in reversing the classes of power such that underlings revolt and subsequently become the oppressors of those who formerly ruled over them. Instead, Paul teaches that, in Christ, a new reality is born in which we can become servants of one another (see Rom 12:10; Gal 5:18; Phil 2:3–8). Those who are in Christ become the servants of each other, and of the world God intends to redeem.
22Wives, submit yourselves to your own husbands as you do to the Lord.	The word "submit" does not actually appear in this verse. It has been added by the translators to aid the flow of the text. This shows that wives' submission to husbands is only one way that Christians should "submit to one another." Wives should submit to their husbands because this is a way that they, in their position, can follow the example of Christ. They should serve their husbands as an act of service to the Lord. Paul tells slaves to do the same with their masters in 6:5–6 and in Colossians 3:22. In this time period in the Roman Empire, husbands were the legal authorities of their wives, just as masters were of their slaves. This command by Paul that wives submit to their husbands is, thus, in the same vein as his directives that Christian citizens submit to human governments as well as slaves to masters elsewhere in his letters.

Table 6.1—A Summary Explanation of Ephesians 5:21–33

Text	Explanation
23*For the husband is the head of the wife as Christ is the head of the church, his body, of which he is the Savior.* 24*Now as the church submits to Christ, so also wives should submit to their husbands in everything. (See also Col 3:18.)*	While Paul elsewhere tells Christians to submit to human governments and slaves to submit to masters, he only introduces the head-to-body analogy in the case of wives' submission to husbands. This is significant in light of all that Paul has taught about the church's participation in Christ previously in his Epistle to the Ephesians. The church, in fact, shares in all the riches and even authority of Christ because the church is Christ's body. Thus, by drawing a parallel between husband-and-wife and head-and-body, Paul is *not* subordinating the wife under her husband, but is rather exalting the wife to a shared role of authority *with* her husband. "In Christ," a new reality has opened up. God is restoring God's original plan for the male-female relationship described in Genesis 1 and 2. In a Christ-centered marriage, a wife sees herself as one flesh with her husband. She is united to him in a way that is analogous to how the church is united to Christ. This is not to her disadvantage, but to her advantage.

Table 6.1—A Summary Explanation of Ephesians 5:21–33

Text	Explanation
25Husbands, love your wives, just as Christ loved the church and gave himself up for her 26to make her holy, cleansing her by the washing with water through the word, 27and to present her to himself as a radiant church, without stain or wrinkle or any other blemish, but holy and blameless. 28In the same way, husbands ought to love their wives as their own bodies. He who loves his wife loves himself. 29After all, no one ever hated their own body, but they feed and care for their body. (See also Col 3:19.)	Here, as in every place in the New Testament, husbands are told to follow the example of Christ in their behavior toward their wives. As Christ sacrificially gave himself for the church, so husbands should serve their wives. Paul does not call husbands to take on a leadership role over their wives. Instead, he calls them to be servants. The idea of servant-leadership, helpful as it is, does not appear in this passage. Thus, Paul is telling wives and husbands to serve each other. One might wonder why Paul did not say the same to masters and slaves. But in his Epistle to Philemon, Paul actually does just that. Though the church has been all too slow in recognizing it, the gospel undermines slavery as an institution. Slavery runs counter to God's created design for humanity. However, in Paul's view, marriage does not. Rather than undermining it fundamentally as he does the institution of slavery, Paul sets the stage for a restored understanding of marriage that agrees with its portrayal in Genesis 1 and 2. "In Christ," marriage is not a contract that binds a lord and his underling, but unites the two representative parts of a whole humanity in a "one flesh" relationship. Marriage, in Paul's theology, is a sacred sign pointing to God's reconciling of all things in Christ. Christ's victory over the powers of darkness resulted in *their* subjugation; but those who are "in Christ," astonishingly, share in that same victory. Likewise, in Christ, husband and wife share equally in the original authority that God gave them at the beginning of creation.
just as Christ does the church— 30for we are members of his body.	Paul adds a reminder here that he has still not departed from the head-to-body analogy that he previously described regarding Christ and the church. Sometimes the word "headship" is used to describe man's relationship to woman. However, this is only half of the analogy. It should be "head-and-body-ship" (if it wasn't for the awkwardness of saying it that way). Neglecting the full, dual analogy Paul is drawing upon results in a top-down hierarchy instead of a bottom-up view of men and women that emphasizes mutual dependence, mutual service, and oneness.

Table 6.1—A Summary Explanation of Ephesians 5:21–33

Text	Explanation
31 *"For this reason a man will leave his father and mother and be united to his wife, and the two will become one flesh." * 32*This is a profound mystery—but I am talking about Christ and the church.*	Paul here quotes Genesis 2:24. He seems to do this for two reasons. First, this verse helps Paul emphasize the oneness of husband and wife in Christ. They are not separate parties arranged in a hierarchical order but one flesh, a unit restored in Christ who, together, rule over a renewed creation. Second, it supports what Paul has just told husbands to do for their wives. In the beginning, God declared that the man would leave his family and homeland—that is, his interests—and cleave to his wife. The man is not to serve himself, but his wife. Paul is connecting his commands to Christian husbands with God's original design as portrayed in the Genesis creation story. The purpose of all of this is to provide a sign pointing to Christ and the church's relationship.
33*However, each one of you also must love his wife as he loves himself, and the wife must respect her husband.*	This verse repeats what Paul has just taught. By telling husbands to love their wives, Paul is not suggesting that there is no need for wives to love their husbands (see Titus 2:4). Likewise, by telling wives to respect their husbands, Paul is not suggesting that there is no need for husbands to respect their wives (see 1 Pet 3:7).

Table 6.3—A Summary Explanation of 1 Peter 3:1–7

Text	Explanation
1*Wives, in the same way submit yourselves to your own husbands*	The phrase, "in the same way," refers to what Peter had just finished saying to slaves in 2:18–25. There, Peter identifies the suffering of a Christian slave with the sufferings of Christ. Likewise here, Peter is speaking to wives who, in this time and place, were under the legal authority of their husbands. Some of these women would have been obliged to suffer abuse at the hands of their husbands. The phrase, "in the same way," signals to the reader that Peter is telling wives to react to their husbands in the same way and with the same spirit with which he had exhorted slaves to react to their masters in the previous passage.

Table 6.3—A Summary Explanation of 1 Peter 3:1–7

Text	Explanation
so that, if any of them do not believe the word, they may be won over without words by the behavior of their wives, ²*when they see the purity and reverence of your lives.*	Peter is by no means providing a master plan for the ideal Christian marriage in this passage. Rather, he is encouraging wives, some of whom were suffering oppression, to identify their own suffering as one with Christ's. Peter hopes that their endurance through suffering will point even their oppressors toward him. Peter's ultimate goal is the transformation not only of the oppressed, but also the oppressor.
³*Your beauty should not come from outward adornment, such as elaborate hairstyles and the wearing of gold jewelry or fine clothes.* ⁴*Rather, it should be that of your inner self, the unfading beauty of a gentle and quiet spirit, which is of great worth in God's sight.*	The word translated "gentle" here is the same that Jesus uses in The Sermon on the Mount (see Matt 5:5) to describe those who will "inherit the earth." It is a quality that all Christians should cultivate, not only women. Jesus uses the same word to describe himself in Matthew 11:29 (see also 21:5). The word translated "quiet" in this text is also a virtue after which all Christians should seek (see 1 Tim 2:2). While Peter's instructions in these verses are directed to Christian women specifically, Christian men would also do well to heed them.
⁵*For this is the way the holy women of the past who put their hope in God used to adorn themselves. They submitted themselves to their own husbands,* ⁶*like Sarah, who obeyed Abraham and called him her lord. You are her daughters if you do what is right and do not give way to fear.*	This passage leaves us modern readers with unanswered questions. Peter refers to Sarah as the model of an obedient wife, and says that she called Abraham "lord." However, according to the biblical account, Sarah and Abraham's marital relationship was quite rocky, to speak liberally. The only time that Sarah calls Abraham "lord" is in the context of her laughing at God's promise that she would have a child (Gen 18:12). Thus, Peter could not have been deriving what he says about Sarah from the Bible. However, the fact that Peter simply refers to Sarah without alluding to a particular passage in the Hebrew Bible may provide a clue that he is referring to an extrabiblical tradition about her. It turns out that, in some extrabiblical literature, Sarah *was* portrayed as an ideal, obedient wife, and she was *also* portrayed as calling Abraham her lord. The best available way to understand this passage, therefore, is to see it as a reference to a popular view of Sarah. Peter is not claiming that "the Bible says Sarah was this way." Instead, he is telling his readers to conform to a popular view of her in their interactions with their husbands.

Table 6.3—A Summary Explanation of 1 Peter 3:1–7

Text	Explanation
[7] *Husbands, in the same way be considerate as you live with your wives, and treat them with respect as the weaker partner and as heirs with you of the gracious gift of life, so that nothing will hinder your prayers.*	The phrase, "in the same way," shows that Peter wants Christian husbands to act in the same spirit as Christian slaves and wives. In the same spirit, then, husbands should respect their wives as heirs with them of life in Christ. Christian wives should see their Christian husbands the same way. While Peter addresses these instructions to husbands specifically, all Christians will do well to apply them in their lives.

Table 7.1—A Summary of Explanation A of 1 Corinthians 11:2–16

Text	Explanation A
[2] *I praise you for remembering me in everything and for holding to the traditions just as I passed them on to you.*	This comment must be sarcastic because Paul has nothing to commend in the following passage.
[3] *But I want you to realize that the head of every man is Christ, and the head of the woman is the man, and the head of Christ is God.*	(Explained in ch. 8)

Table 7.1—A Summary of Explanation A of 1 Corinthians 11:2–16

Text	Explanation A
⁴*Every man who prays or prophesies with his head covered dishonors his head.* ⁵*But every woman who prays or prophesies with her head uncovered dishonors her head—it is the same as having her head shaved.* ⁶*For if a woman does not cover her head, she might as well have her hair cut off; but if it is a disgrace for a woman to have her hair cut off or her head shaved, then she should cover her head.*	This part of the passage is notoriously difficult for modern interpreters to understand. It should be noted for our purposes, however, that no matter how one interprets it, there is nothing in these verses that could be used to subordinate women to men, much less to silence them in church. These verses have to do with head coverings and their propriety for men and women. The explanation we are proposing here is that, while the men of Corinth wanted women to uncover their heads, the women did not deem this appropriate, and were thus resisting. Paul defends the women's desire to cover their heads in church, noting that to not do so would be disgraceful. The issue is about hair. Thus, Paul uses exaggeration to show the absurd logical outcome of the men's failing to respect the women's wishes—doing so would be tantamount to forcing them to shave their heads. Paul is not advocating the forced head-shaving of women, but is using an argument from exaggeration (*reductio ad absurdum*) to show that requiring women to remove their head-coverings would be logically equivalent to forcing them to cut off all their hair.
⁷*A man ought not to cover his head, since he is the image and glory of God; but woman is the glory of man.* ⁸*For man did not come from woman, but woman from man;* ⁹*neither was man created for woman, but woman for man.*	(Explained in ch. 8) Paul seems to make this statement in order to set the stage for verse 11.
¹⁰*It is for this reason that a woman ought to have authority over her own head, because of the angels.*	The word "symbol" does not appear in the original text, as is reflected in the NIV's accurate translation. The authority referenced here is the woman's own. The wording and grammar do not allow for any other conclusion. Paul is not saying that women should wear a sign of *someone else's* authority on their heads. Rather, women have authority over their own heads. This is the only mention of authority in this passage, and Paul says it belongs to women themselves.

Table 7.1—A Summary of Explanation A of 1 Corinthians 11:2–16

Text	Explanation A
[11]*Nevertheless, in the Lord woman is not independent of man, nor is man independent of woman.* [12]*For as woman came from man, so also man is born of woman. But everything comes from God.*	The word translated "nevertheless" (*plēn*) signals the conclusion to an argument. While a great deal of what he has said previously is difficult to follow for us modern readers, this verse is crystal clear. It is a statement of male-female interdependence and mutuality—a mirror reflection of the teaching about male and female in Genesis 1 and 2.
[13]*Judge for yourselves: Is it proper for a woman to pray to God with her head uncovered?* [14]*Does not the very nature of things teach you that if a man has long hair, it is a disgrace to him,* [15]*but that if a woman has long hair, it is her glory? For long hair is given to her as a covering.*	This part of the passage poses several interpretive problems for what we are calling "Explanation A," but which are addressed somewhat more satisfyingly in "Explanation B" below.
[16]*If anyone wants to be contentious about this, we have no [such] practice— nor do the churches of God.*	The word translated "practice" almost certainly refers to the practice of using head coverings. Paul seems to be relativizing the whole issue of head coverings, which reminds us readers that verse 11 should be seen as the basis for any practical application of this passage. Verse 11 leaves the authority in question in the hands of women, not men.

Table 7.2—A Summary of Explanation B of 1 Corinthians 11:2–16

Text	Explanation B
2_I praise you for remembering me in everything and for holding to the traditions just as I passed them on to you._	The comment is *not* sarcastic (in contrast to how we interpreted it in "Explanation A"). On this reading, Paul is actually content with the fact that the Corinthian women are not using head coverings in the church.
3_But I want you to realize that the head of every man is Christ, and the head of the woman is the man, and the head of Christ is God._	(Explained in ch. 8)
4_Every man who prays or prophesies with his head covered dishonors his head._ **5**_But every woman who prays or prophesies with her head uncovered dishonors her head—it is the same as having her head shaved._ **6**_For if a woman does not cover her head, she might as well have her hair cut off; but if it is a disgrace for a woman to have her hair cut off or her head shaved, then she should cover her head._ **7(a)**_A man ought not to cover his head, since he is the image and glory of God;_	It is highly unlikely that this reflects Paul's own thinking as a Jewish man, for the many reasons noted at the beginning of chapter 7. Paul is here summarizing a Corinthian idea, which he will then correct.

Table 7.2—A Summary of Explanation B of 1 Corinthians 11:2–16

Text	Explanation B
7(b)*but woman is the glory of man.* 8*For man did not come from woman, but woman from man;* 9*neither was man created for woman, but woman for man.* 10*It is for this reason that a woman ought to have authority over her own head, because of the angels.*	The conjunction "but" signals that Paul is now responding to his quotation or summarization of the Corinthians' mistaken notion found in verses 4–7a. The term "glory" is parallel to "image" in 7a. By means of this parallel, Paul corrects the notion that only men are made in God's image. If the woman is the man's glory, she must share the man's status. Verses 8 and 9 must be taken together with verses 11 and 12, and together seem to be an allusion to verse 3 and to Paul's revised Shema in 1 Corinthians 8:6. Verse 10 is like a hinge: it is a practical instruction placed between two important theological statements. Verse 10 says clearly that women ought to have authority over their own heads. However we understand Paul's statement that the woman is the "glory" of man, it must lead logically to this conclusion. The question of whether or not this passage can be used to teach the subordination of women under men does not depend on whether or not this passage reflects Paul's thinking (as opposed to an incorrect Corinthian idea). This is because the only mention of "authority" is in verse 10. The word "symbol" does not appear in the original text of this verse. The authority referenced here is clearly the woman's own. The wording and grammar do not allow for any other conclusion.
11*Nevertheless, in the Lord woman is not independent of man, nor is man independent of woman.* 12*For as woman came from man, so also man is born of woman. But everything comes from God.*	The word translated "nevertheless" (*plēn*) signals a conclusion to an argument that *contrasts* with or qualifies something that was just said. It means something like, "the point is . . ."[1] However we interpret Paul's argument in the previous verses, therefore, this is the conclusion to which he arrives, and it is a clear statement of male-female interdependence and mutuality—a mirror reflection of the teaching about male and female in Genesis 1 and 2.

---

1. Peppiatt, *Women and Worship*, 102.

Table 7.2—A Summary of Explanation B of 1 Corinthians 11:2–16

Text	Explanation B
13*Judge for yourselves: Is it proper for a woman to pray to God with her head uncovered?* 14*Does not the very nature of things teach you that if a man has long hair, it is a disgrace to him,* 15*but that if a woman has long hair, it is her glory? For long hair is given to her as a covering.*	This part is almost certainly sarcastic. Paul shows the absurdity of reasoning that women's long hair implies a "natural" need for a head covering by noting (sarcastically) what this would imply about men's hair. The fact is, men have long hair too (unless they cut it off). This eliminates the possibility that the Corinthians could argue "from nature" that women should cover their hair.
16*If anyone wants to be contentious about this, we have no [such] practice— nor do the churches of God.*	Explanation B makes better sense of this verse than does Explanation A. It states that the issue of head coverings is not worth being contentious about. Paul relativizes the issue completely. This interpretation agrees well with verse 10.

Table 9.1—A Summary Explanation of 1 Timothy 3:2–7

Text	Explanation
2*Now the overseer is to be above reproach, faithful to his wife, (see also Titus 1:6a)*	The phrase, "faithful to his wife," is more literally translated, "one-wife/woman man." Paul assumes that elders will be married men. However, being a married man should not be taken as a stipulation. Paul himself was unmarried, as was Jesus, and Paul encouraged singleness, at least in some circumstances (see 1 Cor 7). Rather, the qualifications of an elder concern a person's character.
temperate, self-controlled, respectable, hospitable, able to teach, 3*not given to drunkenness, not violent but gentle, not quarrelsome, not a lover of money. (See also Titus 1:7 and 8)*	Elders should be people of good Christian character. An elder should be a "one-wife/woman man" because, assuming he is a married man, this would be the fruit of Christian virtue.

Table 9.1—A Summary Explanation of 1 Timothy 3:2–7

Text	Explanation
⁴*He must manage his own family well and see that his children obey him, and he must do so in a manner worthy of full respect.* ⁵*(If anyone does not know how to manage his own family, how can he take care of God's church?) (see also Titus 1:6b)*	The elder should be a person not only of good character, but also of ability and of good reputation.
⁶*He must not be a recent convert, or he may become conceited and fall under the same judgment as the devil.* ⁷*He must also have a good reputation with outsiders, so that he will not fall into disgrace and into the devil's trap. (See also Titus 1:9)*	An elder should be an experienced person. Paul seems to assume that a person who has been a Christian longer will have acquired knowledge. This will leave him less vulnerable to diabolical deception. Even though Paul assumes elders will be men, he is still concerned about the possibility of deception. Being male is not a safeguard against the devil's influence. In his letter to Titus, Paul also says an elder should be a person who has sat under teaching so that he can discern between good and bad doctrine and respond appropriately.

Bibliography

Amar, Joseph. *A Metrical Homily on Holy Mar Ephrem by Mar Jacob of Sarug*. Patrologia Orientalis, Tome 47, Fascicule 1, no. 209, Turnhout, Belgium: Brepols, 1995.

———. "Women Are Proclaiming the Word: The Evidence from Syria." *Commonweal Magazine,* July 21, 2020. https://www.commonwealmagazine.org/women-are-proclaiming-word.

Asdourian, Donna Rizk. "Women for the Church." *Public Orthodoxy,* January 9, 2018. https://publicorthodoxy.org/2018/01/09/women-for-the-church/.

Bailey, Kenneth E. *Paul through Mediterranean Eyes: Cultural Studies in 1 Corinthians*. Downers Grove, IL: InterVarsity, 2011.

Barr, Beth Allison. *The Making of Biblical Womanhood: How the Subjugation of Women Became Gospel Truth*. Grand Rapids: Brazos, 2021.

Bauckham, Richard. *Jesus and the God of Israel: God Crucified and Other Studies on the New Testament's Christology of Divine Identity*. Grand Rapids: Eerdmans, 2008.

Belleville, Linda. "Teaching and Usurping Authority: 1 Timothy 2:11–15." In *Discovering Biblical Equality: Complementarity without Hierarchy*, edited by Ronald W. Pierce et al., 205–23. Grand Rapids: IVP Academic, 2005.

Boomsma, Clarence. *Male and Female One in Christ: New Testament Teaching on Women in Office*. Grand Rapids: Baker, 1993.

Bordewich, Fergus M. *Bound for Canaan: The Underground Railroad and the War for the Soul of America*. New York: Amistad, 2005.

Calvin, Jean. *Sermons of Master Iohn Calvin vpon the Booke of Iob. Translated out of French by Arthur Golding*. London: Lucas Harison and George Byshop, 1574. Text Creation Partnership, 2011. http://name.umdl.umich.edu/A69056.0001.001.

Carson, D. A. and G. K. Beale, eds. *Commentary on the New Testament Use of the Old*. Grand Rapids: Baker Academic, 2007.

Cavanaugh, William T. *The Myth of Religious Violence*. Oxford: Oxford University Press, 2009.

"Characteristics of Public School Teachers." *National Center for Education Statistics,* May 2021. https://nces.ed.gov/programs/coe/indicator_clr.asp.

Clouse, Bonnidell, et al., eds. *Women in Ministry: Four Views*. Downers Grove, IL: InterVarsity, 1989.

Cohick, Lynn H. *Ephesians: A New Covenant Commentary*. New Covenant Commentary Series. Eugene, OR: Cascade, 2010. Kindle.

Coleman, Colette. "How Literacy Became a Powerful Weapon in the Fight to End Slavery." *History.com,* June 17, 2020. https://www.history.com/news/nat-turner-rebellion-literacy-slavery.

Culver, Robert. "Let Your Women Keep Silent." In *Women in Ministry: Four Views*, edited by Bonnidell Clouse et al., 25–52. Downers Grove, IL: InterVarsity, 1989.

Davids, Peter H. "A Silent Witness in Marriage." In *Discovering Biblical Equality: Complementarity without Hierarchy*, edited by Ronald W. Pierce et al., 224–40. Grand Rapids: IVP Academic, 2005.

Elliot, Elizabeth. "The Essence of Femininity: A Personal Perspective." In *Recovering Biblical Manhood and Womanhood*, edited by John Piper and Wayne Grudem, 461–67. Wheaton, IL: Crossway, 2021.

Erickson, Millard. *Who's Tampering with the Trinity? An Assessment of the Subordination Debate*. Grand Rapids: Kregal Academic & Professional, 2009.

Foh, Susan T. "The Head of the Woman Is the Man." *In Women in Ministry: Four Views*, edited by Bonnidell Clouse et al., 69–105. Downers Grove, IL: InterVarsity, 1989.

France, R. T. *Women in the Church's Ministry: A Test-Case for Biblical Hermeneutics*. Eugene, OR: Wipf & Stock, 1995.

Frymer-Kensky, Tikva. *In the Wake of the Goddesses: Women, Culture and the Biblical Transformation of Pagan Myth*. New York: Ballantine, 1993.

Glahn, Sandra L. "The First-Century Ephesian Artemis: Ramifications of Her Identity." *Bibliotheca Sacra* 172 (October-December 2015) 450–69.

———. "The Identity of Artemis in First-Century Ephesus." *Biblitheca Sacra* 172 (July-September 2015) 316–34.

Grudem, Wayne. *Biblical Foundations for Manhood and Womanhood*. Wheaton, IL: Crossway, 2002.

———. "Foreword." In *Radical Womanhood: Feminine Faith in a Feminist World*, by Carolyn McCulley, 9–14. Chicago: Moody, 2008.

———. "The Myth of Mutual Submission." CBMW News 1.4 (October 1996) 1. https://cbmw.org/wp-content/uploads/2013/05/1-4.pdf.

Haddad, Mimi. "Women Leaders in the Early Church." *Sojourners*, February 16, 2009. https://sojo.net/articles/women-leaders-early-church.

Harvey, Susan Ashbrook. "Singing Women's Stories in Syriac Tradition." *Internationale Kirchliche Zeitschrift* 100.3 (2010) 171–89.

Heiser, Stuart. "The Majority of U.S. Medical Students Are Women, New Data Show." *American Association of Medical Colleges (AAMC)*, December 19, 2019. https://www.aamc.org/news-insights/press-releases/majority-us-medical-students-are-women-new-data-show.

Hübner, Jamin. "Revisiting αὐθεντέω in 1 Timothy 2:12: What Do the Extant Data Really Show?" *Journal of Paul and His Letters* 5.1 (Summer 2015) 41–70.

Hunter, David G., ed. *Marriage and Sexuality in Early Christianity*. Philadelphia: Fortress, 2018.

Jones, Robert P. *White Too Long: The Legacy of White Supremacy in American Christianity*. New York: Simon & Schuster, 2020.

Keener, Craig S. "Learning in the Assemblies." In *Discovering Biblical Equality: Complementarity without Hierarchy*, edited by Ronald W. Pierce et al., 161–71. Grand Rapids: IVP Academic, 2005.

———. *Paul, Women & Wives: Marriage and Women's Ministry in the Letters of Paul*. Peabody, MA: Hendrickson, 1992.

Kimbrough, S. T., Jr., ed. *Orthodox and Wesleyan Ecclesiology*. Crestwood, NY: St. Vladimir's Seminary Press, 2007.

Knight, George W., III. "Husbands and Wives as Analogues of Christ and the Church." In *Recovering Biblical Manhood and Womanhood: A Response to Evangelical Feminism*, edited by John Piper and Wayne Grudem, 215–32. Wheaton, IL: Crossway, 2021.

Krasinski, John, dir. *A Quiet Place*. Hollywood, CA: Paramount Pictures, 2018.

Lewis, C. S. *Mere Christianity*. New York: HarperOne, 2012.

Marshall, I. Howard. "Mutual Love and Submission in Marriage." In *Discovering Biblical Equality: Complementarity without Hierarchy*, edited by Ronald W. Pierce et al., 186–204. Grand Rapids: IVP Academic, 2005.

McCulley, Carolyn. *Radical Womanhood: Feminine Faith in a Feminist World*. Chicago: Moody, 2008.

McKnight, Scot. *The Blue Parakeet: Rethinking How You Read the Bible*. Grand Rapids: Zondervan, 2018.

McVey, Kathleen. "Ephrem the Kitharode and Proponent of Women: Jacob of Sarug's Portrait of a Fourth-Century Churchman for the Sixth-Century Viewer and Its Significance for the Twenty-First-Century Ecumenist." In *Orthodox and Wesleyan Ecclesiology*, edited by S. T. Kimbrough Jr., 229–53. Crestwood, NY: St. Vladimir's Seminary Press, 2007.

———. "Jacob of Saruge on Ephrem and the Singing Women." *American Foundation for Syriac Studies*, October 11, 2007. http://www.syriacstudies.com/AFSS/Syriac_Articles_in_English/Entries/2007/10/11_Jacob_of_Saruge_on_Ephrem_and_the_Singing_Women_-_-_Dr._Kathleen_McVey.html.

Miller, Donald. *Blue Like Jazz: Nonreligious Thoughts on Christian Spirituality*. Nashville: Thomas Nelson, 2003.

Moo, Douglas. "What Does It Mean Not to Teach or Have Authority Over Men?" In *Recovering Biblical Manhood and Womanhood: A Response to Evangelical Feminism*, edited by John Piper and Wayne Grudem, 233–52. Wheaton, IL: Crossway, 2021.

Moon, Ruth. "Should Christian Colleges Let Female Faculty Teach Men the Bible?" *Christianity Today*, May 14, 2014. https://www.christianitytoday.com/ct/2014/may/should-christian-colleges-let-female-faculty-teach-men-bibl.html.

NCR Editorial Staff. "Editorial: Ordination of Women Would Correct an Injustice." *National Catholic Reporter*, December 3, 2012. https://www.ncronline.org/news/parish/editorial-ordination-women-would-correct-injustice.

Ortlund, Raymond. "Male-Female Equality and Male Headship: Genesis 1–3." In *Recovering Biblical Manhood and Womanhood: A Response to Evangelical Feminism*, edited by John Piper and Wayne Grudem, 119–42. Wheaton, IL: Crossway, 2021.

Padgett, Alan G. *As Christ Submits to the Church: A Biblical Understanding of Leadership and Mutual Submission*. Grand Rapids: Baker Academic, 2011.

Peppiatt, Lucy. *Women and Worship at Corinth: Paul's Rhetorical Arguments in 1 Corinthians*. Eugene, OR: Cascade, 2015.

Princeton Theological Seminary. "President Barnes Preaches on Exodus 20:7–11 | March 5, 2020." *YouTube*, 12:17. March 11, 2020. https://www.youtube.com/watch?v=PGBAku3H5tE&list=PLjSFe-2r4QfuAUR8pQMPI8hSL7ON038WS&index=1.

QABible. "Is It Wrong for Guys to Listen to Female Speakers? (John Piper Q&A)." *YouTube*, 3:15. January 26, 2013. https://www.youtube.com/watch?v=Rmar_uBUD1U.

Ritchie, Guy, dir. *Sherlock Holmes*. Burbank, CA: Warner Bros. Pictures, 2009.

Rosenthal, Jake. "The Pioneer Plaque: Science as a Universal Language." *The Planetary Society*, January 20, 2016. http://www.planetary.org/blogs/guest-blogs/2016/0120-the-pioneer-plaque-science-as-a-universal-language.html.

Šeper, Franjo. "Declaration *Inter Insigniores* on the Question of Admission of Women to the Ministerial Priesthood." *The Vatican*, October 15, 1976. https://www.vatican.va/roman_curia/congregations/cfaith/documents/rc_con_cfaith_doc_19761015_inter-insigniores_en.html.

Shakespeare, William. *As You Like It*. Durham, NC: Duke Classics, 2012.

Spencer, Aída Besançon. *Beyond the Curse: Women Called to Ministry*. Grand Rapids: Baker Academic, 1985.

Stackhouse, John G., Jr. *Partners in Christ: A Conservative Case for Egalitarianism*. Downers Grove, IL: InterVarsity, 2015.

Thompson, John L. *Reading the Bible with the Dead: What You Can Learn from the History of Exegesis That You Can't Learn from Exegesis Alone*. Grand Rapids: Eerdmans, 2007.

Thurman, Howard. *Jesus and the Disinherited*. Boston: Beacon, 1976.

Tisby, Jamar. *How to Fight Racism: Courageous Christianity and the Journey toward Racial Justice*. Grand Rapids: Zondervan Reflective, 2021.

Tutu, Desmond Mpilo. *No Future without Forgiveness*. New York: Doubleday, 1999.

Van Marter, Jerry L. "Middle East Churches Assembly Issues Final Communiqué." *PC(USA) News*, January 15, 2010. https://www.pcusa.org/news/2010/1/15/middle-east-churches-assembly-issues-final-communi/.

Waltke, Bruce K. *An Old Testament Theology: An Exegetical, Canonical, and Thematic Approach*. Grand Rapids: Zondervan, 2008.

Weintraub, Melissa. "Torture and Torah: Defense of Dignity and Life in Jewish Law." In *Torture Is a Moral Issue: Christians, Jews, Muslims and People of Conscience Speak Out*, edited by George Hungsinger, 123–44. Grand Rapids: Eerdmans, 2008.

Westfall, Cynthia Long. "The Meaning of Αὐθεντέω." *Journal of Greco-Roman Christianity and Judaism* 10 (2014) 138–73.

———. *Paul and Gender: Reclaiming the Apostle's Vision for Men and Women in Christ*. Grand Rapids: Baker Academic, 2016.

CPSIA information can be obtained
at www.ICGtesting.com
Printed in the USA
BVHW061411300122
627306BV00005B/10